CW01498459

A Deadly Marriage

*How Molly Martens' obsession with
her stepchildren cost her husband,
Jason, his life and legacy*

BRIAN CARROLL

SANDYCOVE

an imprint of

PENGUIN BOOKS

SANDYCOVE

UK | USA | Canada | Ireland | Australia
India | New Zealand | South Africa

Sandycove is part of the Penguin Random House group of companies
whose addresses can be found at global.penguinrandomhouse.com

Penguin Random House UK,
One Embassy Gardens, 8 Viaduct Gardens, London SW11 7BW

penguin.co.uk

Penguin
Random House
UK

First published 2025

001

Set in 13.5/16pt Garamond MT Std
Typeset by Six Red Marbles UK, Thetford, Norfolk
Printed and bound in Great Britain by Clays Ltd, Elcograf S.p.A.

The authorized representative in the EEA is Penguin Random House Ireland,
Morrison Chambers, 32 Nassau Street, Dublin D02 YH68

A CIP catalogue record for this book is available from the British Library

ISBN: 978–1–844–88684–5

A Deadly Marriage

Investigative journalist and documentary producer Brian Carroll is a law graduate. He is a former crime correspondent, news editor and deputy editor of the *Irish Examiner*. He has reported from around the world for the *Irish Daily Mail* and has been a profile writer for the *Sunday Times*. He has researched and produced transnational investigative documentaries for Netflix (*A Deadly American Marriage*), TNT/HBO Max (*Dirty Moneyball: Cuba's Ransomed Stars*) and RTÉ (*The Many Lives of Kevin McGeever*). He has also contributed to the BBC and Virgin Media. He reported on the killing of Jason Corbett for the *Irish Times*. *A Deadly Marriage* is his first book.

For my wife, Karen, daughters,
Molly and Ava, and my parents, Tom and Pauline.

Contents

CONTENTS

List of key participants in the events of 2 August 2015

The Corbett family: 160 Panther Creek Court, Meadowlands, Davidson County, North Carolina

Jason Corbett (39) An Irish citizen, Jason was manager of a packaging plant in Lexington, North Carolina. The father of two was beaten to death in his home on 2 August 2015 by his wife and his father-in-law.

Molly Martens Corbett (31) A housewife and part-time swim coach, Molly was stepmother to Jason's two children for seven years. Before marrying Jason, Molly had been employed as the children's nanny. Molly admitted hitting Jason with a brick but claimed she acted in self-defence.

Jack (10) and Sarah (8) Jason's children from his first marriage. They were in the house, sleeping upstairs, on the night of the killing. They subsequently spent fifteen days living with their father's killers while a US court determined who should get custody of them, Molly or Jason's sister, Tracey.

The Martens family: 12500 Comblain Road, Knoxville, Tennessee

Tom Martens (65) A former FBI agent, Tom was in his daughter Molly's North Carolina home staying overnight when he and Molly killed Molly's husband. Tom admitted hitting Jason with a baseball bat but claimed he acted in self-defence.

Sharon Martens (65) A mathematics teacher at Pellissippi State Community College in Knoxville, Tennessee, Sharon was present on the night of the killing. Sharon told police she saw Tom go upstairs with the bat. However, she then went back to sleep.

Bobby Martens (35) A federal agent with the Inland Revenue Service, Bobby was the first-born of Tom and Sharon's four children. After the killing, Jack and Sarah stayed with Molly at Bobby's house in Monroe, North Carolina, for fifteen days pending a guardianship ruling on whether the children's future lay in America or Ireland.

Stewart (24) A mechanical engineer, Stewart was working as a construction manager in Atlanta, Georgia, at the time of the 2015 killing. Tom Martens told police the bat he used to strike Jason was previously owned by Stewart, a former college baseball player.

Connor (22) In 2015 Connor was entering the final year of his bachelor degree in Economics at the University of the South. He campaigned for Tom and Molly's release from prison and helped to administer their various online fund-raising efforts.

The Corbett-Lynch family, Limerick

Tracey (43) General Manager of Tait House, a community enterprise in Limerick, Tracey was Jason's sister. Tracey travelled to America to fight for custody of Jack and Sarah. She and her husband, David Lynch, were named as guardians in Jason's will. They have raised Jack and Sarah in Ireland since August 2015.

David Lynch (45) Manager of Treaty Steel in Limerick, David was Jason's brother-in-law and close friend. When Jason married his first wife, Margaret Fitzpatrick, David was his groomsman. David and Tracey have two sons, **Dean and Adam**, who were twenty-four and fourteen at the time of the killing.

The Fitzpatrick family, Limerick

Margaret 'Mags' Fitzpatrick Jason's first wife, and mother to Jack and Sarah. She died in November 2006, eleven weeks after giving birth to Sarah. Jack was two years old. Family and friends say Mags was Jason's 'soulmate'.
Catherine Fitzpatrick Mags's sister. The night Mags died, Catherine witnessed her sister having an asthma attack, and Jason rushing her to hospital. The Martenses would later contest Mags's autopsy and allege that Jason killed his first wife.

The Earnest family, Alexandria, Virginia

Mike Earnest (63) Only brother of Sharon Martens. A former special agent for the Naval Criminal Investigative Service, Mike was working as a federal agent in Washington DC for the Special Inspector General for Afghanistan Reconstruction at the time of the killing. He played a key role, beginning the day after the killing, as an advocate and spokesperson for the Martenses.

Investigators at Davidson County sheriff's office

Sheriff David Grice The most senior law enforcement officer in Davidson County, which had a population in 2015 of approximately 163,000. Grice visited the crime scene hours after the killing and immediately believed Tom and Molly Martens were lying.

Lt Wanda Thompson Head of the Criminal Investigations Division. The most senior investigating officer, she interviewed Molly Martens hours after the killing.

Detectives Brandon Smith and Michael Hurd They interviewed Tom Martens hours after the killing and tracked down witnesses who revealed Molly's troubled past.

Detective Nathan Riggs He took a statement from Sharon Martens at 6.34 a.m., hours after the killing, in the basement of Jason and Molly's house.

Lt Frankie Young Chief of Crime Scene Investigations. He took more than 600 photographs at the crime scene.

Corporal Clayton Dagenhardt The first officer from the sheriff's office to reach the scene. He had experience of more than 200 bloody crime scenes. He noticed the blood was pooled and congealed, not runny, as it should be when fresh.

Corporal Rusty Ramsey He and Dagenhardt woke Jack and Sarah from their beds and escorted them downstairs, careful to have them shield their eyes as they passed the blood trail leading from the master bedroom.

Deputy David Dillard He heard Molly crying and saw her rubbing her neck. She was making crying noises, but he didn't see any visible tears.

Emergency medical services

Sgt Barry Alphin When attempting to save Jason in the back of an advanced life support ambulance, Alphin's hand went inside Jason's shattered skull. 'I called the code and stopped life support.'

David Bent The first paramedic on the scene, alongside

Alphin. Bent noticed streaks of blood caked into Molly's blonde hair and a slight redness on her neck.

Amanda Hackworth Qualified eleven years, she noted dried blood and that the body was cold. She asked: 'How long did they say they waited before they called 911?'

Carley Lane A paramedic who attempted chest compressions on Jason in the life support ambulance.

Social workers

Sheila Tyler Interviewed the children at Bobby's house the day after the killing.

Brandi Reagan Interviewed Jack and Sarah at Dragonfly House Children's Advocacy Center, four days after the killing. Reagan was trained to interview children who were suspected victims of child abuse or domestic violence.

Andrea Huckabee A licensed clinical social worker specializing in childhood trauma, she interviewed Jack and Sarah eight days after their father's death.

Heidi Mathis Interviewed the children at Bobby's house twelve days after the killing, and one day before the guardianship hearing. Mathis questioned Molly about concerns over her mental health.

The custody case

Kim Bonuomo Lawyer representing Tracey and David at the guardianship hearing. She worked 18-hour days for almost two weeks preparing the case.

Brian Shipwash The presiding judge in the guardianship hearing. He said Molly 'had this deranged entitlement to the children'.

Prosecutors

Garry Frank District Attorney for Davidson County. Frank successfully oversaw Tom and Molly's prosecution for second-degree murder, but he later refused to sanction a retrial when the Martenses won their appeal.

Greg Brown Assistant district attorney, he led the prosecution team in the courtroom for the 2017 trial of Tom and Molly Martens for second-degree murder. It was his last case before retiring.

Alan Martin Assistant district attorney, he gave a powerful closing statement in the 2017 trial, his speech punctuated by the sound of a baseball bat hitting the prosecution table twelve times, to echo the number of blows sustained by Jason on the night of the killing.

Ina Stanton Assistant district attorney. In a Skype interview with Stanton, Jack said he and Sarah were told to lie about their father being abusive.

Criminal defence attorneys

David Freedman Tom's lead attorney, Freedman was widely considered the top criminal defence attorney in North Carolina. Freedman settled on a strategy of putting the victim, Jason, on trial. He filed court papers alleging that Jason may have killed his first wife.

Walter Holton Molly's lead attorney, Holton was a former prosecutor. His client did not take the stand in her own defence. Holton accused the prosecution of withholding key evidence, including a long blonde hair which disappeared after being photographed between the fingers of Jason's right hand.

Key witnesses

Shannon and Charlie Grubb Neighbours of Jason and Molly in Meadowlands, and friends of the couple. They invited both to their house for a party two days before Jason was killed. At the party Molly was witnessed loudly insulting Jason about his weight.

Melissa Sams A child custody lawyer, Sams was a Meadowlands neighbour who met Molly through the neighbourhood book club. Molly told Sams she was being abused by Jason but she wouldn't leave because she didn't want to lose Jack and Sarah. Sams advised her to secretly record Jason being abusive and send her the tapes.

Billy June Jacobs A Meadowlands neighbour. In 2014, almost eighteen months before the killing, Molly told Jacobs she was the victim of 'physical, mental and emotional abuse'.

Jennifer Turner Another Meadowlands neighbour. Molly called in person to Jennifer Turner's house one evening, saying she had been in a really bad fight. 'She was crying and saying she couldn't leave because she loved the kids.'

Helen McCormac A nurse who lived next door to Molly's brother. She witnessed Jason being jealous and controlling around Molly, dictating the clothes she could wear.

Tori Adkins Molly and Sarah's horse-riding instructor. Molly told Adkins that Jason controlled her movements and wouldn't allow her any money. Molly and Sarah spent part of the afternoon before the killing with Adkins.

David Fritzsche Next-door neighbour. He spent the afternoon of 1 August 2015 drinking beers in his driveway with Jason. Hours later Jason was dead. Police brought Molly to Fritzsche's house at 5.30 a.m., some two and a half hours after the killing.

Lynn Shanahan Sarah's godmother, and friend of Jason and his first wife, Mags. Molly told Lynn she had reconnected with an ex-boyfriend and didn't love Jason any more.

Paul Dillon Jason's best friend. Jason told Paul over the phone that he was planning on leaving Molly and returning to live in Ireland with Jack and Sarah.

Wayne Corbett Jason's twin. A week before the killing, Wayne overheard Sharon and Molly talking about how Jason would not let Molly adopt the children.

Marilyn Corbett Jason's sister. She witnessed Molly physically abusing Jack.

Preface

In the winter of 2019, a politician asked me if I would meet with Tracey Lynch and provide her with some communications advice. Tracey was general manager of Tait House, a publicly funded community enterprise which provides training and employment opportunities for people in economically disadvantaged areas in Limerick, Tracey's native city in the south-west of Ireland.

As I was going into the meeting, the politician mentioned that Tracey's brother was Jason Corbett, the 39-year-old Irish packaging executive who was killed in his North Carolina home by his wife, Molly Martens, and her father, Tom. It had been four years since the killing.

I was only vaguely aware of the case. I had not followed the coverage closely on television or in the print media. My superficial takeaway from what I had seen online was that Molly and her father killed Jason because he was a domestic abuser.

At the time of writing, ten years after the 2015 killing of Jason Corbett, this remains a view held by many. Others believe Jason Corbett was an entirely innocent victim of an orchestrated campaign by Molly Martens to falsely depict him as a domestic abuser so that she could get custody of his two children, Jack and Sarah, who were then aged ten and eight.

After my Tait House business with Tracey concluded, she asked if I would meet with Sarah to help her prepare for an interview with Ryan Tubridy, Ireland's most prominent broadcaster, on his radio show on RTÉ, Ireland's national broadcaster. Sarah had written a children's book, *Noodle Loses Dad*, about dealing with childhood grief. Ryan Tubridy was going to feature Sarah's book on his show.

I met with Tracey and Sarah, who was thirteen at the time, in their Limerick home. We discussed how to deal with nerves, although I remember thinking that Sarah didn't appear to have any.

Sarah was remarkably mature and articulate. She still spoke with the trace of an American accent. She was worried Ryan Tubridy might ask about what happened in North Carolina. She didn't want to talk about that publicly, but she did want to talk about her dad.

Sarah's book, inspired by Jason, tells the story of a child who loses her dad and as a result moves house and becomes part of a new blended family. Sarah wrote the book to help other children who were dealing with grief. She did book readings at schools, donated part of the proceeds of the book to the Children's Grief Centre in Limerick and featured on Ireland's most popular television talk show, *The Late Late Show*. Sarah's home city honoured her courage in writing the book by naming her Limerick Person of the Month in February 2020.

Sarah certainly knew about grief. Her mother, Margaret 'Mags' Fitzpatrick, had died suddenly when Sarah was eleven weeks old. Sarah's dad then hired Molly Martens through an online recruitment agency as a nanny to help him raise Sarah and her brother, Jack, who was two years old at the time of his mother's death.

Molly Martens moved to Ireland from her native Tennessee in March 2008. Jason married Molly three years later in 2011, and they moved to Meadowlands, an upscale golf enclave in Davidson County, North Carolina. It was an American adventure and a second chance at happiness for them all.

Four years later, on 2 August 2015, Jason was beaten to death in the master bedroom of his Meadowlands home. Six hours after Tom and Molly Martens admitted killing Jason, they were sent home without charge and handed his children. Jack and Sarah were kept in the custody of their father's killers for fifteen days while a court adjudicated on who should be granted guardianship – Molly or Tracey.

In his will, Jason had named Tracey and her husband, David, as his preferred guardians for Jack and Sarah in the event of his death. Molly challenged the will's legality in America and sought sole custody, as she had been the children's stepmother for seven years.

The media on both sides of the Atlantic were enthralled by this international 'tug-of-love' story featuring two Irish children who had been orphaned by their beautiful stepmother and her father, a former FBI agent who had spent half his career in counterintelligence, protecting the United States from Russian, North Korean and Chinese spies.

During those fifteen days in the custody of their father's killers, Jack and Sarah were interviewed by American social workers on four occasions and they alleged their father had hit, pushed and shoved Molly. They depicted their father as angry, jealous and controlling. The children's allegations offered some corroboration for Molly and Tom's claims to police that they acted in self-defence – that Jason was the aggressor on the night, that he had been choking Molly and had told Tom that he was going to kill his daughter.

However, after Tracey won guardianship and the children returned to Ireland Jack and Sarah changed their stories. The children started to remember disturbing details not just from those fifteen days but also from their four years living with Molly in Meadowlands. They wrote about these memories in their diaries, extracts of which were sent to investigators and the district attorney in Davidson County in 2017.

Jack had officially recanted his allegations against his father in a Skype interview with the district attorney's office in May 2016, nine months after the killing and five months after the district attorney had decided to bring second-degree-murder charges against Tom and Molly Martens. The children now said they had been coached and threatened into making false accusations against their father. They said Jason was not the abuser in the house, Molly was.

The Martenses countered that Jack and Sarah had been brainwashed by Tracey from the moment they returned to Ireland. Molly was a victim of domestic violence who had lost everything, they said, including the two children she had loved and raised as her own. According to the Martenses, Molly was the only mother the children had ever really known.

At the time of my first meeting with Tracey in late 2019, Tom and Molly Martens were in prison, serving sentences of twenty to twenty-five years for second-degree murder.

In early 2020, Tracey told me that she had been approached by numerous production companies in the United States and Ireland, all looking to make a documentary about her brother's killing. Tracey sought my advice on whether she should give an interview for any of these proposed documentaries. The North Carolina Court of Appeals was about to rule in February of 2020 on Tom and Molly Martens' appeal against their 2017 convictions. The appeal court would decide whether the Martenses would be freed or spend most of the next two decades in prison.

Tracey had already helped to restore her beloved younger brother's reputation in a book, *My Brother Jason*, which she co-authored with the *Irish Independent* journalist Ralph Riegel. Published in 2018, the book gave a powerful insight into the incredible ordeal that Jason's family had endured.

By February 2020, however, three months after our first meeting, Tracey felt that Jack and Sarah's lives were about to be upended again. If the North Carolina Court of Appeals overturned the Martenses' convictions, judgement would fall on Jason once more. Tracey was forced to weigh up whether it was better for the world to hear her and the children's stories in their own words, rather than risk these proposed new documentaries telling only the Martenses' version of events.

Tracey was understandably wary of the media. The US television network ABC aired exclusive interviews with Tom and Molly Martens two days after their convictions in August 2017. The interviews, pre-recorded before the trial, were explosive.

The ABC 20/20 show specialized in true-crime stories and drew audiences of 4 million viewers for its most high-profile shows. The millions who watched the episode about Jason Corbett's killing were told by Tom and Molly Martens that Jason was a serial domestic abuser who choked Molly during forced sex and may also have killed his first wife.

The Lynch family had decided not to give an interview to ABC in 2017. Tracey did subsequently give an interview to CBS, which produced a more balanced documentary as a result. Despite this, social media continued to fester with allegations that Jason was a domestic abuser.

Supporters of the Martenses continued to post and share the domestic abuse allegations in support of their campaign to have the Martenses released as victims of a miscarriage of justice. Then, in February 2020, the Martenses' convictions for second-degree murder were overturned.

Tracey felt that she needed to take part in one definitive documentary to ensure Jason's story, and that of Jack and Sarah, was accurately portrayed. She asked me if I would help her.

I had been a reporter for more than twenty-five years,

fifteen of them working as an investigative journalist. I had moved from print journalism into documentaries and had researched and presented a high-profile documentary for RTÉ. The documentary was the product of a 3-year investigation I had carried out into the kidnapping of an Irish property developer. *The Many Lives of Kevin McGeever* exposed him as an international fraudster who had faked his own kidnapping and starved himself for eight months to avoid repaying $70 million owed to duped property investors. The documentary revealed the kidnapping was just the latest in a 30-year career of frauds on four continents. McGeever had even established a fake bank in Liechtenstein and duped American investors out of $8 million.

After watching this documentary, Tracey asked me if I would be interested in producing a documentary about Jason Corbett's killing. I pitched the documentary to Netflix, who commissioned me to co-produce the documentary with a UK production house, Sandpaper Films.

Sandpaper felt that an Irish producer would not be acceptable to the Martenses, so it was agreed that I would produce the Irish end of the story and feed into the investigations on the US side but a non-Irish producer would interview Tom and Molly Martens.

I have conducted more than eighty hours of interviews with people on both sides of the story. I interviewed Jack and Sarah multiple times, meeting with them regularly throughout their teenage years, helping them prepare for their Netflix interviews and their ongoing interactions with detectives and prosecutors in the United States.

Over the course of four years – from February 2020 to November 2023 – the children found themselves in a truly extraordinary situation. Their father's killers won their appeal and were freed because the appeal court judges, and later the North Carolina Supreme Court, ruled that the allegations

Jack and Sarah had made to the social workers during their fifteen days in the custody of their father's killers should have been put to the jury in the Martenses' 2017 trial.

The trial judge in 2017 had weighed up the children's condemnation of their father and their subsequent recantations of those allegations once back in Ireland and had adjudicated that the jury should not hear either. This was the principal reason why the supreme court upheld the overturning of the Martenses' convictions and declared that they were entitled to a retrial.

Jack and Sarah were already dealing with the loss of their father, and the loss of Molly, whom they had once loved. They had been uprooted from their American lives, had started in a new school and were living in an entirely new family unit. Now, on top of this, they had to somehow live with the guilt of knowing their condemnation of their father had ultimately led to his killers' release from prison.

Jack and Sarah were insistent that they lied about their father in those fifteen days because they were coached and coerced into doing so, by Molly. Both children carried that guilt throughout their teenage years, but supported by the selfless love of Tracey, David and their new brothers – Tracey and David's sons, Dean and Adam – they showed extraordinary resilience and bravery. They were determined that when a retrial took place they would take the witness stand and tell the world the truth of their unique experience.

As readers will discover, the path to the truth of this story was long, arduous and, in so many ways, cruel on these two children.

Jack and Sarah were aged fifteen and thirteen when I first spoke to them about what happened in Meadowlands. They were aged nineteen and seventeen by the time they got to finally stand in open court in November 2023 and have their say.

By the time of that hearing I had been working on co-producing the Netflix documentary for three years. We had filmed interviews for the documentary with Jack and Sarah and with Tracey and David. Tracey had approached me in June 2023 saying US publishing houses were interested in a book on the case. She asked me if I would be interested in pitching a book.

I agreed to write a book objectively assessing the facts of the case, using my law degree and my experience carrying out investigative journalism internationally. The book, like the documentary, would be impartial, and I would follow the evidence where it led me.

I was eight months into writing and researching this book and had already conducted numerous interviews in America when, in February 2024, Tracey decided that her family no longer wished to cooperate with it. This was disappointing, but understandable. What Jack and Sarah wanted from the outset was the opportunity to have their say – they got that when they delivered victim impact statements to a North Carolina court in November 2023, and when they sat for filmed interviews for Netflix. Sarah had decided to write her own book, a memoir called *A Time for Truth: My Father Jason and My Search for Justice and Healing*, which she published in the spring of 2025.

For this book, I have used quotes from Jack and Sarah where those quotes pertain to facts already in the public domain, via the children's victim impact statements, court documents, transcripts and exhibits, or comments made on social media and in traditional media. I have also used comments Jack and Sarah made to me during our interviews to inform my analysis, particularly in relation to the events in the story which are contested, with Jack and Sarah having one perspective, and the Martenses another.

As readers will discover, Jack and Sarah are central to this story. They were the victims, orphaned by their stepmother, but they were also the alleged motive – detectives believed Jason was killed because he was planning to leave Molly and return home to Ireland with his children.

Molly and Tom Martens made Jack and Sarah the central plank of their self-defence argument. They say the children were witnesses to domestic abuse in the house. The Martenses' legal team produced multiple neighbours and friends of Molly's who claimed to have witnessed Jason's controlling and abusive behaviour. The Martenses would go on to allege that Jason killed his first wife – Jack and Sarah's mother, Mags – and that Molly and Tom feared Molly was next.

To complete the character assassination of Jason Corbett, the Martenses were prepared to weaponize his children against him. The guilt or innocence of the Martenses, and of Jason, too, rests to a large degree on what Jack and Sarah remember.

A Deadly Marriage is told in three parts. Part One deals with the killing and the fifteen days Jack and Sarah spent waiting for a judge to rule on whether their futures lay in America or Ireland. I have treated the days which Jack and Sarah spent in the custody of their father's killers as the crucible of this story. Part Two deals with Jack and Sarah's return to Ireland and the criminal trial. Part Three covers the extraordinary aftermath, where eight years after the killing Jack and Sarah found themselves sitting across a courtroom aisle facing off against the woman who had reared them as a mother for seven years.

I conclude the story with my own findings and an analysis of how these new findings raise fresh questions about what really happened in the master bedroom of Jason and Molly's Meadowlands home on 2 August 2015.

I have reviewed tens of thousands of pages of court

documents, social worker case files, detective case files, affi-davits, search warrants and transcripts and used these to recreate the killing of Jason Corbett.

Molly and Tom Martens refused interviews for this book, but I have used their police interviews, Tom's court testimony, Molly's online comments, defence exhibits and witness testi-monies to provide a balanced assessment of the arguments on both sides of this case.

I spent six weeks in North Carolina and Tennessee researching the book and interviewing key people involved in the investigation and subsequent court cases. Any scene or descriptive detail provided is based on interviews con-ducted by myself or others. Where I have used interviews conducted by others – for example interviews given to other journalists or comments made online – I credit the source material in footnotes. Where possible, I have used court documents, police files or social worker case notes to sub-stantiate claims made by interviewees.

I have used first names for the principal characters and for any witnesses who were not acting in an official capacity. Those acting in official capacity, such as detectives, pros-ecutors, attorneys or social workers are referred to by their surnames. Material is styled in standard Irish/UK English, apart from US documentation (e.g. transcripts of police interviews, court transcripts, media reports), where US spell-ings are retained.

The story of the killing of Jason Corbett encapsulates themes of motherhood and family and features sensitive issues such as domestic violence, mental illness and sup-pressed memories. This story also explores how money, politics, status and influence can tip the scales of justice. Ultimately, it is a tragedy that I have sought to explain as conscientiously and respectfully as possible.

PART ONE

1. A Death in Davidson County

Sgt Barry Alphin and his partner, David Bent, sped out of the emergency medical services base in Winston-Salem, hurtling north on North Carolina Highway 109. A heart had stopped in Meadowlands.

Alphin watched the pine trees flash red as he and Bent turned off Motsinger Road on to Meadowlands Drive and careered towards Panther Creek Court, one of twelve exclusive neighbourhoods making up the Meadowlands golf community.

After half a mile, the trees flanking Meadowlands Drive gave way to a clearing where an artificial lake, a feature of the private Meadowlands golf course, was visible in the moonlight, shrouded in a low, drifting mist. The ambulance travelled on for a further mile, through 50 acres of parkland, past manicured lawns and upscale homes.

At 3.10 a.m., eight minutes after the 911 call, the paramedics turned into a horseshoe-shaped cul-de-sac of six homes and reversed down the sloped driveway of 160 Panther Creek Court.

They ran along a shrub-lined concrete walkway towards a barefoot, tall, grey-haired man in his mid-sixties who was waiting under the porch light, on the phone to 911, with the front door open behind him.

Dressed in a red polo shirt and white check-patterned boxer shorts, Tom Martens calmly led the paramedics inside, directing them immediately left into a low-lit ground-floor master bedroom. Here Alphin and Bent found Tom's 31-year-old daughter, Molly, on her knees, sobbing out a count – one, two, three, four.

She was attempting cardiopulmonary resuscitation (CPR) on a naked, heavy man about six foot tall lying on his back next to the bedroom door. His face, beard and chest were caked and matted in flaky, dried blood. Tom called his distraught daughter away and told her to let the paramedics do their job.

Alphin and Bent sidestepped a bloodstained lamp on the floor and separated on either side of the prone man, each falling to one knee as they ripped 'quick pads' from their packaging and slapped them on the bloodied chest. The quick pads were connected to an electrocardiogram monitor which read 'asystole', a flatline showing no cardiac rhythm.

The paramedics were taken aback. They had arrived expecting an entirely different scene. The 911 dispatcher had misclassified the emergency as a cardiac arrest and only updated the incident to an assault minutes later. Alphin and Bent had missed the update and were shocked to find blood all over the carpet and walls.

Two fire officers arrived to help them, but the room was dark and the space was confined, so Alphin weighed up moving the body. He called out to the woman who had been attempting CPR.

'First thing I wanted to know,' Alphin recalled later, 'was how long had this been going on. After so many minutes or hours, there's no chance for resuscitation. We try to get a really quick game plan. I remember asking just in general, "How long has he been down?" and I think the lady told me: "Since we called you."'

The patient was a 262-lb man, aged in his late thirties, lying motionless between the open bedroom door and the south wall to the right. A blood-smeared black vacuum cleaner stood upright behind the supine body, its black cord trapped under the man's head, further limiting Alphin's room to manoeuvre.

Alphin raced outside to get a backboard. He met Corporal Clayton Dagenhardt running in. Dagenhardt was the first police officer to receive the 911 call but only activated his siren two minutes later, once the incident was upgraded to an assault. He reached the house in twelve minutes.

Alphin warned Dagenhardt: 'It's bad in there, real bad, horrible scene. It is not just CPR.'

Dagenhardt encountered Tom and Molly Martens in the hallway immediately outside the master bedroom. Tom was closest to the bedroom door, with Molly to his left.

Dagenhardt entered the bedroom, where fire officers were attempting CPR, frantically battling to bring the man back to life. Dagenhardt went to close the bedroom door, but one of the fire officers called out for him to watch out, there was blood smeared on the inside of the door.

Alphin returned with the backboard. He shouted: 'Slide him on the board, get him in the truck immediately.' Turning to Dagenhardt, he said: 'If you are taking pictures, you better do it now. We are leaving here.'

Dagenhardt pulled out his cellphone and took two photographs of the victim. He noted several areas of 'puddled' blood next to the body. Fresh blood is runny, but this was 'congealed like Jell-O' and was starting to harden. There was another congealed pool of blood next to the left eye socket; dried blood on the chest; and drying blood on the walls and on the bed.

The paramedics and fire officers heaved the man on to the backboard and then on to a stretcher. Judiciously avoiding the large bloodied brick on the cream carpet, they rushed the victim out to the advanced life support ambulance. Leaving the room, Alphin spotted a 28-inch-long baseball bat resting against the bedroom dresser. Bent touched the victim's body. It felt cold. He also noted that the blood was dried.

Dagenhardt closed the master bedroom door and moved

his torchlight over the scene. He took care not to step on a glass photo frame which lay shattered beneath a fallen table lamp just inside the door. The lamp, still lit, was about 12 inches tall. The shade was tilted like a broken neck and had blood flecks cast up one side.

The lamp sent a low, coned shadow up the magnolia walls, shading them a light orange. The walls were blood-spattered and gouged. Dagenhardt traced the lamp cord to a plug behind a 6-foot-wide cedarwood dresser to the left of the bedroom door as he entered. Some of the dresser drawers were out an inch or so, pushed closed with such little care that clothing items were trapped and sticking out.

Either the users of these drawers were untidy by nature or some of the drawers had been opened and closed in haste. The dresser had nine drawers in total. The three drawers on the right-hand side were out an inch or so.

The picture frame must have fallen from the dresser first. Then the lamp crashed down on top of it. For blood to stain the lampshade, the victim had to have been pretty low down when struck. Even if the blood had got under there when the lamp was still on the dresser, the victim had to have been beneath it. There was blood spattered across the large mirror over the dresser.

Dagenhardt zoned in on the picture frame beneath the lamp and, in particular, on the bride photographed beneath the smashed glass. Dagenhardt recognized the woman he'd just seen in the hallway. She looked exuberant in a white sleeveless wedding dress.

Dagenhardt had lived his entire life in North Carolina. If asked to pick one place in Davidson County where there might be a homicide, Meadowlands would not have been high on the list.

On average there were three murders a year in Davidson

County, and typically they were not who-done-its. The killings were often the homicidal tipping point of domestic violence. Drugs or alcohol were usually involved. And they didn't occur in neighbourhoods like Meadowlands, a luxurious community where the residents and lawns were equally well manicured.

There was open access to Meadowlands, so strictly speaking it was not a gated community, but it wore its privilege in the private tennis club and swimming pool for residents and the sprawling beauty of its nature park and walking trails. Many residents owned golf buggies to take them to and from the Meadowlands golf course.

Neighbours in Meadowlands could be vigilant about noise violations or failure to keep one's lawns mowed regularly, but such misdemeanours were rare. Meadowlands tended to be a monochrome, conservative place. It had a book club and a bible-study group. If safe, middle-class, conservative America was soft wind chimes in the porch light, then Meadowlands saluted that flag. Life here was far removed from the one lived in Davidson County's 350 trailer parks.

Patrol officers like Clayton Dagenhardt were often the first responders at homicide scenes. As such, Dagenhardt had been walking into crime scenes for fourteen years. About once a month, he would enter a crime scene where blood had been spilt.

After witnessing about two hundred such scenes over the years, Dagenhardt was sure of one thing, reaffirmed for him the minute he walked into the master bedroom at 160 Panther Creek Court: there was a whole world of difference between blood spilt and blood spattered. The master bedroom was spattered with rage, fear and survival.

As experienced as these paramedics were, Dagenhardt did not believe they could save the victim.

Still in the blood-spattered bedroom, Dagenhardt called the sheriff's office. He instructed the lieutenant in charge to wake Lieutenant Wanda Thompson, the head of Davidson County's Criminal Investigations Division (CID) and alert her to a homicide. He talked her through the scene and detailed the blood-soaked brick and the bloodstained baseball bat.

Dagenhardt then opened the door, to be faced by Tom and Molly, who were standing immediately outside in the hallway.

Molly – slight and blonde-haired in blue pyjamas – was crying between rapid shallow breaths. Dagenhardt noted some dried blood in Molly's hair, but otherwise she, like Tom, had no obvious injuries. He asked them if there was anyone else in the house.

Tom told Dagenhardt in a clear, steady voice that there were two young children upstairs and that his wife, Sharon, was asleep downstairs in the basement.

Dagenhardt told Corporal Rusty Ramsey and Deputy David Dillard, who had arrived shortly after him, to escort Tom and Molly outside the house. The father and daughter sat together on the steps of the porch and watched as Dillard ran crime-scene tape around the perimeter.

Meanwhile, Dagenhardt and Ramsey ascended the wooden stairs to wake the children in their first-floor bedrooms.

Ramsey told 10-year-old Jack that he was a policeman and that something had happened downstairs. He was going to bring him downstairs to his grandma. Jack had to promise to close his eyes and keep them shut.

Ramsey took Jack up in his arms and kept the boy's back to the stairs as they turned left down sixteen steps. Boots scrambled over the hardwood hallway floors below. Loud voices echoed up the high walls of the living room, then suddenly silenced.

Jack's sister, 8-year-old Sarah, was below Jack on the stairs, gathered in the arms of Corporal Dagenhardt.

'Eyes shut real tight now,' Dagenhardt said as they rushed right, then right again, the police officer walking backwards at this point so Sarah's back was to the ground-floor master bedroom door and the trail of blood leading from it out the front door. They walked through a galley-kitchen door and down a second flight of steep wooden steps to the basement.

Dagenhardt tried the basement door handle, then pressed his shoulder into it before it opened with a creaking sound. He peered through the darkness.

To his immediate left was a bathroom and a damp-smelling games room. He noted shot glasses laid out on a bar counter, a couch, a television, an Irish tricolour flag, a karaoke machine, a pool table, and then, straight ahead, a black Everlast boxing bag hanging from the roof of a cluttered storage room.

Finally, his eyes settled on the thin line of lamplight under a bedroom door. The door opened and Sharon Martens stepped into the frame.

Dagenhardt put Sarah down and she ran to Sharon, or 'Seecu', as Sarah called her. Corporal Ramsey told Jack he could open his eyes.

Sharon didn't fire questions at the policemen. She didn't ask if anyone was hurt, or if her husband and daughter were safe upstairs. Instead, Dagenhardt noted, she appeared remarkably calm and merely asked if everything was okay.

Dagenhardt told Sharon there was an active investigation and that he needed to leave the children in her care. He asked her for some shorts and shoes that he could give her husband, then instructed her not to leave the basement until officers returned to get them.

The police officers left. They closed the basement door behind them and returned upstairs.

*

Jack described for me several years later how, of the three people missing that night, an instant sense of foreboding told him it was his dad who was hurt.

Outside the basement window, a torch beam roamed the deck at the back of the house, before settling on sixteen bricks stacked in twos beneath the exterior wooden porch.

Jack had needed to be persuaded to call Molly Mom.

He remembered Sharon once muttering under her breath how he was just a god-awful, horrible person because he wouldn't call Molly Mom or Sharon Seecu. Sharon didn't want to be called Grandma, Granny, or any of those names. She said she wasn't that old.

Jack's biological mother, Margaret 'Mags' Corbett, had died in November 2006 – almost nine years previously – when Jack was two years old and his sister, Sarah, was eleven weeks old. At that time they were living in Limerick, in the south-west of Ireland, with no thought of ever moving to America.

Then Molly arrived in March 2008 from Tennessee. She was brought in as a nanny to Jack and Sarah, who were by then three years old and eighteen months old respectively. Molly was only expected to stay six months but, within weeks, Sarah was calling her Mommy.

Molly stayed in Ireland for three years. Then she married Jack and Sarah's father, Jason, in June 2011, when they all moved to North Carolina.

Since Jack was three years old, Molly was the only mother he'd known, but that didn't make Sharon Grandma. Not in Jack's eyes.

In the basement after the policemen left, Sharon, holding Sarah in her arms, told Jack to go out to the playroom.

'Play your computer games,' she said. Then Sharon

whispered in Sarah's ear. 'Princess, Mommy's gone with *her* daddy to help the police. Tom knows what to do.'

As Jack searched the basement for his computer games, he thought of Sharon whispering secret instructions to Sarah only last month.

'Just call,' she'd said, 'and when I answer, or Tom answers, say the password and hang up.'

Jack could not find his Xbox or Wii games. Some game covers were lying around, but not the discs, which was strange because that was one of the latest rules on the chores list for Jack: all his computer games had to be stacked neatly in their covers.

Jack wondered if the discs were upstairs in the bag he had seen packed by his father's bed last night. It was much bigger than the usual travel bag his father used on business trips.

Jack prayed his dad was okay. He thought: Sarah must have called Sharon with the emergency code word she told us to use. Why else did Tom and Sharon show up here out of the blue last night, when they lived a 4-hour drive away?

Outside in the ambulance, Barry Alphin and David Bent were frantically working under the bright LED lights to bring Jack and Sarah's father back to life. Two further paramedics joined them to assist – Amanda Hackworth and Carley Lane.

Alphin, sitting behind the victim's head, could see heavy bleeding around the face and skull.

'His eye sockets had a lot of gel blood,' Alphin said afterwards. 'His ear had a lot of gel. I tried to clean him up to find the source of the bleeding.'

Bent was on the victim's right side, trying to insert an IV into his hand. Lane was on the victim's left, doing chest compressions. Hackworth, wearing a short-sleeved uniform, leant over to attach the 'five lead' to get a better reading on the cardiac monitor. Her arm brushed the man's naked torso.

'He's cool,' she said. 'How long has he been down?' Hackworth noted dried blood around Jason's broken nose and black eye.

She asked again: 'How long did they say they waited before they called 911?'

'The minute he went down,' Alphin replied. 'That's what they said.'

Alphin used his bare forearm to touch the victim's arm and chest to check for himself. He recalled, 'He did feel very cool to me.'

Alphin frantically cleaned the head, chest and torso to see if the victim was still bleeding. Then, when attempting a last-ditch intubation, he placed his gloved left hand under the victim's chin and his right hand under the head: 'As I did, all of my fingers went inside the skull. My right hand was just mushy. At that point, I realized there was severe trauma to the back of the head.'

Bent and Hackworth tried shocking the body. The EKG monitors stayed in flatline. They jolted him with another 30-amp current, then stopped. Alphin called time of death: 'From a combination of how long it had been since we had been working CPR and the coolness of his body, the amount of blood loss and the trauma on the head, I concluded there was no way of any life sustaining. That's when I called the code and stopped life support.'

Jason Paul Corbett, born 12 February 1976, was pronounced dead at 3.24 a.m. on 2 August 2015. There was never a moment when the paramedics could have got him back. There had been no pulse and zero electrical activity. So, he was dead when the paramedics got there. That was about as much as they could say with absolute certainty.

David Bent left the advanced life support unit and saw Molly Martens, Jason Corbett's wife, lying on her right side, curled into a foetal position on the immaculately cut grass. Wearing flip-flops, she had a 6-foot-long brown fur blanket draped loosely over sleeveless sky-blue pyjamas with a white paisley-style pattern.

Earlier, in the bedroom, Bent had witnessed Molly on her knees performing 'ineffective' chest compressions. Now, up close to her 5-foot-6 frame, he saw how elfin-thin she was, about 110 pounds, less than half the weight of the man lying cold on a gurney in the back of the ambulance.

Bent noted dried-blood smears across Molly's forehead and right cheek, streaks of blood caked into her blonde hair and an exiguous redness, like faint sunburn, on her neck. He examined her eyes using a pen light but did not detect abnormalities. He noted some blood discoloration spots on her pyjamas, around the waist and legs. The heart rate for a normal adult is between 60 and 100. Molly's was 120. She was clearly in shock, but when he asked if she would go to a local hospital she refused. Bent had her sign a waiver form confirming that she had declined medical treatment.

In the presence of Sgt Alphin, Molly said her neck was sore because she had been choked. Later, when Bent was alone with Molly, she said Jason was 'intoxicated from drinking a lot that night' and that this was 'not the first time he had hit her'.

After securing the perimeter with crime-scene tape, Deputy Dillard consulted with Deputy Matt Collins, who was charged with logging the entry and exit times of everyone at the scene. Over the course of the next seven hours, Collins would make thirty-two entries on the log.

After being instructed to separate the father and daughter, Dillard took Molly from the porch to the front passenger seat of his patrol car across the street. He left the passenger door open and stood sentry beside it for just shy of an hour and twenty minutes. 'I was to observe her and to make sure she didn't have contact with anybody else,' he said. He saw dried blood in Molly's hair and on the side of her face, but otherwise she appeared uninjured.

Dillard witnessed Molly being examined by emergency medical services (EMS) personnel on two occasions, with a 5-minute interval between them. During these intervening minutes, he heard Molly crying and saw her rubbing her neck: 'She was making crying noises, but I didn't see any visible tears. She was also rubbing her neck in a scrubbing motion. It wasn't constant. She would do it and stop and do it and stop while continuing to make the crying noises.'

Dillard noted that Molly changed her story between the two EMS examinations: 'While answering questions [to EMS], she also stated that Jason woke up because her daughter had woken up from a bad dream and was crying. But she then changed that by saying he was mad because a barking dog had woken him up. When EMS asked her where she was hurt or where Jason had hit her, she responded by saying "my throat is sore" and "he may have elbowed me in the right side of my face."'

Molly's father, Tom Martens, was escorted about 50 yards down the road to the junction of Panther Creek Court and Red Hawk Lane, where Dagenhardt had moved his patrol car. Tom was placed in the front seat and was shown how to use the heater and the radio.

Tom seemed cooperative and calm, even when subsequently refused access to the house to use the bathroom. Dagenhardt explained the house was now a preserved crime scene. Tom proposed urinating against a nearby tree. Instead, Dagenhardt opened the two doors of the patrol car on the passenger side and let Tom urinate between them.

At 5 feet 11 inches tall, Tom was just an inch shorter than his now deceased son-in-law, but he was 100 pounds lighter. Up close, Dagenhardt could make out some dark spots in the fabric of Tom's red top, but otherwise the 65-year-old bore no signs of having just survived a violent altercation with a much stronger man twenty-six years his junior.

On foot of Dagenhardt's alert, Lieutenant Thompson, the CID chief, was woken from a sound sleep in Salisbury, some 40 miles away.

Thompson made four calls. She dispatched detectives Brandon Smith, Michael Hurd and Nathan Riggs to the scene, along with Lieutenant Frankie Young, the supervisor of Crime Scene Investigations (CSI) in Davidson County.

Young parked his Ford 150 outside the scene at 4.35 a.m. and went immediately to the ambulance. He took photographs of the victim's broken nose, black eye, open scalp wounds, severely bruised left hand and a single long strand of blonde hair trapped perfectly between the curled fingers of Jason Corbett's bloodstained right hand.

Sgt Alphin closed Jason's eyes, and Young left in search of Molly. He took her from Dillard's patrol car so that he could photograph her and record any injuries. He got her to stand close to one of the fire engines. He wanted to get a full-length shot of her.

As he was preparing his camera, he noticed how Molly 'continually tugged and pulled on her neck with her hand'. After several requests to stop, she complied. Lt Young observed blood on her cheek, forehead and hair, but he did not notice any injuries.

Shortly before 5 a.m., Detectives Smith and Hurd arrived in their unmarked county cars. They entered the crime scene, where Young's camera clicked and shadow-flashed over the blood pooled in the cream carpet and spattered across the south wall to the right of the bedroom door.

To the left of the south wall there was a hallway leading to an en suite bathroom. The walls on either side of the hallway were smeared and spattered with blood.

The detectives tried to get a sense of flow. Was the victim struck going to the bathroom or coming from it? Young snapped the spatter up the left-hand hallway wall. Then, he saw something at his feet on the right-hand side and bent down for a closer view. He photographed two clumps of brown hair and pink flesh.

Young was 2 to 3 feet from the bathroom door. Inside the bathroom, the light fitting was blood-smeared and smashed. There was a circular impression on the bathroom wall less than 12 inches above the light fitting. It was white with no traces of blood.

Young moved back out to the bedroom, the main theatre of violence. There was a similar white, round impression on the south wall, an impact point where the magnolia paint had been smashed in.

Pooled blood had stained the cream carpet carmine. The bloodstains centred in intensity in an area between the inside of the bedroom door and the wall 4 feet to the right. Small blood puddles had coagulated into a jellied form.

The detectives wondered if the victim had been attacked while still in the bed. There was some blood sprayed across the cream underside of the quilt. Young shone a light on the inside of the bedroom door and followed blood smears going left to right across it, three quarters of a handprint on one side, and wet bloody fingerprints beneath the door handle. Someone had been desperately trying to escape.

Young waited for Smith and Hurd to finish examining the room before he began measuring the distances between the floor and the impact points on the wall. Inches above the skirting board there was a rectangular shape where something had hit the wall with such force the plasterboard had impressed and cracked the paint into the perfect facsimile of the end face of a brick.

When detectives later lifted a bloodstained brick from the bedroom floor, they found it was covered on multiple sides with blood, hair and human tissue. The brick was 6 inches long, 5 wide and 3 deep. The carpet beneath it was soaked with blood, which had seeped from the concrete and left a macabre brick-shaped stain. There were drops of blood on the inside eave of the master bedroom door, indicating the door was open at some point during the bloodshed.

When Wanda Thompson arrived she examined the body for herself, before going to Dagenhardt's patrol car and introducing herself to Tom Martens as the lieutenant supervising the investigation.

She asked if Tom was willing to come down to the station and answer a few questions about what had happened. She started to explain that he was not under arrest, when Tom interrupted. 'He just said, "I'm a lawyer, I understand,"' Thompson recalled. 'He was calm and cooperative.'

Next, Thompson went to talk to Molly. She discovered that Molly wasn't in Dillard's patrol car. Molly had asked to use the bathroom, so Dillard had escorted her to neighbour David Fritzsche's house, next door to the crime scene. It was 5.30 a.m., but the 45-year-old was awake. He had risen two hours earlier to use the bathroom, seen blue and red lights flashing outside Jason's house and couldn't return to sleep.

As Molly used David's downstairs bathroom, Dillard gave little away except to say there was an active investigation. David told Dillard about spending the previous afternoon with Jason. After helping Jason to mow his lawn, they had spent about five hours drinking beers together on David's driveway. 'We shared about eight beers each,' David said. Molly had joined them after collecting Sarah from horse-riding. Molly had one drink with them and then she made a comment to Jason, asking how he would feel if her parents showed up. Then, ten minutes later, Molly's parents, Tom and Sharon, arrived in Jason's driveway.

Jason helped them unload the car. 'He was not impaired in any way,' David noted afterwards. 'That was the last time I saw him. We went off to dinner at 8.30 p.m.'

Thompson entered the hallway to the Fritzsche house. She was quietly furious at Dillard for allowing Molly to use the bathroom, as she later recounted. 'Dillard said, "What was I supposed to do, let her pee in the street like Tom?" I told him there were evidence cups in the trunk of all the patrol cars and Tom should have been asked to pee in an evidence cup, too. What if alcohol or drugs were an issue in this?

'The first thing I noticed when I spoke to Tom in Dagen-hardt's patrol car that night was a strong smell of alcohol. I told Dillard that Molly should never have been left behind a closed bathroom door to wash up or do whatever she liked in there.'

Thompson remembers Molly sobbing, asking for 'her children'. She agreed to escort Jack and Sarah over for a few minutes while a detective took a statement from Sharon Martens in the basement.

For years afterwards, Sarah would harbour a deep-seated resentment about Lt Thompson telling her that night that no one was hurt.

'She took us out the back door of the basement, past all the bricks under the porch – all of them except the one Molly had Jack put in her bedroom a few days before. I remember looking at the trees flashing blue, white and red at the back of our garden. As we walked across the grass to the Fritzsches', we saw an ambulance, but every time we asked, they told us no one was hurt. Molly was hysterical in the Fritzsches'.'

Jack remembers Molly sitting in the Fritzsches' living room. 'She didn't say anything about Dad being hurt. She looked really raggedy and was acting confused like she was on something. She seemed out of it.'

When Thompson opened the front door of the Fritzsches' house to let the children leave ahead of her after their brief visit with Molly, David Fritzsche heard the crime-scene tape flapping in the dark, and everything seemed suddenly very real.

Dagenhardt's 12-hour shift was coming to an end. He received a radio call to say the Third Squad of the Patrol Division were about to begin their 6 a.m. shift and take over. Dagenhardt said he would save them the trip and deliver Tom to the station himself, then clock out. Lt Thompson transported Molly to the station.

Hurd and Smith also returned to the sheriff's office, having spent approximately one hour at the scene.

Jack and Sarah were left in the care of Sharon Martens. They were instructed to remain in the basement as the CSI chief and several of his officers continued to photograph and catalogue the bloody scene in the master bedroom overhead.

When escorting Tom back to the station Dagenhardt noted that he appeared calm until the corporal rolled his window down and began to vape.

Almost immediately, Tom complained of the cold. Dagenhardt did not like his tone, so he ignored him. Even though it was a relatively short journey, less than a 25-minute drive, Tom could not hide his pique. He asked where they were going and, later, with growing impatience, if this station they were going to was even in the same county.

Tom was shivering and rubbing his hands together by the time Dagenhardt signed him over to Detective Hurd, who showed him to a seat in Interview Room Number One at 6.31 a.m.

It was sunrise in Davidson County, not that you could see it inside the windowless room, where Tom Martens was eager to get this over with.

2. A Mysterious Death or Two

Detective Michael Hurd laid out a yellow A4 pad on the interview desk, then sat into one of two chairs arranged opposite Tom Martens, turning his chair a fraction so that he was sitting slightly sideways on to Tom.

Tom rolled his shoulders and sighed. It was cold and he'd been up at least half the night. He knew the interview wouldn't start until that empty chair was filled.

Tom's thirty years working for the FBI had made him an interrogation expert. It had been forty years since he'd qualified as a lawyer, but the basics of interrogation hadn't changed. The next guy through the door would be interviewing him. Hurd was the junior here.

Hurd looked even younger than his twenty-seven years. He had a gun holstered to his right hip and a sleeve tattoo down to his right elbow.

Tom was not a fan of tattoos. Molly's hippy, Jesus-obsessed ex-boyfriend, Jeremy Taylor, had loads.

Molly had been through several boyfriends over the years, but apart from Jonathan DeBerry, her high school sweetheart, Tom had not overly warmed to any of them. Least of all, the guy he had just killed.

At least Jonathan DeBerry had come from what Tom considered good stock. Like his wife, Tom believed you could judge a man's character by his family and social standing.

Tom and Sharon had thought Molly and Jonathan were a perfect match. It was such a pity Molly had been unable to keep it together in her teens. Tom did not blame Jonathan, or

Jon, as he called him. Even Tom struggled to cope with his only daughter's psychiatric issues.

In the interview room, Detective Hurd asked Tom, 'Are you from here?'

Tom answered immediately. 'No. I live in Knoxville, Tennessee.'

'Ahuh . . . And with your daughter being here, you is originally from here?'

'No,' Tom said. Then he left a long pause, like he was still deciding how to play this – give them all the information he had or stick to yes-or-no answers. He was not under arrest. No one had read him his Miranda rights. He had come voluntarily and had not asked for a lawyer. This whole thing was a mess, but he could see a way out of it. He would tell them the whole story, as soon as that empty chair filled. Two minutes of complete silence followed. Then, Detective Brandon Smith entered and offered Tom something to drink.

'Cup of coffee would be great,' Tom said, adding how he liked it 'black at the top'.

Smith went off, ostensibly to get the coffee. Outside, he listened to Tom on the 911 call. Tom's voice remained remarkably calm.

'My, my daughter's husband, uh, my son-in-law, got in a fight with my daughter. I intervened, and I, I think, um, and, he's in bad shape. We need help.'

The 911 operator, Karen Capps, asks Tom what he means by 'in bad shape'. Tom, briefly agitated, replies: 'He, he's bleeding all over and I, I may have killed him.'

Capps instructs Tom to roll the man on to his back so they can verify his breathing. Tom tries, but he doesn't have the strength.

'He's a big heavy man, I can't do it,' he says. Capps asks

if there is anyone there who can help. 'My daughter,' Tom replies, 'and she's in terrible shape.'

'Okay,' Capps says. 'Someone needs to get him on his back. We need to verify he's breathing.'

Tom, a little testily, replies: 'I'm trying, lady, hang on.'

The 911 operator tells Tom to put the phone on speaker. Molly is then heard in the background saying: 'I think he's still alive.'

Tom hadn't said a word since Smith left to get the coffee. After three minutes had passed, Hurd attempted some chitchat.

'I used to drink coffee, but I'm on energy drinks now. I guess I was drinking so much of it, it wasn't affecting me.'

Tom answered: 'Correct.' Then, he didn't say another word for five minutes.

Hurd returned to scrolling. He had worked violent scenes, but nothing quite like what he'd encountered at 160 Panther Creek Court.

Tom's body language betrayed him with each crossing of his legs, each folding of his arms, every exasperated heavy breath. Hurd knew Tom had barely slept and was desperate to start.

Tom bowed his head, barely concealing his contempt. 'We don't need to go to Colombia to start,' he said.

Hurd ignored the sarcasm about Tom's delayed coffee and kept thumbing through his phone. He noted Tom variously resting his chin on his hand, staring to the side at the floor, occasionally breathing heavily through his nose and clearing his throat. He watched Tom fold his arms, stare at the roof and yawn too loudly.

At last Smith returned with the coffee. Tom had been sitting there for seventeen minutes. He picked up the Styrofoam cup and ensured the detectives noticed his hands.

'I'm already shaking,' he said.

Smith took his seat opposite Tom. Smith was a more experienced detective than Hurd, but only by one year.

The FBI's instruction bible for homicide cases is called Managing Death Investigations. The 627-page tome says it takes two years for most officers to become proficient in homicide investigations.

Smith was just shy of two years in the job, and this was, potentially, his and Hurd's first murder inquiry.

Smith: You said you're retired, is that correct?

Tom: I'm a retired FBI agent for a number of years and now I'm employed as a contractor for the UT-Battelle Corporation, which runs the Oak Ridge National Laboratory.

Smith: What did you do with the FBI?

Tom: First half of my career was criminal. Second half of my career was counterintelligence. I was a supervisor and general manager for all but about five years.

Smith: And currently with the company, what do you do with them?

Tom: Counterintelligence.

Smith: You all still currently live in Knoxville, come here together to visit. When did you all just arrive?

Tom: We arrived around 8.30.

Smith: And the two children is their kids?

Tom: The two children are his kids by a former marriage. And perhaps it would be helpful if I just kind of launched into a story . . . 'cause it will contribute to my state of mind. He's an Irish citizen. He was married in Ireland. He had those two children and his first wife died in mysterious circumstances. The finding was that she had an asthma attack in his car. She died of asphyxiation. Molly saw an advertisement for a, what do you call 'em, not a babysitter, my mind's not too sure right now . . .

Smith: A nanny.

Tom: A nanny. And so she answered that ad and she went to work for Jason in Ireland and they subsequently developed a romantic relationship. And he got transferred here to Winston-Salem to a packaging plant.

The detectives were intrigued by the news of Jason's first wife choking to death. Tom had claimed on the 911 call that Jason was choking Molly. Maybe this, their first homicide investigation, would turn out to be a big case.

Tom said Jason was drunk. Jason had insisted on driving to collect Jack from a neighbour's house where he was attending a friend's birthday party. Molly offered to drive.

'But he wasn't having any of that. So that was just kind of his attitude. When he got back, we went to bed. And I guess we'll get to the nitty-gritty,' Tom said.

'A lot of this evening is a blur to me. Whenever I woke up, I heard arguing and thumping going on on the floor above me, and it sounded bad. And again, I'm trying to give you some context here. Ah, I would say their marriage has not been a good one.

'That's, you know, Dad speaking – pretty hard to ever measure up to my daughter's standards in Dad's eyes. But he was abusive. Usually, to my knowledge, not physically abusive, but I mean he'd grab her or whatever and I don't think she told us everything.

'But he was very controlling and abusive. He needed to see her phone, he needed to analyze anything on her computer. I would go play golf with the guy and he would send texts, I mean hole after hole, which I didn't get to see. But – and she didn't talk to me much about this – but she would talk to her mother, Sharon, about how cruel and abusive and controlling he was. I know this sounds like a big excuse, but this is my mindset.'

It was not lost on the detectives that Tom had now referred to both his 'state of mind' and his 'mindset'.

It was the lawyer coming out in him, maybe his FBI experience, too. In order to prove self-defence, a defendant needed to show they were in real fear for their lives and acted not out of malice but to save themselves.

The detectives sensed Tom was trying to control the interview.

In the basement back at the house, Jack felt groggy. Later he would recall that Molly gave him two tablets the night before his father's killing – one red, one white. She said they were for his asthma, but he had never taken asthma pills. He hadn't had an asthma attack for two years.

Sarah kept slipping in and out of sleep, nestled beside Sharon in the basement bedroom. Jack was too scared to close his eyes. He tried to think of anything else, but his mind kept reverting to the crime-scene tape he'd seen flapping in the breeze as they had left the Fritzsches' house earlier, when they'd been brought over to see Molly.

The blue lights had stopped flashing now, but there was still no sign of his father.

Jack tried not to think of the worst thing imaginable, but every time he asked Sharon if his father was okay, she told him they would have to wait for the police to come back.

Jack could hear police officers upstairs in Jason and Molly's bedroom. Another officer was out on the back deck, wearing blue latex gloves and white plastic covers on his shoes. He was photographing the bricks stacked neatly outside the kitchen door.

Jack focused on what had happened the day before.

He'd risen early to work through his chores list, starting with the shoe shelf in the garage, where he straightened the wellingtons, trainers and shoes so they were all uniform.

He washed dishes and cleaned the kitchen counters, then folded the clothes piled in the laundry basket.

His dad was mowing the lawn, or cutting the grass, as every Irish person called it. Molly, however, was determined to get rid of Jack's Irish accent and idioms: 'You'll be saying "mowing the grass" from now on, Jack. That's what we agreed, isn't it?'

Jack remembered running glasses of water out to his dad as he mowed the lawn in 90-degree heat. Sarah had joined him. She was eight years old and her hands were so small most of the water had spilt before she reached their dad.

Jason held the glass up to the sun and said, 'Honey, you don't have to bring me water, I'll just come in.' Sarah ran off to get some more. Jack remembered his father pretending to chase Sarah, then winking at him.

Jack was excited. Molly would be taking Sarah horse-riding soon. Then, it would be just him and Dad. They planned to pick out their fantasy football teams – soccer, not American football. Both wanted Liverpool players. Jack was a Liverpool fan because his dad was.

After that, Jack was due at a friend's birthday party. The plan was: movies first, then pizza and ice cream.

Jack didn't get to enjoy treats like that as often as other children. Molly insisted that Jack consume up to twenty-five baby carrots a day as part of his swimming regime. She encouraged Jack to eat broccoli, chicken and boiled rice if he wanted to be a champion swimmer.

Molly had made sacrifices, practised and listened to *her* mom about what she could eat. Even though she was a great swimmer, a star at Farragut High and Clemson University and had been on the fringes of the US Olympic swimming team, repeated foot surgeries had destroyed her dreams.

Is that what you want, Jack, that kind of disappointment? Some days, Jack had baby carrots for breakfast.

Jack had already won five gold medals, been a triple event

winner and been voted the best swimmer on his team twice in his four years swimming, but Molly warned him the competition would get stiffer now against kids from High Point and Greensboro.

If he showed discipline, he could improve. He was only ten. But now was the time for real commitment. If he started something, he had to finish it. He had to chew his food thirteen times before swallowing and not just wolf it down like his Irish relatives. Molly did not like waste or quitters. In truth, she was not too fond of the Irish, either.

Molly would collect Sarah and Jack from school and take them swimming. The children recall having to eat their broccoli, chicken and boiled rice in the car en route.

Sometimes, Molly was in such a hurry Jack would have to climb into the trunk to put on his swimming Speedos while Sarah changed in the back seat. Jack would practise in the pool first, then, while Sarah was swimming, he would do his homework.

Sarah struggled with reading and writing at school, so Molly promised to help. But, by the time they returned home after swimming, the children were often exhausted. They remember being under orders from Molly to say a quick goodnight to their father, then go straight to bed.

'Your father doesn't like to be bothered,' she would say.

Molly regularly completed Sarah's homework for her at the breakfast table before school.

Molly's swimming and dietary regime for Sarah was stringent, too, until one day Sarah finished next to last in a swim meet. Molly put Sarah back in with the 4-year-old beginners.

After that, Sarah didn't have to eat so many carrots. Molly dressed Sarah in party dresses with big bows, and they spoke about her new ambition – to be a veterinarian married to some rich farmer.

*

At ten forty-five on the night before Jason was killed, Meadowlands neighbour Melissa Sams opened her front door to Molly and Jason. At that point, Jason had less than four hours to live.

He and Molly were there to pick up Jack from his friend's birthday party. Melissa was surprised to see Molly, as she had texted her at 10.14 p.m. to say Jason would collect Jack in twenty minutes.

Molly had been at Melissa's house for book club, once. Afterwards Molly had a 'wine-induced headache' and texted Melissa to apologize for being 'outspoken and overbearing'. Melissa assured her that she was not.

Melissa was this beautiful, accomplished lawyer, but at book club she seemed so nice, so interested in Molly's opinions.

Melissa led Jason and Molly into the living room, where they chatted with her husband, Jim, a senior AT&T account executive. Jason appeared drunk to Melissa, who later recalled his eyes being glassy and his colouring being off.

While Jack got himself ready the two couples talked about Jason's afternoon drinking beers in the Fritzsches' driveway. When Tom and Sharon's sudden arrival was mentioned, Melissa joked about in-laws spending the night.

As they returned home, Jack sat behind the driver's seat in Jason's Honda Accord so he could see his father's face in the passenger seat when he told him about *Pixels*, the Adam Sandler movie they had seen in the Palladium in High Point. Also, Jack did not want Molly looking at him when he said the part about the pizza in Mario's, or the ice cream he had from the Cold Stone Creamery afterwards.

Jack was surprised to find Molly's parents at their house. He didn't like them. Unless you were talking about golf or baseball, talking to Tom was like talking to a school principal.

*

It would later emerge that Tom had brought two presents for Jack that evening – a second-hand baseball bat, which had previously belonged to Tom's son Stewart, and a tennis racket – but he didn't give either of them to Jack on the night.

Investigators were immediately suspicious about this detail. They were sceptical that any grandfather would bring a gift for his grandson and not give it to him immediately. They also considered it strange that any grandparent would bring a gift or gifts for their grandson but nothing for their granddaughter.

Detectives needed an explanation from Tom about how that bat, which he brought as a present for Jack, ended up covered in blood in the master bedroom.

At the house, talking to her parents that night, Molly seemed hyper to Jack, listing off in that sing-song voice of hers what Jack was doing in baseball, swimming and school like she was running through a checklist of conversations. 'He's got fifth grade coming up. Science is Jack's favourite subject, but he doesn't care much for math, even though I taught him how to do all his multiplications real quick, quick enough so he could solve fifty problems in under sixty seconds.'

When afterwards Jack tried to think of anything unusual that happened, nothing sprang to mind. Molly had made mojitos, but she was always drinking those. Jason and Molly had some, but Jack could not recall if Tom did. Sharon liked her wine.

Sarah was already upstairs in bed, and his dad wasn't saying much, so Jack said goodnight. His father went into his and Molly's ground-floor bedroom, and Sharon, Tom and Molly went down to the basement.

Usually when they visited, which was not often, maybe two or three times a year, Tom and Sharon would sleep in the guest bedroom on the same floor as the master bedroom.

But this time, on a hot August night, they chose the cooler climes of the basement.

Jack remembered coming downstairs from his bedroom around midnight. He wanted to say a proper goodnight to his father. When he got to the bottom of the stairs he heard Molly, Tom and Sharon talking in the basement.

Jason was sitting up in bed watching a Japanese golf tournament on TV. Jack's dad loved golf. They both did.

Jack remembered seeing a black Nike bag packed in the corner of his dad's bedroom. He worried his dad might be going on another business trip. He didn't like it when his father went away. The atmosphere in the house would change.

He had never seen that Nike bag before. And he would never see it again. It disappeared from the master bedroom before the police arrived.

Jack was certain he had seen it as he said goodnight to his father. It was packed so full the white logo looked distorted. The size of the bag had made Jack worried that his father was going away for a long spell. At the time Jack didn't raise his concerns with his dad.

All he remembered Jason telling him was that he loved him. 'See you in the morning, buddy,' he said.

In the basement, Sarah dozed and then startled awake, trying to piece together the night before.

She remembered Molly giving her tablets to take before bed. Molly said the tablets were to treat a yeast infection. And Molly knew best. After all, Molly was the one who discovered Sarah was lactose-intolerant and needed to eat gluten-free foods. Even the doctors missed that.

Sarah blamed the tablets for the nightmare she subsequently had about her sheets. She had awoken convinced the pink ballerinas on her sheets were live lizards and spiders.

She had gone downstairs to Molly and Jason's bedroom. Dad was asleep, with his back to her, facing the window. She remembered Molly rushing out of bed in a long white T-shirt to bring her back upstairs.

Sarah had a secret code with Sharon. She had practised real hard that week, calling and saying, 'Peacock'. She must have called Sharon's number at least three times a day.

Lieutenant Wanda Thompson was Davidson County's 57-year-old head of criminal investigations. Known for her good humour, she more than held her own in the testosterone-fuelled world of detectives. In one colleague's words, Thompson could, if necessary, 'kick doors down for breakfast'.

When Thompson arrived in Meadowlands, she went straight to the ambulance. 'When I get there, they said, "He's gone." And one of the paramedics said, "I went to tilt his head back to open his airway, and my hand slid into his brain."

'I thought it kind of odd,' said Thompson, 'that they're into a fight, and he's buck naked. Then I went inside to the bedroom, and I was like, holy crap. There were impressions on the wall, down, toward the floor. It looked like somebody's head hit that wall. There's a lamp on the floor. There's the ball bat. A brick.

'There was blood, blood splatters, and I'm like, dang, there's a lot of blood. There was blood on the blankets and the comforter and the bed, and it was on the walls and the blinds, and I was like, holy moly. So just the horrific nature of the scene struck me. This was a hell of a fight.'

Thompson tried to get a sense of momentum. The violence seemed to have started in the bed and finished with a bloody handprint on the bedroom door. Anyone leaving that room would be traumatized, even her own officers.

*

At 6.45 a.m., in Interview Room Number Five in the police station, Thompson began her interview with Molly. Molly was sobbing so hard her shoulders were closing in on her ribs, reducing her voice to an anguished whisper.

Using the present tense, Thompson asked Molly for her husband's name, date of birth and occupation. If Molly wondered whether Jason had survived, she did not seek any clarity on the matter. Thompson assured her that she was not under arrest and she could leave any time she wanted.

Severely agitated, Molly crossed and uncrossed her arms, alternately enveloping herself or hunching forward and back in apparent discomfort. She kept rubbing her neck, wringing her hands and clasping her throat.

Molly said they were fighting. There was a history of domestic violence. Asked how long for, she replied: 'Forever'.

Thompson asked if Molly had ever called the police or gone to the hospital. It was commonplace for domestic violence victims to be reticent, but with Jason dead, there seemed little point in Molly holding back.

She had been to the hospital a 'couple of times'. Pressed for details, Molly said she went to a hospital in Kernersville in spring 2015. She did not tell the doctors there about the domestic abuse. She said she was experiencing headaches and thought she might need an MRI. They refused her one.

During her police interview Molly avoided eye contact, focusing on the floor while she wrung her hands. Thompson had seen similar signs of shame in many domestic violence victims.

Thompson: What were you fighting about tonight?

Molly: My daughter had a nightmare. She thought the fairies [they were actually ballerinas, not fairies] on her sheet were insects and spiders. She woke up, so he was angry that he was woken up.

Thompson: So that's what started it?

Molly: And then a dog barked, and he was angry that the dog barked.

Thompson: What happened?

Molly: I said she'd just had a nightmare. He choked me. Told me to shut up. I screamed.

Thompson elicited more details. Molly said Sarah came downstairs and called her from outside. Molly went upstairs, changed Sarah's bedsheets and returned to Jason.

'He said that Sarah was too old to be coddled. He started choking me and . . . and then I screamed.'

Thompson tried to tie down where exactly Molly was when the violence started, but Molly seemed confused about whether she was lying in bed, sitting up or standing. She then asked why Molly kept grabbing her neck.

Molly: I'm sorry. It hurts.

Thompson: Did the paramedics look at you at the house?

Molly: Yes. My throat hurts.

Thompson: So, you laying on the bed or sitting on the bed or what?

Molly: I don't know if I was laying or sitting. I couldn't breathe any more. I thought I was going to die, so he let go a little bit, and I screamed.

Thompson: Was he lying on the bed?

Molly: No, he was sitting up on the bed.

Thompson: Were you laying down or sitting up?

Molly: I don't remember if I was sitting up or laying down.

Thompson: How was he choking you?

Molly: First, with his hand pressed really hard here [touching her neck]. He does that a lot. And then with his arm around my neck.

Thompson: Was he sitting down or standing?

Molly: Sitting down and standing up. Maybe he was standing up by the end of it. I don't know. Can we stop? Please stop.

Molly buried her head in her hands and cried.

The CSI chief, Frankie Young, arrived to photograph Molly. When Molly removed her fleece top Thompson noted the delicate silver bracelet on her right wrist. Young photographed it, her arms, neck, back and legs, and then, instructed by Thompson, he snapped a yellowing bruise on Molly's right arm.

Asked if Jason had caused this bruise on another night, Molly said yes.

Thompson: Are you feeling a little better now?

Molly: Not really.

Thompson: So you guys were arguing?

Molly: He grabbed my throat and then he put his arm around it when he heard me screaming. Then he let go for a second and I screamed really loud. I can't remember next until my dad came in.

Thompson: When your dad came in what happened?

Molly: He had a baseball bat and he hit Jason or tried hitting him and Jason got the baseball bat and tried to hit my dad and might have missed and I, and I hit him on the head with a brick on my nightstand. A decorative garden thing.

Thompson: You had a brick on your nightstand, what was that for?

Molly: The kids and I were going to paint these bricks and flowers around the mailbox. Sarah brought one in to ask if we could do it and I said we didn't have time and it was still there.

Thompson: So, it was there for a couple of days or a couple of weeks?

Molly: Just a couple of days.

Thompson: So, your dad comes in, Jason and him get into it and what happened then?

Molly: I was screaming 'help' and he was screaming 'I'm going to kill you' or 'I'm going to kill her' and [breaks down].

Thompson: You picked up the brick and you hit him on the head?

Molly: I'm not sure if I hit him on the head or the shoulder.

Thompson: What happened then?

Molly: My dad got the bat. He [Jason] tried to grab me and my dad hit him again.

Thompson: How many times did you hit Jason?

Molly: I don't know. I don't know. I shouldn't have screamed.

Thompson: Why shouldn't you have screamed?

Molly: I don't know.

Thompson: Were you afraid for your safety?

Molly: Yes.

Thompson: Did you need help?

Molly: Yes.

Thompson: Then, why shouldn't you have called for help?

Molly began wailing. Thompson asked if Jason had been drinking. Molly told her about Jason drinking all afternoon. He loved beer. When they lived in Ireland, Jason would binge-drink, she said, staying out on Friday nights after work until the early hours.

Thompson: I know that the Irish people are known for drinking.

Molly: Yes, they are.

Thompson asked Molly again how many times she had hit Jason, and how many times Tom had hit him. Molly said she did not know. Thompson asked her to write a statement about what had happened. Molly asked if she had to, if she could do it later, and if she had to do it in the sheriff's office.

Thompson: Yeah, in sheriff's office is where we do it.

Molly: So the kids are back at the house?

Thompson: They're downstairs with your mom.

Molly: So when we go back is it going to be clean?

Thompson: We try and minimize that for the children. There's going to be quite a bit of blood. Your husband bled a lot. There's quite a bit of blood in the bedroom, and from the bedroom leading out of the house.

Molly: And that's going to be there for the kids?

Thompson: Yes, unfortunately. We can put you in contact with companies that do crime scene clean-ups and that kind of stuff, but there's going to be several days, especially with it being Sunday morning.

The interview had been under way for more than forty-five minutes and Thompson noted that Molly hadn't asked about Jason.

Thompson: You know your husband didn't survive his injuries?

Molly: I didn't think so.

Molly started sobbing about how she was scared of Jason's family, frightened they would try to kill her or take the children. Thompson's heart sank. This was when she discovered that the children were not Molly's.

'I thought we'd made a huge mistake,' she later told me. 'I'd brought the children over to see her [Molly] at the neighbour's house. I'd seen Molly whispering in the children's ears.

She could have just been comforting them, but she also could have been instructing them what to say.

'If we'd known at the scene that Jack and Sarah were not Molly's, and that she hadn't adopted them, then we would have kept them apart. We wouldn't have left the children alone with Sharon. The protocol in these situations is the children should be taken into temporary care while we establish who the next of kin is.'

During the interview, Thompson confirmed Molly's worst fears: 'If you haven't adopted those children, then there's a real possibility the children will be taken back to Ireland.'

Molly became hysterical, her chest heaving as she sobbed uncontrollably. Thompson could see the distress was real. This was a woman who, only twenty-four hours earlier, seemed to have everything: children, a husband, a house, a car and money. Now, she could lose her whole family. Thompson could see that no one would take Jack and Sarah off this woman without a fight.

At 7.55 a.m. Molly signed a short statement:

My husband Jason Corbett was upset that he awoke and an argument ensued with him telling me to 'shut up' (etc) and he applied pressure to my throat/neck and started choking me. At some point I screamed as loud as possible. He covered my mouth and then started choking me again with his arm. My father Tom Martens came in the room and I cannot remember if he said something or just hit Jason to get him off me. Jason grabbed the bat from him and I tried to hit him with a brick (garden decor) I had on my nightstand. I do not remember clearly after that.

Thompson: Okay, Molly, we'll collect all the evidence, take all the witness statements and stuff. Then we'll go to the DA's office and talk with the DA's office about what happened. The DA will make the determination whether any criminal charges are appropriate in this case. At this point, having talked to your dad, and talked to you, it looks like this is going to be self-defence, okay? I don't think there's going to be any issue with that.

Thompson told Molly she was free to leave. One of her colleagues would deliver Molly and her father back to the children.

Readers will likely grapple with trying to understand how Sarah and Jack were left in the care of the people who had just killed their father, especially as Thompson had realized at this point that an error had been made. It has never been officially explained, but sources told me that the detectives did not feel Jack and Sarah were in any physical danger from Tom, Molly or Sharon after they had interviewed Tom and Molly.

From a criminal investigation perspective, it would have been better to isolate the children and interview them, but it was felt that the investigation should take second place in priority to the welfare of the children. They were about to learn that their father was dead, so immediately taking them away to emergency custody could have exacerbated the trauma.

Over the next twenty-four hours the police would learn more worrying details about Molly – from Jason's family. But for now, it was decided it was safe for Jack and Sarah to be left with the Martenses.

Back in the basement, while the police interviews were being conducted, Sharon calmly read her book, *The Ringer*, a novel by Jenny Shank about two families from opposing cultures forced together through a violent death.

Sharon told Jack and Sarah it could be several hours before Tom and Molly returned. She did not mention their father.

It would later emerge that Sharon was informed shortly

after six that morning that Jason was dead, when Detective Nathan Riggs was sent to the basement to take a statement from her.

Riggs recalled: 'She had not been informed about what had occurred upstairs and did not know that Jason was deceased. I explained to her what had occurred and that Jason had not survived. She became emotional and started to cry.'

Sharon decided to wait until Molly's return before informing the children. In the interim, she suggested they pass the time playing solitaire on Sarah's iPad.

Before Tom left the sheriff's office he asked Smith what would happen next. Smith said that would be up to the DA.

'Gotcha,' Tom replied.

When they were back at the house in Meadowlands, Tom turned to Sheriff David Grice and asked him what would happen next.

'I told him the DA would look at it and probably send it to a grand jury. He winced. He thought we'd just accept self-defence and that would be it.'

Sarah remembers Molly and Tom coming to the door of the guest bedroom in the basement. Sarah ran into Molly's arms.

Molly called Jack to her, but he demanded to know where his father was. Tom said there had been an accident. Molly said she and Jason had argued. Jason had choked her, and she hit him, and he fell and hit his head, and, well, he's dead.

Sarah screamed. Jack remembers everyone crying, except Tom. Jack tried to catch his breath and scream, but between the panicked beats the words came out defeated, staccato and strange.

Molly tried to pull Jack into her embrace, but he ran straight for Tom, pounding him with his small fists.

3. Case Histories

Ice-cold showers were good for losing weight, an obsession of Molly's since she was fifteen. But today, after returning to the house from the sheriff's office, she needed warm water to wash her husband's blood from her hair.

Case Histories, the book Molly had been reading in the bath on Friday, was still lying beside the shower door. Molly liked detective stories. She could lounge for hours, letting the bathwater go tepid as she sipped wine and absorbed the adventures of Jackson Brodie, a detective who specialized in investigating infidelity.

After showering, Molly returned to the basement. The children recall Molly and Tom arguing over two things: their passports, and the need to inform Jason's family that he was dead. The police had taken Jason's passport from the bedroom the night before, but the children's passports were missing.

Tom told Molly that she needed to inform Jason's family. Molly said Wanda Thompson had offered to contact the Irish police if necessary, but Tom said no, the last thing they needed was Jason's family finding out on the news.

Molly's older brother, Bobby, arrived at the house. Molly put Jack and Sarah into Bobby's white Toyota Celica sports car. She was staying behind in Meadowlands with Tom and Sharon.

In the car, Sarah was cuddling her stuffed toy dogs, Clover and Snowball. Molly had packed her favourite doll, Annabel, too. Jack was surprised to find among his clothes a framed photograph of his dad and his real mom, Mags – Molly must have retrieved it from the guest bedroom, where she had locked it away in a rage weeks before.

Bobby turned around in the driver's seat and softly said, 'I'm sorry.' Then they took off for Union County. Bobby turned on the radio. Otherwise, the 90-minute journey south passed in silence.

After Jason moved to America to marry Molly in 2011, his twin brother, Wayne, regularly took his annual holidays in Meadowlands. He had spent the weekend before the killing in Washington DC with Jason, Molly, the children and Sharon. They stayed in the $730,000 Virginia home of Sharon's brother, Mike Earnest. Tom bowed out, citing work commitments.

Mike took everyone to see the Pentagon, where he had a security pass through his work as a federal agent with SIGAR – the Special Inspector General for Afghanistan Reconstruction. After the Pentagon, they saw the White House, Ford's Theater – where President Abraham Lincoln was assassinated – and Capitol Hill.

Wayne noticed some tension during lunch in an Irish bar. He overheard Sharon and Mike's wife, Mona, talking with Molly about how things would be so much easier 'if Jason would just sign those papers'. Wayne assumed they meant adoption papers. For four years, Molly had been pleading to adopt the children.*

Jason heard Mona, Molly and Sharon talking about 'those papers' over lunch, but ignored them. Later that evening, in Mike's home, the adoption question was raised again. Jason said it was not an appropriate time or place to discuss *his* children.

* In an interview with *Elle* magazine, published on 24 March 2021, Molly Martens claimed that Jason never followed through on his promise to let Molly adopt the kids as part of the wedding ceremony or afterwards.

Wayne recalled: 'Jason asked me a few days before I left if I could stay for another week. But I couldn't afford it. I wish I had stayed. Maybe things would have been different, but I couldn't have known what was going to happen.'

His last conversation with Jason was while Wayne was waiting for a connecting flight from New York to Shannon in Ireland. Jason knew Wayne had a few hours to kill. 'It was typical Jason,' Wayne recalled later. 'He was worried I'd drink too much and not be allowed on the flight. He was always checking on me like that. Mags [Jason's first wife] was the same. I was born a few minutes before him, but Jason was always protective, like an older brother.'

Though some friends and family members later suggested that Jason was planning to leave Molly and return to Ireland in late August 2015, according to Wayne he never discussed this with him.

'I knew he was planning to come for my father's eightieth birthday. He texted me when I was in JFK. "Wayne, it was really good to see you and I appreciate you coming over. We'll have a pint in August." I replied to that and then he texted at 8.27 p.m. "Cheers bro, stay safe." That was the last word I had from him.'

Six days later, on 2 August, Wayne was in Lahinch, a seaside resort 70 kilometres north-west of Limerick, when he saw he had a missed call from Molly. 'She'd never ring me,' he later observed. 'It was very unusual. I said, there's something wrong here. I think I did try to ring her back, but I couldn't get through. I went home to Limerick.'

In fact Wayne tried to call back three times, but Molly would not answer.

Returning that day from Lahinch to his parents' Limerick council estate house, where he was living, his phone rang again. 'It was ten past six in the evening, Irish time. That was ten hours after they killed Jason. I saw Molly's number and I answered, expecting Jason or Molly, but I got Sharon. It was a short call.'

Sharon's tone was as curt as the call. 'She said, "Jason and Molly had an argument. Molly pushed Jason. Jason fell and hit his head. Jason's dead." I couldn't believe it. I demanded to talk to Jack and Sarah. She said, "No. They're too upset." I asked to speak to Molly and she said "No," and hung up. It was all over in seconds.'

Wayne ran home thinking of how Jason and he would make this race as kids, sprinting to see who could be first in the door. It was a battle for dinner when they were growing up in a family of eight children. Six boys – John, Michael, Stephen, Christopher, Wayne and Jason – and two girls, Marilyn and Tracey, all being fed from the wage of a truck driver with the Shell petroleum company.

Wayne's father, John, was upstairs when Wayne got in. Rita, Wayne's mother and John's wife of fifty-five years, was in the kitchen. Wayne called his father down and told them both the devastating news. Rita remarked afterwards that her husband was never the same again.

That August bank-holiday weekend Jason's sister Tracey was in Saint-Jean-de-Monts in France with her husband, David Lynch, their 14-year-old son Adam, Tracey's niece Kate, and a 12-year-old girl whom Tracey and David had fostered just three months previously.

Tracey was nineteen and David twenty-one when they had their first born, Dean, in 1991. The road ahead would be hard, but they had the full support of their families, and especially of Jason, who at fifteen years of age was first in line with offers to babysit.

By the time Tracey and David's second son, Adam, was born a decade later, Jason was an integral part of the Lynch family, best friends with both David and Tracey, and considered more of an older brother to Dean and Adam than an uncle.

Having been parents at such a young age, neither Tracey nor David had gone to university. They took night classes and progressed, much like Jason, into management positions in their respective careers. David was the manager of the Treaty Steel plant in Limerick, and Tracey was the general manager of Tait House, a social enterprise which provided training, education and childcare services to people from disadvantaged backgrounds.

France that August 2015 was the first trip overseas for the girl Tracey and David were fostering. Tracey watched her join Adam and Kate digging a grave-sized trench on the beach. Adam lay down in it and allowed the two girls to cover him with sand. Tracey's new family unit was forming, with the foster girl a loved addition. They were about to mark the end of their fourth day on holidays with a barbecue when Wayne phoned David.

Wayne told David to step away from Tracey because he had some bad news. Tracey saw David's eyes and caught the tone in his voice. She knew.

The previous night, she had woken from a nightmare in which a baby was crying. The dream was so vivid she had woken David in distress. She had carried a sense of foreboding with her all day.

In fact, Tracey had been worried for several weeks that she had made a mistake in not travelling that summer to see Jason, as she often did. She knew he was considering leaving Molly. She'd left a message on his phone a fortnight previously, telling him to come home.

David walked towards her. 'Tracey, it's Jason.'

Before David could even finish, she began retreating into the mobile home, humming a nursery rhyme her father had taught her to recite in times of stress: 'One, two, three, four, five, once I caught a fish alive . . . six, seven, eight, nine, ten. Then I let it go again.'

David whispered, 'Tracey, listen to me, Jason's dead.'

Tracey screamed. She had never suspected Molly was capable of killing her brother, but after years of lies and fantasies, and strange, inexplicable events, Tracey knew to question whatever story Molly and Sharon were peddling now.

Tracey tried to call Molly but couldn't get through. She eventually reached Sharon, who told her that Jason had been drinking for nearly twenty-four hours before he attacked Molly. In a brisk, cold tone, Sharon said her daughter had defended herself, pushed Jason away, and he fell, striking his head. This was not the first time Jason had attacked Molly, Sharon said. She claimed the police had been called on six previous occasions.

Tracey knew Jason and Molly's marriage was an unhappy one, but the Jason that Sharon was describing was nothing like the brother she knew. Tracey asked to speak to Molly, but Sharon refused to put Molly on the phone. Exasperated and in shock, Tracey asked if Molly had been arrested. Sharon, indignant, questioned how Tracey could dare to ask such a thing. The line went dead.

Tracey packed her bags while David tried to book her on the next available flight to Ireland. She kissed her kids goodbye, not knowing it would be weeks before she would see them again.

It was a 5-hour drive to Paris. While David drove, Tracey made repeated attempts to contact Molly. There was no answer. At 7.50 p.m. – they were six hours ahead in France – Tracey texted Molly: 'Molly, your mam hung up on me. Why don't you ring me or tell me where my brother is and what happened?'

Phone records show Molly had arrived at her brother Bobby's house by the time this text was sent, having travelled there in her own car after she sent Jack and Sarah off with Bobby in his car.

With no response forthcoming to her text, Tracey texted Molly again, two hours later, at 9.53 p.m.: 'Molly, please. How can you be so cruel and not contact me or my family to let us know. What happened to Jason?'

An hour and twenty minutes later, at 11.12 p.m., an exasperated Tracey sent Molly one final text. It read: 'I need you to ring me and explain what happened to my brother. How could you be so cruel not to contact his family? If you do not contact me, I will begin ringing and contacting all his friends and work colleagues. I also want to speak to my niece and nephew.'

Earlier that day, driven by Bobby, Jack and Sarah arrived at Bobby's $600,000 house. Bobby was a federal agent like Tom had been, but he worked for the Inland Revenue Service.

Jack and Sarah were greeted by a cacophony of strangers, some of them speaking Spanish. Bobby's wife, Elynette, was Puerto Rican. Everyone called her Ely. Ely's parents, sister, nieces and nephews had just arrived for a holiday. Some of their suitcases were still dotted around the open-plan living room and kitchen.

Bobby's daughter, Gabby, rushed to greet Sarah. She was seven years old, a year younger than Sarah, and they had always got on well. Gabby took Sarah by the hand and ushered her out through the large, tented backyard patio, past the hot tub and the fixed barbecue grill and cook-out area to a huge swimming pool where Gabby's Puerto Rican cousins were frolicking in the lunchtime sun, oblivious to Jack and Sarah's changed world.

Sarah was shown the bedroom she would share with

Molly. There were no boys of Jack's age. He was brought to Bobby's office and shown the large brown couch where he would sleep. With so many visitors in the house, there was no bed for him.

There was a suitcase on the floor, open, with the lid upright against the end of the couch. Jack remembers peering inside, wondering if somebody else would be sharing the room. He recalled seeing notebooks, manilla folders, USB sticks and computer hard drives.

Jack was told that Molly's younger brothers, Connor and Stewart, would be arriving soon, and the following night he would have to sleep in a small storage room off the kitchen.

He recalled afterwards how in Bobby's house, every time he thought about his dad, his breath seemed to disappear between the rapid, panicked beats of his heart. He didn't want to be on his own in the house, but when he walked into a crowded room he seemed to bring silence with him. People were arguing or whispering everywhere he went, only to go mute on seeing him.

Molly, Tom and Sharon had spent two hours at the crime scene before driving in separate cars to Bobby's house, arriving around 1.30 p.m.

After Sharon's call informing Wayne of Jason's death, there was a flurry of calls to Molly's phone and to Sharon's. Twenty minutes after Wayne was informed, Molly's phone rang and she picked up. It was Catherine Fitzpatrick, Mags's sister.

Catherine later recalled: 'I asked [Molly], where were the kids and were they okay? Molly just said: "He is gone. He is gone" and then, hung up.' Molly's cellphone records show this call lasted one minute and twenty-four seconds.

An hour and twenty minutes later, Molly called Catherine back. When Catherine asked Molly if Jack and Sarah were in the house when everything happened, Molly said they were.

She added that it was not the first time they had witnessed Molly and Jason arguing.

Molly told Catherine she was frightened of Jason's family. She claimed Jack was scared because he had heard Tracey on the phone to Molly, threatening to come and take the children.

'Molly then said she would get someone to ring me the next day to speak to the children. Molly then hung up,' Catherine said.

According to Tracey and Jack's recollections, it was several hours later before Molly finally allowed Tracey to briefly speak to Jack. So, Molly could not have known by the time of her phone call with Catherine Fitzpatrick that Tracey was 'threatening to come and take the children'.

Jack recalls that the phone call with Tracey took place while the children were in Molly's Honda Pilot around 6 p.m. (11 p.m. Irish time). It was still Sunday, the day on which their father had been killed in the early hours. They all went to a Mexican restaurant, which had been booked as a get-together for Ely's vacationing family.

Jack and Sarah both remember being en route to the restaurant when Molly told them about her plans to buy a new apartment and a new car. Jack said later: 'I remember her showing me a green Kia Cube car on her phone. She talked about an apartment, and the school I would go to. I just remember her saying that I can have all of this if I would just tell everyone, anyone who asks, that my dad hit Molly. If I didn't say that, I'd be taken away.'

Molly's phone pinged with a text from Tracey. Molly called her back, sobbing.* Molly said she had hit Jason after he

* Molly appears to have been using somebody else's phone for this call – possibly Sharon's – because it is not recorded in the cellphone records later

tried to strangle her. He fell, and hit his head. When Tracey asked what she hit him with, she refused to answer. Tracey demanded to speak to Jack and Sarah.

Molly passed the phone to Jack, whispering: 'Tell her not to come.'

Jack remembers Tracey telling him how sorry she was, that she loved them and would be there soon. Jack told her there was no need.

'Molly was whispering: "Tell her not to come. Tell her not to come." So, I told Tracey not to come, that we were okay. Then Molly took the phone and hung up.'

All through the meal at the Mexican restaurant Jack kept thinking of a fire that had taken place at Bobby's house on Christmas Eve in 2009, when they were on a visit from Ireland. It was eighteen months before Jason and Molly got married. Jack had just turned five. The fire was one of his earliest memories.

Someone had put a smouldering log into the trash. Sharon was upstairs with her dog, and her grandchild, Gabby, then aged two, was in an upstairs room watching a movie. Sarah, then aged three, was on her way up the stairs to join Gabby when someone shouted about the house being on fire. Sarah ran outside. Jason ran back inside to help get Gabby, Sharon and Sharon's dog.

'We had to spend Christmas Eve in a local hotel,' Sarah recalled. 'All our presents went up in the fire. I remember my dad went out and somehow managed to get presents and a tiny tree that he spray-painted white. When we woke up on

---

produced on foot of a search warrant. Molly's phone records for 2 August 2015, reveal nine calls between Wayne and Molly – seven of them incoming calls from Wayne, of which five are listed as lasting for zero seconds, indicating that they went unanswered. The records don't indicate any connected calls between Molly and Tracey's cellphones.

Christmas morning, the tree was there with tiny baubles on it, and there were presents all around the hotel bed.'

After returning from the Mexican restaurant Jack and Sarah both recall Molly and Sharon sitting with them around the living-room table, Sharon at one end, Jack at the other, like the 10-year-old was now the man of the house. Jack remembers Sarah and Molly were sitting together to Sharon's right.

Sharon gestured for Tom to take a seat opposite Molly, but he was in a surly mood and instead hovered nearby before, according to Jack, walking away as soon as Sharon and Molly began warning the children about their Irish relatives.

Jack and Sarah both say that they were warned that the Lynches were going to try to kidnap them. If they wanted to live in a big house in the sunshine, and keep swimming, horse-riding, playing baseball and all the other nice things they could do in America, then they needed to listen carefully and do exactly what Molly and Sharon said.

Some people were going to come and ask them questions. All they had to do was tell the truth. They loved Mommy, right? You don't want to be taken into care, do you? Then, just tell the truth. Just tell whoever asks that you love Molly and that Daddy hit Mommy. Mommy's all you have now, so you want to stay with Mommy, don't you?

David dropped Tracey outside Charles de Gaulle Airport at 2 a.m. She spent the night in the ghostly airport, searching the internet for contacts. At 4.53 a.m. she sent John Young, Honorary Consul of Ireland for North Carolina, an email with the subject 'Suspicious death – support needed urgently'.

Tracey outlined her grave concerns about Molly's mental health problems, telling Young that Molly was 'bipolar'. Tracey told Young that Molly was not Jack and Sarah's biological mother, and she had not adopted the children. She said Molly's family was not providing any information.

Tracey asked the Irish consul for his assistance in getting Jack and Sarah, and Jason's remains, home to Ireland. She had no idea then that she would spend most of the following decade trying to get answers about how and why her brother was killed.

Tracey's son, Dean, collected her at Dublin Airport and, after a 2-hour car journey, delivered her to her parents' home in Limerick around 1 p.m. on Monday.

The house was packed with Jason's siblings and friends, but there was an extra poignancy to the sight of his mother, Rita, holding hands with Marian Fitzpatrick, Mags's mother.

Brendan O'Callaghan, best man at Jason's wedding to Molly, recalled how frantic everyone was.

'At one point Tracey booked flights [to the US] costing eighteen thousand euros. It was a mistake obviously, but that just shows you how panicked everything was.'

Tracey organized a flight for 9 a.m. the following day. Her sister, Marilyn, and Jason's best friend, Paul Dillon, would accompany her.

Tracey later wrote in her book, *My Brother Jason*, that Rita told Tracey: 'Bring my baby boy home to me.' Tracey went on to write: 'Marian Fitzpatrick told me she and Rita then linked arms. Marian recalled saying: "Bring those two children home safe to us where they belong."'

Brendan, who was Jack's godfather, said everyone was suspicious of the Martenses' story, but especially Paul Dillon, who was Sarah's godfather. Brendan was with Paul when David called to tell them Jason was dead.

'Straight away, Paul said: "She killed him."'

4. Mr Type-A Personality

At 10.23 a.m. on Monday, 3 August 2015, Shelly Lee was assigned case file 37698.

Lee was a social worker in Davidson County's Department of Social Services (DSS). The case file contained a brief homicide report, timing the incident as having started at 2.30 a.m. with Sarah's nightmare. It stated that Molly was informed by law enforcement that she was 'not supposed to give the children any details about what happened'.

Within twenty minutes of being assigned the file, Lee took a phone call from Tracey. Tracey told Lee that Molly was bipolar, on strong medication, and she drank margaritas frequently. Lee asked Tracey about any history of domestic violence. Tracey said she wasn't aware of any.

Lee notes on the file: 'Tracey is worry [*sic*] about the children as Molly has not been responsive to the family's call/text. Tracey was able to speak with Jack for about 30 seconds. She hasn't spoken with Sarah yet. She wants to make sure the children are okay.'

Lee assured Tracey they would meet the children and assess their safety. At this point in time, neither the DSS nor the sheriff's office had an address on file for where the children were, just a phone number for Bobby Martens.

Lee called Molly but got her voicemail. Next, she called Bobby's number. He said Molly was in a meeting. Lee then spoke with John Young. According to Lee's notes, the Irish consul told her that Molly was requesting 'cremation as soon as possible. Mr Young doesn't know what he can do to stop the cremation from occurring but he is working on this.'

It is unclear who informed Young that Molly was trying to get Jason cremated. His body was still at the medical examiner's office. Phone records show Molly had contacted JC Green Funeral Home on Sunday, 2 August, less than twelve hours after the killing, at 1.16 p.m., and had spent seven minutes discussing funeral arrangements.

After talking to JC Green, there were three calls to the sheriff's office from Molly's phone, but it's unclear if these were about releasing the body. Tom would have been acutely aware that an autopsy would have to take place prior to any cremation.

Lee's case notes indicate that there was uncertainty over whether Jason's will – which declared Jason's sister, Tracey, and her husband, David, as Jack and Sarah's legal guardians in the event of Jason's death – would be valid in the United States. During his phone call with Lee, Young asked her if social services could take custody of Jack and Sarah while the issue was resolved.

After the call with Young, Lee spoke with Lt Thompson. The police had not been overly concerned about Molly leaving Davidson County only twenty-four hours earlier. But Tracey's warnings in the interim, about Molly being bipolar, had heightened Thompson's concerns over the children's welfare.

Thompson could not simply dispatch Union County cops to seize the children. First, they would have to establish that the children were in danger. So, Thompson needed Shelly Lee at Davidson County DSS to take the lead and work with Child Protective Services in Union County to get a safety assessment done immediately.

When Lee had first received the file on Jack and Sarah at 10.23 a.m. that Monday morning, she was tasked with delivering an investigative response within seventy-two hours.

Within the space of a few hours, having talked to Tracey, Wanda Thompson and representatives of the Irish government, Lee deemed the case required immediate action.

After speaking with Lt Thompson, Lee asked her boss, Olinithia Tate-Fielding, if DSS should take the children from the Martenses. Tate-Fielding advised that 'the Department will likely not consider filing for custody.' Instead, Lee was instructed to fax Union County social workers for immediate assistance.

Lee did so and outlined how the initial 72-hour response time no longer applied: 'Due to the nature of this report and the concerns that Molly Corbett, stepmother, may leave to Tennessee with the children we ask that you assist us in initiating this case TODAY (08/03/2015).'

Lee called Molly again. Molly explained that she was trying to organize a lot of things, including a priest for Jason's funeral. She had left Jack and Sarah at Bobby's house with Sharon while she made arrangements.

Lee informed Molly that a Union County social worker would be calling to meet her and the children. They were not to leave North Carolina until CPS had completed their investigation. Molly told Lee that law enforcement had not placed any restrictions on her movements, 'other than she needed to be able to respond, upon their request, within an hour'. Nonetheless, she agreed not to leave North Carolina.

Lee and Molly then discussed Jack and Sarah. Lee wrote in her notes, 'The children are doing as well as they can.' Lee's note continued: 'Mrs. Corbett reports that Sarah doesn't understand things as much as Jack does. Currently, Sarah thinks that she's on vacation as she is surrounded by family members at the moment.'

Lee also wrote: 'Molly was emotional stating that Jack and Sarah are her children. She's raised them for about eight years. Molly states that she's the only mother the children know . . . Molly reports that she is not willing to give her children up. She will consult with an attorney.'

Sheila Tyler, a social worker in Union County, was asked to conduct an unannounced visit to Bobby's house.

Tyler arrived there at 5.45 p.m. on Monday but found Molly was out. Tyler called Molly but was told she was two hours away, meaning the social worker would have to return that evening. The element of surprise was lost.

In an interview with me in 2023 Thompson said the police wanted to interview Jack and Sarah immediately on that Monday but could not do so because the children were outside of Davidson County. Bobby's house was in Union County.

Thompson told me she was concerned that she and the sheriff's department had made a major error in allowing the children to be kept in the care of the people who had killed their father. The children should have been put in the temporary custody of the DSS – as was requested that Monday by the Irish consul.

Jason's death was being reported within twelve hours, but the involvement of a former FBI officer in the killing had not leaked yet.

Sheriff David Grice was quoted in media reports stating that a man had died following a 'domestic disturbance' and they were not looking to interview anyone outside the home. Grice added that there were 'persons of interest' within the family.

Tom knew it would only be a matter of time before Corporal Dagenhardt's 'incident/investigation report' was logged and placed on the public record. It was common practice for the crime-beat reporters to access such reports, and they would quickly learn about his 911 call.

Tom was due at work that Tuesday morning at the counter-intelligence unit at Oak Ridge National Laboratory (ORNL). Oak Ridge was one of two sites for the Second World War Manhattan Project – the development of the atomic bomb.*

These days, Oak Ridge was at the forefront of innovations in supercomputing, national security and secret energy sources. It had an annual budget of $2.4 billion and employed 5,700 people, including more than 2,000 scientists and engineers. In addition, more than 3,000 guest researchers used ORNL facilities every year.

A lot of Tom's work in the counterintelligence unit involved security checks on these guest researchers, and security briefings for any ORNL scientists going overseas to work on collaborative licensing arrangements.

As a senior counterintelligence officer (SCIO), Tom was paid approximately $150,000 a year. He would soon face crippling legal bills without this 6-figure salary.

Tom called his employers to allay their concerns. He told them he had acted in self-defence to protect his daughter, like any father would, and he had no case to answer. But he knew there was no room for controversy, even the whiff of it, in his job.

Every SCIO had to submit to a lie-detector test – 'a counterintelligence scope polygraph examination' – before taking up their position, and afterwards, at any time of their employer's choosing. Tom had to sign up for regular drug-testing. He was subject to a background check at a minimum of every five years.

Tom knew his employers would ask him to step aside, for now. There would be an internal investigation, a formal

* The second, better-known site was Los Alamos.

interview and then they would permanently revoke the Q-level security clearance he had held for forty years. Tom's Q clearance had previously allowed him to access 'Top Secret Restricted Data' relating to America's atomic and nuclear energy secrets.

Tom knew instinctively that his distinguished career in counterintelligence was over. His employers immediately suspended him on full pay, pending an internal investigation.

Tom took great satisfaction from counterintelligence work; he once orchestrated an undercover sting to foil a contractor at Oak Ridge who was attempting to sell secrets about enriched uranium (which is used to make nuclear weapons) to foreign spies.

Tom knew he would never enjoy such power again, and that a new reality beckoned for the 65-year-old. He would remain suspended on full pay until 1 December 2015, when, he says, he retired.

To fully understand the impact of this blow to Tom's social and professional status, it is useful to examine the findings of a forensic psychiatrist, Dr George Corvin, hired in 2023 to provide a psychological assessment of Tom.

Dr Corvin concluded that he was a classic type-A personality* who, while not totally devoid of emotions, was

---

* The idea that all humans fall somewhere along the continuum between type-A and type-B personalities was first posited in the 1950s by two American cardiologists, Meyer Friedman and Ray Rosenman. The cardiologists were looking to establish links between certain personality traits, such as anxiety, and heart disease. They were inspired to carry out their study by a porter in their clinic who pointed out that all the chairs in the waiting area were only worn out on the arms and the front edge of the seat. The cardiologists reasoned that this meant most of their patients (all needing cardiology consultations) were anxious people, getting up frequently from their seat, or otherwise sitting impatiently on the edge of their seat. They set out to show that there was a link between certain personality types and a higher incidence of heart

nonetheless emotionally stunted. Type-A personalities are outgoing, ambitious, rigidly organized individuals who are highly status-conscious, impatient, anxious, proactive and concerned with time management. They are often work-aholics and aggressive.

Tom's personality exhibited a lot of type-A traits. Dr Corvin found Tom to be 'meticulously responsible, rules-driven, a man who liked order and organization'. The one type-A trait he possibly lacked, however, was being outgoing, although he could be friendly as required. While Tom was generally polite, he was a naturally taciturn man outside of, and sometimes even within, his own family.

Tom could be sociable, especially with those whom he considered of his class and status. Work colleagues at Oak Ridge, for example, could engage in casual chat with Tom about their families, their weekends, or even esoteric inter-ests such as women's basketball. Some colleagues had been invited to Tom's $525,000 home for dinner parties hosted by the ever-sociable Sharon.

With those Tom considered to be beneath his social status, however, he was less sociable. He would play along, observ-ing social conventions, while reserving judgement. This had been his approach with Jason, and most if not all of Jason's Irish family and friends. In Tom's words, with Jason he 'played nice'. But in the privacy and sanctuary of the counterintelligence unit Tom told some colleagues, including JoAnn Lowry, how he 'hated that son-of-a-bitch son-in-law'.

Tom was unflappable in a crisis, but there was a coldness to this self-control. When two colleagues in the counterintelligence

---

disease in later life. The links to heart disease have since been questioned – not least because Friedman and Rosenman's original study was funded by tobacco companies – but the categorization of people into type-A and type-B person-alities has endured.

unit had an affair, it split opinion among the thirteen counter-intelligence officers, with Tom being openly condemnatory.

Tom later told his criminal defence attorney, David Freedman, about the affair and how it might be exploited to question the credibility of anyone from his unit who spoke to the district attorney's office – the prosecutors in the upcoming case against Tom – in negative terms about him.

Counterintelligence involves second-guessing your enemy's future actions, putting yourself in your enemy's shoes, asking yourself what it is your enemy wants from you and how they might go about getting it.

A good counterintelligence officer formulates a defence to counter his enemy's aims.

Asked by detective Michael Hurd to explain his work at Oak Ridge, Tom replied: 'It's basically spy versus spy.'

Tom told Hurd how much he enjoyed 'pitting his wits' against foreign agents.

Prosecutors at the DA's office would later argue that Tom also enjoyed pitting his wits against the comparatively inex-perienced detectives who interrogated him on the night of the killing. What Tom didn't appreciate was that Hurd and Smith were engaged in counterintelligence tactics of their own – letting Tom believe that he was in control of the interview so that he would keep talking and thereby elabor-ate on details which could later be subjected to independent verification.

Details like the dinner date he cancelled in Tennessee. During their interview with him, Detectives Smith and Hurd had found it suspicious that Tom had undertaken an impromptu 4-hour drive to Meadowlands the day before Jason's killing. Tom had said that he and Sharon had no plans that Saturday and just decided to visit the children before the new school year.

Detectives would later discover that he and Sharon had suddenly cancelled dinner plans with Tom's boss, Selin Warnell, a former CIA station chief, in Tennessee that night. He had also requested Monday off. These were minor discrepancies, but a red flag for detectives.

After informing Warnell on Sunday morning of what he framed as his defensive killing of his son-in-law, Tom next sought out lawyers, should Garry Frank, the DA, decide to press charges.

David Freedman was widely considered the top criminal defence attorney in North Carolina.* He represented all sorts – from cop killers to corrupt politicians. In thirty-three years, he had yet to lose a case. Plenty of his clients went to prison, but usually on a lesser charge. When he represented a man charged with the first-degree murder of a Winston-Salem police officer, no one gave Freedman's client a chance. Yet the killer escaped with a second-degree murder conviction.

Freedman, then aged fifty-nine, was well connected politically. The DA for neighbouring Forsyth County considered him to be his 'blood brother', and the two often lifted weights together at the YMCA on Saturday mornings.

On Monday, 3 August, the day after Jason's killing, Tom walked into Freedman's offices, knowing criminal defence attorneys billed out at between $200 and $400 an hour and that he would likely need four of them. Freedman was at the upper end of the fee scale.

Tom and Molly would eventually generate close to a million dollars in fees, and the law firm of Crumpler, Freedman, Parker & Witt would pay Freedman a tidy bonus for

---

* A graduate of the University of North Carolina law school, Freedman had been named the state's best criminal defence attorney by *Business North Carolina* magazine and was listed for nine straight years by Best Lawyers of America.

its share. In addition to the fees, the case would also generate lucrative nationwide and international publicity. Small wonder that Freedman greeted the former FBI man's travails with open arms.

Molly would need separate representation. Freedman recommended Walter C. Holton.

Holton was something of legal royalty in Winston-Salem. In 1878, his great-aunt, Tabitha Holton, became the first female attorney to be licensed to practise law by the North Carolina Supreme Court. Holton's father, uncle and grandfather had practised law in Winston-Salem. Holton himself was a former assistant district attorney for Forsyth County and a former US attorney for the Middle District of North Carolina. Appointed by President Bill Clinton, he was the chief federal prosecutor for the Middle District for seven years.

A father of four, Holton had testified before both the House and Senate judiciary committees on curbing gun violence. He was a strong advocate for reducing the high incarceration rate among young African Americans through increased investment in education.

It's unlikely Tom Martens would have shared such sympathies for the young, black and incarcerated, but if Molly wanted a lawyer with liberal political credentials and connections, a family lineage spanning 125 years of practising law in the North Carolina courts and Christian community roots as a member of the Home Moravian Church, then Holton was her man. He was an expensive choice, perhaps, but a wise one, given the jeopardy Molly faced.

Freedman and Holton made for a good double act, a legal yin and yang: the conservative, balding Freedman appealing to moneyed and middle-class jurors, while the handsome, homespun and coiffed Holton won over the minorities.

Right from the beginning, Freedman and Holton could see a strong self-defence case for the Martenses, especially for Molly, seeing as Tom was taking the rap in his police interview and on the 911 call. Freedman saw obvious positives in Tom's distinguished career with the FBI. However, Freedman could also see a potential downside to Tom's personality. Tom did not lack in self-righteousness, something easily confused with arrogance, and neither trait would play well with a folksy Davidson County jury.

Molly, on the other hand, was a beautiful, articulate middle-class mother, desperate to keep hold of 'her children' – exactly the type of victim or perpetrator the media loved to obsess over. Holton, sharp as a tack, took an early note on Molly's case: after questioning, the cops drove Tom and Molly straight home. As Holton would later tell a jury: 'In a murder case, they drive you to jail.'

Molly returned to 160 Panther Creek Court some time before 11 a.m. on Monday. She was witnessed by a neighbour who appears to have contacted Tracey.

Tracey left a voicemail with social worker Shelly Lee at 11.12 a.m. to tell her that the children were now back at their Meadowlands home. This was an error – in fact Molly had returned to Panther Creek alone. The children remained in Bobby's house.

While in Panther Creek, Molly called Advanced Bio Treatment, a company specializing in crime-scene clean-ups. The company spent the day scrubbing blood and brain matter from the master bedroom walls. Molly had Jason pay for it – the $5,000 fee came from their joint account, not from Molly's personal account. She had already called her home-insurance providers to see if she could claim the cost back.

In the two weeks after the killing she withdrew $17,500. This was to finance legal counsel on the issue of custody of the children, which was separate to her criminal defence lawyers. In this regard, she was well prepared. She had been planning to make an emergency application for custody for at least eight months prior to Jason's killing.

While Molly concentrated on the custody battle ahead, Tom focused on the criminal case. He knew the DA would be meeting with the detectives soon to discuss their interviews and whatever else they had gleaned from the crime scene and Jason's autopsy.

5. B15-2636

At 10.05 a.m. on Monday, 3 August 2015, pathologist Dr Craig Nelson unzipped the body bag containing Jason Corbett. He created a unique body identification number: B15-2636.

Often in such cases a victim's hands are bagged – sheathed in plastic to preserve any hair, blood or bodily tissue trapped under the nails – but this was not required here. The CSI chief, Frankie Young, had judged at the scene that there was no need to bag the victim's hands.

When the body was removed at the medical examiner's office, the single strand of blonde hair, photographed trapped between Jason's fingers at the crime scene, was missing. Perhaps the hair was washed away by the abundant blood in the body bag.

Years later, in the criminal proceedings that followed, the Martenses' defence lawyers took a more sinister view. To create an ellipsis of reasonable doubt, they seized on this missing hair.

The defence lawyers would argue that the hair photographed between Jason's fingers at the scene was Molly's hair, and that this offered proof that Jason had been choking Molly that night. They would argue that Young had been negligent in not bagging Jason's hands or preserving this hair. They would suggest at trial that the missing hair was just one of a number of pieces of evidence withheld from the jury.

Dr Nelson's report did not provide an explanation for each injury, but prosecutors later considered whether each was likely caused by brick or bat.

The multiple fractures to Jason's nose, for example, were likely caused by a brick. The nose was flattened right to left, by a weapon wide enough to break the nasal bones and cause bruising from above the bridge and over the length of the nose. A bat or brick could have done that. However, a red half-inch scrape mark inside purple bruising on the right side indicates the weapon was likely sharp-edged.

Tom had admitted hitting Jason multiple times with a bat. However, he appeared during his police interview to know nothing about the brick. He was careful never to verbally confirm even seeing it.

When Detective Smith said to Tom during his police interview, 'There's a cement-type block in the bedroom,' Tom opened his arms out like he knew nothing about it. Smith asked: 'Do you know where it came from?'

Tom didn't offer a verbal answer, he merely shook his head. Smith tried again: 'So the only thing you struck him with was the baseball bat?'

Tom replied: 'Yep. This sounds so defensive on my part. He's a big, strong guy, he's got me unmatched. I know he's a martial arts guy, a boxer. I tried to stay a bat's length away from this guy, I'm scared to death.'

Smith asked again: 'But you don't recall anything about the cement block?' Once again, Tom shook his head. The detectives moved on and the subject of the brick was not revisited.

Molly admitted she 'tried' to hit Jason with the brick. The blood, hair and tissue on multiple sides of the brick indicate she succeeded.

Dr Nelson said an instrument with a 'corner or edge' (such as a brick) is more likely to leave a linear laceration, especially where it overlies an area of bone. Linear lacerations were found on Jason's head. Given that Tom never so much as saw the brick, Molly must have struck these blows. Either that, or there was another mystery attacker in the bedroom.

Jason appeared to be defending himself from the brick on one side and the bat on the other: multiple half-inch red scrapes, cuts and bruising were found on his right hand, whereas only bruising was found on the left forearm and hand.

There were large areas of bruising on the left and right legs. On the left upper thigh, irregular-shaped bruising measured 4 by 3 inches. The right thigh was impacted by a jagged edge, leaving a linear red scrape flanked by multiple scrapes which marginally punctuated the skin. Below these, there was bruising on the right knee and shin, and scrapes on the toes. One explanation for these injuries is that the victim was on his back, raising his right foot to defend himself, as a brick was swung down towards his groin.

The fatal blows were all administered to the head. Jason was struck in ten locations on either side of the head at the front, centre and back of the skull. Two of the impact sites had been battered multiple times, so there were at least twelve blows in total. When Dr Nelson pulled back the scalp, pieces of skull bone fell out from the top right-hand side, leaving a large triangular area of exposed brain.

A weapon hit the back of Jason's head with such force it cut through the scalp, penetrating it by at least an inch, then fractured the skull bone, the force radiating outwards, parting the bone like an iceberg breaking, causing a bridging effect.

The cracked skull bone was forced upwards, which in turn caused the already ruptured scalp above and around it to part and jut up and outwards like the points of a star.* The sheer

* Dr Nelson said this wound was a 'coarsely stellate, complex, branched, full-thickness, laceration with partial avulsion. The branches individually range from ½" to 2" in length. There is undermining around the wound up to 1" in

force applied was evident from the body's reaction to it: the scalp points rose by up to 2 inches.

Inside this wound there was a further one-and-a-quarter-inch laceration with exposed brain tissue, indicating that more than one blow (and possibly more than one weapon) struck this exact location at the top of the head on the back right-hand side of the skull.

Given the location, and the ferocity of the blow(s), the probability is that the victim was facing away from the weapon(s) at the point of impact. If not already unconscious, the blow or blows to this location would certainly have knocked the victim out.

On the top left side of the skull there was another huge wound, measuring 6 by 4 inches, the impact so forceful it tore through the hair, skin and tissue, cracking the skull, the bone partially separating like earthquake fault lines. The ferocity of the blow(s) was evident from the ripple effect, which undermined the scalp for 2 inches above and below.

These injuries would also have rendered Jason unconscious. Dr Nelson found that any one of eight impact sites on the skull could have knocked Jason out.

On the left side of the head, above the ear, there was a laceration that again exposed brain tissue. There were other half-inch jagged wounds beside it. The only part of the head to escape haemorrhage was the right front region – another indication that the bulk of the blows were delivered while Jason was facing away from the weapons.

At least one of the twelve blows was delivered when Jason was already dead. 'There's very little bleeding of that injury, suggesting it happened after the heart had stopped,' Dr Nelson said.

---

depth. The edges have abrasion and tissue bridging is evident. Skull fractures are visible in the depths of the wound.'

Dr Nelson's 4-word cause of death – extreme blunt-force trauma – scarcely did justice to the detail of the suffering.

At 12.52 p.m. that Monday, Dr Nelson handed Det. Sgt Tony Yon three evidence bags containing hair, a blood card for DNA analysis and Jason's silver wedding ring.

The body was then prepared for release to Jason's next of kin, Molly Martens.

Jason had ensured that Jack and Sarah still saw Mags's family regularly, even when they moved to the US. On his last trip home in December 2014, Jason had told Mags's mother, Marian, that Jack and Sarah would go to secondary school in Ireland.

'He wouldn't let Molly adopt Mags's children,' Marian said later. 'I was glad about that.'

Sarah remembers being called out of the swimming pool at Bobby's on Monday, 3 August to talk to her aunt Catherine on the phone. She and Jack had been left in Sharon's care at Bobby's house while Tom and Molly were out from early Monday morning until 8 p.m.

Catherine had called Molly the previous day, as soon as she heard Jason was dead. Molly had hung up, then called back, promising she could speak to the children the next day. When no one called, Catherine rang Sharon, who claimed she couldn't make international calls.

Sharon told Catherine that Sarah had greeted Jason's death by saying: 'He can't hurt you any more, Mommy.'

As Sharon put Sarah on the phone, Catherine overheard her warning the child: 'You are not touching my phone with wet hands, missy.' Catherine spoke briefly to both children.

Sarah remembers playing hide-and-seek with Gabby on the evening of that Monday. Sarah hid inside a wardrobe in the bedroom she was sharing with Molly. Sharon and Molly entered. Sarah couldn't hear exactly what they were saying, but Sharon repeated questions and Molly answered.

As we know, when social worker Sheila Tyler had attempted an impromptu visit to Bobby's house several hours previously, she had been turned away because Molly wasn't there. Tyler was under specific instructions to interview Molly as part of her safety assessment.

When Tyler returned after 8 p.m. she found Molly present with a lawyer, Kelley Gondring. Gondring said Molly would not discuss the events of 2 August as a criminal investigation was pending.

Tyler moved the children out of earshot from Molly, before interviewing each individually.

At Bobby's house, Tyler was told by the Martenses and by the children, in disturbing detail, what life was really like for Molly, Jack and Sarah. Far from being the innocent victim of a mentally disturbed woman, Jason Corbett was, according to his own children, a violent, jealous man.

Sarah accused her father of taking Molly into their bedroom and hurting her. Asked how she knew this, Sarah said Molly had told her. Sarah then said she saw Jason hit Molly and pull her hair.

'They were getting in the car and her mom and dad were in the hall before the door to go to the garage,' Tyler reported. 'She saw her dad smack her mom. Her mom fell, got up and then went to the car.'

Sarah told Tyler that Jason would scream and yell. The most recent argument was after a neighbourhood party two days before the killing, when her dad got drunk.

Sarah told Tyler that her aunt [Tracey] was coming to take her and Jack away but she wanted to stay with Molly.

Jack told Tyler his parents fought 'physically and verbally'. He had once tried to separate them but was accidentally pushed down about three steps in the garage. Jason would get mad when Molly didn't pay bills on time or if lights were left on. Jack said he saw his dad hit his mom a few times 'with his fist anywhere on her body that he can'.

Tyler asked Jack if he could summon a miracle, what would it be? 'Jack stated for his parents to stop fighting and for his dad to be alive,' Tyler recorded.

The children said Molly could only buy two fruits. When Jason saw an orange, apple and bananas he threw the orange and smashed it, then 'went after Molly'.

After speaking with the children, Tyler interviewed Molly, asking her questions from the Non-Offending Parent Domestic Violence Assessment Tool.

The abuse began in America, Molly said, after Jason reneged on promises to allow her to adopt the children. He often grabbed their passports and threatened to leave.

Jason would monitor her phone, spending and clothes. He was so jealous the children learned to lie that Molly wore long tights at the pool. He would drink three times a week. He would place his hand over her mouth and nose during forced sex. She would lose consciousness. Each time, it got worse.

Molly had not made this allegation to Thompson during her police interview. She didn't say anything to Tyler about Jason slapping her across the face or punching her with a closed fist – allegations which Jack and Sarah had made moments earlier, out of Molly's earshot.

In Tyler's DSS case notes, Molly was presented as 'the non-offending parent', while Jason was described as the 'perpetrator'. These assumptions seemed to influence the questions that Tyler asked Molly. For example, Molly was asked about Jason's drinking, but not her own. The DSS case notes contain Tracey's allegations that Molly was on 'heavy medications' for her bipolar disorder, however, Tyler never asked her about this.

It was not Tyler's role to cross-examine Molly. However, the social worker's primary purpose was to establish the safety of Jack and Sarah – an issue of concern to detectives and the DSS. Tracey's allegations about Molly's mental health and alleged substance abuse were surely germane to any such determination.*

The DSS had specifically asked Tyler to interview Tom and Sharon. Tom's absence and failure to interview were not noted in Tyler's report.

Sharon told Tyler that she learned of the physical abuse from the children, but Molly had denied it. Sharon said she had seen the family four times in the past month because Jason would not be violent in her presence.

Tyler interviewed Bobby, even though he was not listed for interview.† Bobby said he had not witnessed any abuse but had heard yelling and screaming at an event at his home. He said it started because Molly was in the hot tub. She was wearing long tights with shorts and a long shirt.

According to Tyler's notes, Bobby said: 'There were kids in the pool; young people, but a few of them. Jason had been drinking and got really upset because Molly was in the hot tub.'

Jason threatened to get the passports and take the kids.

---

* The trial court observed in finding of fact #16: The Union County DSS interviews were conducted 'in regard to alleged alcohol and/or substance abuse by the defendant Molly Corbett and concern about physical abuse of Jack Corbett'.

† The social worker misspelled the surname, Martens, every time, giving three different variations – Robert Martinens, Elynette Martines and Natalia Martins. Having misspelled Jason's name throughout her report, and having at one point called Jack Kevin, it raises questions about the haste in which the report was compiled.

He left the house, and Bobby and his brother went behind him to make sure he did not drive. Bobby said Jason sat in the driveway for a while, then left. He came back later and apologized to everyone for his behaviour.

After Tyler left, Molly took Jack and Sarah out for ice cream. Sarah began to cry. 'Molly told me coldly "your father is dead," Sarah recounted later. "You need to get over it. Life goes on."'

Jack rose early on the morning of Tuesday, 4 August. He recalled seeing a sheet of paper on the kitchen counter with the heading 'David and Tracey Lynch'. Beneath the Lynches' names was a list of accusations: alcoholics, IRA, involved in crime, undesirables in their house.

Alongside the sheet of paper on the kitchen counter, Jack recalled that he saw what he called 'police evidence bags' containing electronic equipment.

Sharon's brother Mike Earnest left Bobby's house that Tuesday morning and travelled with Molly to Jason's office in Lexington, 75 miles away, arriving at the Multi Packaging Solutions (MPS) plant before 9.30 a.m.

After transferring in 2011 to manage MPS's plant in Lexington, Jason proved charismatic, with a flair for team-building and sales. Molly was less popular. Jason's secretary witnessed Molly verbally abuse Jason several times. When Molly attended a company Christmas party dressed in a white ballgown, many staff saw this as typical of her self-aggrandizing behaviour.

Prior to arriving at MPS, Mike called Melanie Crook, the company's regional director of human resources. Melanie recalls that Mike identified himself as a federal agent who was en route to secure Jason's belongings.

Mike denied citing his occupation or conducting an 'illegal

search' of Jason's office. He refused my multiple interview requests, claiming Irish journalists were biased. He used his refusal emails to list allegations against the Lynches, and countered various allegations reported by the Irish media with his side of the story. However, he then told me I was not authorized to use any of these comments.

The one comment Mike would allow was in relation to this allegation that he had misrepresented himself as a federal agent. He told me that in December 2015 he was interrogated by two of his colleagues at SIGAR, on foot of an anonymous complaint.

'The conclusion of the internal investigation,' Mike told me, 'which cost US taxpayers roughly $15,000, was that it was a completely false allegation. I subsequently learned that the anonymous call into the SIGAR hotline came from Ireland.'

When Mike and Molly turned up at MPS, Jason's colleague Melanie Crook recalled Mike being very insistent that he and Molly be allowed entry to Jason's office. Crook called Lt Wanda Thompson to ask if federal agents were investigating Jason's death. Thompson assured her no federal agents were involved and MPS could refuse entry.

'She [Melanie Crook] called me back a few minutes later,' Thompson said afterwards in an interview. 'She said, "They're wanting to come in and search for the children's passports." I said, "They absolutely don't get the passports."' (Thompson believes Molly wanted the passports to stop Tracey taking the children to Ireland.)

Thompson recollected her conversation with Melanie Crook and MPS: 'I said, "Are those kids' passports on your property?" And they said, "I don't know, but Jason has a lockbox in his office. And he's had them here before." I said, "You don't have to release them." She said, "The problem is she [Molly] is his next of kin."'

Molly and Mike were given a box of Jason's possessions.

At MPS, Mike and Molly may also have been seeking information about Jason's life insurance policies as well as looking for the children's passports.

The previous day, less than forty-eight hours after the killing, Mike had called First Unum Life Insurance enquiring about drawing down Jason's policy, which was administered by his employers. Tracey told Thompson that Molly stood to gain $600,000 and the policy had recently been changed online to remove Jack and Sarah as beneficiaries. Thompson now had a strong financial motive for Molly to kill Jason.

After leaving MPS, Molly consulted with her lawyers, then visited a notary public in Forsyth County to initiate guardianship proceedings. Letters were sent to Jason's parents and Mags's parents informing them that Molly had applied for guardianship. Molly also filed petitions for step-parent adoption.

Later, both Mags's parents and Jason's parents observed how they were in complete agreement about never allowing Molly to adopt the children. Marian Fitzpatrick, Mags's mother, later recalled: 'She [Molly] sent these papers. Then, she kept ringing our house as well. And Mike Earnest kept ringing. But we would never have agreed to it.'

Next on that Tuesday, 4 August, Molly telephoned the DSS offices to inform them of the guardianship application. She expected the DSS to immediately grant her full custody. Social worker Shelly Lee asked her to grant Jason's family access to the children. Molly refused. She claimed police had warned her not to speak to the Lynches.

Lee's notes state that: 'Molly was emotional and doesn't understand why anyone would think that removing the children from her care is in the children's best interest.'

*

While Molly was calling the DSS, Tracey, her older sister Marilyn, and Jason's best friend of thirty-three years, Paul Dillon, were en route to North Carolina.

As we know, upon learning of Jason's death, Paul immediately suspected Molly. 'I never trusted her,' he later recalled. 'She never liked me and didn't like Jason being friends with me. I last saw him [Jason] at Christmas 2014. From January 2015 to July 2015, every time I spoke with Jason he expressed his desire to move back to Ireland. He also said Molly was "still crazy".'

Embarking on her US journey, Tracey had barely slept in the previous forty-eight hours. Between being the focal point of her own family and dealing with the Martenses, the US police, social services, the Irish foreign office, US-based consular staff and the media, she was exhausted.

It was 5.30 p.m. on Tuesday, 4 August, when Tracey, Marilyn and Paul landed in North Carolina. Honorary consul John Young met them with bad news. Jack and Sarah would be left in the care of their father's killers.

Back on the other side of the Atlantic, Tracey's husband, David Lynch, was also running on empty. After a 10-hour round trip to Charles de Gaulle Airport in Paris, he had a 17-hour ferry journey to Ireland with the kids.

David was tasked with getting Jason's will. It had been changed in April 2007, six months after Mags died, to make David and Tracey guardians should Jason die before the children's eighteenth birthdays.

Next, David arranged an emergency bank loan. Securing guardianship would go on to incur 6-figure legal fees.

Thompson's case notes record Jason's family's alarm when they called the sheriff's office seeking information. As yet, they knew very little about what had actually happened. The phone call informing Wayne of his twin's passing had lasted fifty-three seconds.

Jason's older brother, Michael, told Thompson the Martenses were not answering any calls at the time. They believed Molly intended to cremate Jason. Thompson said she could only provide further details in person.

It was only when Michael, Tracey, Marilyn and Paul Dillon met Thompson at the sheriff's office on the evening of Tuesday, 4 August, that they learned the full horror of what had happened. Jason had not died from a fall, as Sharon and Molly had both claimed. In fact, he was beaten to death.

Until they heard the recording of the 911 call Jason's family had no idea about Tom's involvement, the baseball bat, or that Sharon had been there, too. Then, they were told about the bloodied brick.

Thompson told the family that the medical examiner had released Jason's body to Molly, as she was Jason's next of kin. Jetlagged and grieving, Jason's siblings and friend began calling the medical examiner's office and funeral homes trying to locate Jason. Then, they went to Jason's home.

By now, the Meadowlands community was rife with speculation. Detective 'door knocks' had already revealed a divide – some neighbours had heard domestic violence allegations; others cited Molly's reputation for lying.

A neighbour spotted the Lynches at Meadowlands and texted Molly. Call logs show that defence attorney Jones Byrd contacted the sheriff's office at 10.19 p.m. that Tuesday asking for a patrol car to respond because Jason's family were 'camping out' demanding to see Jack and Sarah.

'She [Molly] is scared they will do something to her home,' is what Byrd told the sheriff's office.

Before they could even approach the front door of 160

Panther Creek Court, Tracey's phone rang. It was the sheriff's office telling her to leave immediately.

Her brother wasn't yet dead seventy-two hours, but now Tracey was cast into extraordinary circumstances. She faced three immediate challenges: find Jason's body, clear his name, and, somehow, bring his children home.

6. Seeing Wood for the Trees

A nurse at the medical facility where Jason's remains were first brought tipped off his family that Molly had changed funeral homes. Jason's sisters rushed to Cumby Family Funeral Services in High Point and sought access to his body. Cumby's, however, said that to release Jason's remains, they needed Molly's permission as the next of kin.

Marilyn phoned Sharon repeatedly. Sharon answered just once – to tell Marilyn that her lawyers advised her not to speak to Jason's family. Then, she hung up.

Marilyn, who was ten years older than Jason, wondered what they were hiding. She later observed, 'Why wouldn't you let the immediate family see the body, or see two children who just lost their dad? It was so telling.'

The Irish consul, John Young, advised Tracey to engage separate legal counsel to fight the guardianship case, the adoption application and – as was now evident from Sharon's blunt instructions – to negotiate access to Jason's remains.

On the morning of Tuesday, 4 August, the Martenses opened a new legal front. Molly sought an emergency interim order for custody. After being granted emergency custody, she arrived with her uncle Mike at the DSS offices and claimed that Tracey was coming to kidnap the children.

Social worker Shelly Lee's case notes record Molly making allegations about Tracey and David being in, or associated with, the Irish Republican Army (IRA) – a terrorist organization. Several of Tracey's brothers were also in the IRA, Molly claimed.

Also at this time, Molly made the first recorded allegation to the DSS that she had suspicions around the death of Jason's first wife.

Lee's case notes state: 'Jason told her that the mother [Mags] passed away after an asthma attack but Molly read the autopsy report. It stated that they couldn't determine the cause of death. Since the biological mother had asthma they stated that this may be a cause, however, Molly stated that the biological mother haven't [sic] had an asthma attack in years.'

Molly had been unable in her police interview to remember a single instance of physical abuse by Jason. Nor could she definitively date a single hospital visit she had made seeking help for domestic violence. Yet, in the space of seventy-two hours she had sought and gained emergency custody of the children, alleged to social workers in two counties that Jason asphyxiated her regularly during forced sex and planted the suspicion among social workers that Jason had killed his first wife.

Before leaving the DSS offices, Molly was warned to 'stay close to her phone' in case the Dragonfly House Children's Advocacy Center, which specialized in identifying and counselling suspected victims of child abuse, had any additional questions ahead of the children's medical evaluation, which was scheduled for the next day.

Next Molly travelled to High Point, where she purchased a new cellphone from AT&T. Then she went to Bank of America and transferred $15,000 from the savings account in her name to a checking account jointly held with Jason.

When Wanda Thompson and Detectives Smith and Hurd met that week with the district attorney Garry Frank and his assistant DAs Greg Brown and Alan Martin for their first case conference there were four options to consider:

first- or second-degree murder, and/or voluntary or involuntary manslaughter.

There were suggestions that Tom's FBI career might frighten off Frank. However, the DA had a track record of taking on big, powerful figures. He had even brought felony charges against one of the most powerful, maverick and corrupt individuals in Davidson County – his own sheriff, Gerald Hege.

By the time of Jason's death Frank was into his fifth term, seventeen years as DA. However, there were rumblings about his recent record. Five years earlier, in 2010, Frank had prosecuted a wealthy dentist, Dr Kirk Turner, who slashed his wife's throat twice with a 4-inch pocketknife. The wounds were so deep she was semi-decapitated. It was supposed to be a slam-dunk case. But the dentist argued that his wife had stabbed him first, with a 7-foot spear, and that he'd acted in self-defence. His argument was successful and he walked.

The case led to a 6-figure pay-out for the dentist amid allegations that the North Carolina State Bureau of Investigations (SBI) officers had framed him. The crime lab run by SBI was subsequently shut down and replaced by a new entity, the North Carolina State Crime Laboratory.

The Kirk Turner case remained Frank's most spectacular defeat. So, when he met with his assistants and the detectives to first discuss the Jason Corbett killing, the Turner experience underscored Frank's innately cautious approach as a prosecutor.

On initial inspection, the Martenses' self-defence case appeared strong. The truth was, Tom's career was an ace card for the defence. FBI agents and law enforcement were given more credence by juries. Convicting a former FBI man who intervened to save his daughter being strangled by a foreign national would not be easy. It certainly was not a slam dunk.

Frank was initially unconvinced by the merits of murder

charges, either in the first or second degree. Proving premeditation for first-degree murder would be extremely difficult. What would the motive have been?

Detectives outlined how Molly stood to gain close to a million dollars – from a life insurance policy reported by Jason's family to be worth $600,000, and by taking ownership of a mortgage-free house worth $350,000.

The prosecutors were sceptical. Alan Martin had dealt with hundreds of violent crime scenes. He pointed out that the weapons used were not items you would expect to find in a bedroom, to just reach out and grab in a crime of passion. Tom brought the baseball bat, but why was the brick there? That could indicate some advance planning, but would a bat and brick really be weapons of choice in a premeditated murder?

Initially at least, Martin was leaning towards second-degree murder, which didn't require premeditation, just proof of malice. He asked what evidence there was of malice.

Detectives pointed out the shorn clumps of hair and scalp found in the hallway linking the bedroom to the bathroom. The final blows were struck in the bedroom, at the south wall immediately right of the entrance to the bathroom hallway. There was a round, red splash like someone had coated a soccer ball in paint and kicked it at the wall. To the right of this, there was an obvious descending pattern of blows.

The excessive violence, coupled with the provisional findings of the medical examiner, certainly pointed to overkill, which indicated malice. Detectives Smith and Hurd both felt that Tom and Molly's story did not match the crime scene.

Frank's most senior assistant DA, Greg Brown, said a blood-spatter expert would be required to properly interpret the scene. The DA's office would then weigh the expert's conclusions against two narratives – the story Tom and

Molly had told detectives, and the story being told by the crime scene and Jason's remains.

Thompson recalls there being significant scepticism in the room about motive. Each of the prosecutors doubted that Molly was motivated by the prospect of cashing in a $600,000 life insurance policy. Molly wouldn't get a cent if she was criminally responsible for Jason's death. The 'slayer' law prevented murderers from inheriting their victims' estates.

Detectives were asked to keep an open mind and examine what other motives she might have had. Thompson told the prosecutors that she suspected the children were Molly's motivation. According to Thompson's hypothesis, Jason wouldn't let Molly adopt Jack and Sarah. She learned he was leaving her and taking Jack and Sarah back to Ireland. She wanted the children, the house, the money, the lifestyle – everything but Jason. But she hadn't planned things very well, and now she was going to lose those kids. Maybe she only intended to provoke a confrontation while having Tom, a retired FBI agent, at the scene. Maybe her plan was to take Jack and Sarah back to Knoxville and apply for emergency custody, with the former Knoxville FBI supervisor as her star witness.

Thompson recalls her detectives pushing hard for a murder charge at that initial case conference. 'Michael and Brandon said this was clear overkill,' Thompson said. 'The injuries Jason sustained were so severe, the malice was clear. The autopsy had found at least twelve points of impact. So, I remember, I think it was Michael, saying something like "If you pull a gun on me and I shoot you once, that's self-defence, but if I go over and shoot you twelve times in the head, that's murder."'

When the prosecutors listened intently to the 911 call during their conference with Thompson and the detectives, like them, they suspected the Martenses were faking CPR.

Assistant DA Martin had heard hundreds of 911 calls. Tom was too calm, precise and articulate. He wasn't out of breath, and didn't sound terrified, panicked, confused or traumatized. Instead of frantically asking for help, he set out his defence first: how his son-in-law got in a fight with his daughter, and he intervened. He went on to outline how Jason had been drinking.

When Karen Capps, the 911 operator, asked him to roll Jason on his back, he seemed annoyed.

TM: He's a big heavy man, I can't do it.
KC: Is there anyone there that can help you?
TM: My daughter, and she's in terrible shape.
KC: Someone needs to get him on his back. We need to verify he's breathing.
TM: [sounding exasperated] I'm trying, lady . . . hang on.

He's told to put the phone on speaker, and Molly is heard in the background shrieking: 'I think he's still alive.' The line goes quiet for another few seconds.

TM: Okay, I've got him rolled over.
KC: All right. I want you to put one hand under his back, the other hand on his forehead and tilt his head back. Put your ear next to his mouth and tell me if you can hear or feel any breathing.

Thompson reminded the attorneys that one paramedic's fingers had slipped inside Jason's skull. If Tom had really been tilting Jason's head back, he'd be covered in blood. Yet he and Molly had very little blood on them.

On the tape of the 911 call, Tom says he used a baseball bat to hit Jason. Then, he offers more defence: 'He was choking my daughter. He [Jason] said: "I'm going to kill her."'

At the meeting with the district attorneys Thompson noted that it was two minutes into the phone call before Tom and Molly started CPR. Both of them were trained in CPR, but neither attempted it until told to do so by the operator.

KC: Place the heel of your hand on the breastbone on the center of his chest right between the nipple [*sic*].

TM: I'm somewhat familiar with this.

KC: I have to give the instructions. Just go ahead and do it if you know what to do.

Tom hands the phone to Molly. She sounds hysterical. The operator tells her to stay calm because after 200 compressions she's going to have to take over. Tom and Molly alternate CPR without either of them sounding out of breath.

It was their lack of breathlessness that made the operator, Capps, feel that Molly and Tom were faking CPR. She gave the detectives her opinion. Even seasoned EMS workers found CPR exhausting.

TM: I'm not seeing any signs of life here.

KC: We're just keeping the blood circulating, keeping the oxygen in there until we can get some air up there.

Molly Martens: 1, 2, 3, 4 . . . 1, 2, 3, 4 . . . 1, 2, 3, 4.

KC: All right, she's slowing down, you feel like taking over for her?

TM: I'll try.

The paramedics who were first on the scene noted Molly doing 'ineffective compressions'. When detectives canvassed EMS workers who had performed CPR multiple times, the response was universal – Tom and Molly were faking. CPR was physically exhausting and you couldn't count out loud like Tom with that precision, rhythm and monotone while you were doing deep chest compressions on someone twice your weight.

Aside from Tom and Molly, there was one other person of interest to the detectives and the district attorneys.

Martin found it highly suspicious that Sharon was downstairs listening to this explosive event involving people she loved, yet she didn't respond in any way. She didn't go upstairs to her husband, daughter and grandchildren. She didn't call 911. If her statement to Detective Nathan Riggs was to be believed, what Sharon did instead was wake up briefly, then go back to sleep.

It was already evident to DA Garry Frank at that first meeting with Thompson and the detectives that this would be a long, expensive case, regardless of whether they went down the murder or manslaughter route.

The detectives would have to invest significant time and resources into establishing not just what happened on the night but what happened in Jason and Molly's marriage leading up to the events of 2 August 2015. Assistant DA Alan Martin wanted the backstories of everyone involved.

Detectives were instructed to dissect Jason and Molly's marriage, their finances, emails and cellphone activity. Was Jason planning to take the children home to Ireland? Was Jason a wife beater? Had Molly been to hospital with any injuries? Had she reported the abuse to anyone?

The police canvass of Meadowlands was throwing up a mixed picture – neighbours who heard rumours; others who heard about abuse directly from Molly. But there was no one, as yet, who actually saw Jason being physically violent towards Molly.

An investigative social worker, specially trained in how

to interview children who were suspected victims of child abuse, was scheduled to interview Jack and Sarah at Dragonfly House on Thursday, 6 August, four days after the killing. What the children had to say there would be of vital interest. Would they explain how that brick got in the bedroom? Were they planning to paint it, like Molly claimed?

Sharon had told Detective Nathan Riggs about the codewords which the children were to use in the event of an emergency. The detectives were told to instruct the investigative social worker at Dragonfly House to ask the children for more detail about these codewords.

Frank asked detectives to talk to Tom's neighbours, friends and associates. Tom was immersed in the highly secretive world of counterintelligence. Penetrating this world of spies would be difficult.

By the end of that first case conference between Thompson, her detectives Smith and Hurd, and the DAs Frank, Brown and Martin, all four prosecution options – first- or second-degree murder, and/or voluntary or involuntary manslaughter – still remained on the table.

Molly's successful application for emergency custody effectively ended the DSS's capacity to investigate the welfare of the children.

Chris Watford, Attorney for Child Protective Services, later admitted that the DSS disagreed with the manner in which Union County Social Services had dealt with the matter.* The DSS was now, like the Lynches, powerless to intervene.

* 'The investigation for the Davidson County Department of Social Services was effectively ceased when the stepmother sought and achieved an ex parte custody order from the Honorable April Wood,' Watford said at the guardianship hearing, on 14 August 2015.

Molly was also out of contact for approximately twenty-four hours, as she had changed her phone. The DSS case notes indicate that they did not get Molly's new number until Thursday, 6 August, and when they called, it went unanswered. DSS were unable to leave a message as the voicemail had not been set up.

Jack and Sarah would be kept in the care of Molly, Tom and Sharon for the next nine days, until a full guardianship hearing on 14 August. In the meantime, if the Lynches sought to approach the children without consent, they faced arrest.

7. Dragonfly House

On Thursday, 6 August, Molly dressed 8-year-old Sarah in a short-sleeved, white-collared purple dress with intricate multicoloured paisley patterns. She brushed Sarah's shoulder-length blonde hair until it was perfectly straight, then tied it up in a high ponytail, leaving Sarah's neck exposed, in the style Molly herself most frequently deployed.

Ten-year-old Jack dressed himself in a green, navy and white check-pattern shirt with button-down collars. He found the best trousers Molly had packed and put them on. He patted his hair forward, parting it down the middle and palming it down the sides. His fringe came down a half-inch from his dark-rimmed glasses.

The children were getting ready to attend a memorial service for their father.

Also that morning, at 8.45 a.m., Molly texted Marian and Catherine Fitzpatrick, the mother and sister of Jason's first wife, Mags. Molly now sought their support, despite having hung up on Catherine only days before.

'Marian and Catherine, I just wanted to let you know that the kids are doing okay. We have a memorial today and they are going to see a counsellor. I don't know what you are thinking about me with so much slander out there, but I realize I have no control. If the Corbetts have for whatever reason led you to believe that I am keeping them from Jason, I assure you this is not true.

'He had to undergo an autopsy and after finally making it to the funeral home he has not yet been released for viewing.

I am trying to get whatever signed possible for his family to see him and take him back to Ireland.'

Molly's text continued: 'In regards to speaking with them [Jason's family], I cannot do it because of the threats they have made. I implore you to consider the kids. They have lost one mother and now they have lost their father. Please do not aid in taking them from the mother that has nurtured and raised them for the last seven and a half years. Would you truly think that is best for them?'

Jack, Sarah, Molly and Sharon drove 104 miles to a church in High Point. Molly warned that Tracey might try to kidnap them, so Sarah had to hold Molly's hand, while Jack watched out for black SUVs.

On arriving, the children were briskly escorted into the church, past a sentry of security officers. Tracey believed these were off-duty police hired by the Martenses from a neighbouring county to stop the Lynches from entering. Some, however, were High Point police, deployed at Wanda Thompson's request. Molly and Tom had claimed that two of Jason's brothers were IRA terrorists on the no-fly list – a register maintained by the US government of suspected terrorists who are banned from boarding flights to the US. The sheriff's office couldn't verify that, but because of Tom's FBI background and security clearance, the claims could not be ignored.

'I tried to tell Molly, if they're on a terrorist watch list, they can't fly here,' Thompson recalled later. 'She was like, "You don't understand, this family's going to kill me." A lot of the stuff that they gave us just didn't add up.'

At the service in High Point, a Catholic priest blessed an empty coffin. Despite Molly's text to the Fitzpatricks that morning insisting that she was not preventing Jason's family from seeing his body, her lawyers were still negotiating over the release of Jason's remains. While these negotiations continued, Jason's body remained at the funeral home.

Agreement was reached later that day: the Lynches could take Jason's body if they paid the repatriation and burial fees. Tracey agreed, but management at Cumby's warned it would still take twenty-four hours to prepare the body for viewing.

After the 'memorial service', Jack and Sarah were brought to a Chick-fil-A drive-in en route to Dragonfly House in Mocksville. Four days after their father's death, detectives would finally hear the children speak about life with Molly and Jason in Meadowlands.

A forensic interviewer, trained to elicit information from suspected child abuse victims, was due to question Jack and Sarah separately. After that they would each have a full-body medical examination.

Sharon drove. Jack and Sarah recall her talking to them via the rear-view mirror, issuing instructions. They just had to repeat what they had said to the black lady [social worker Sheila Tyler].

Molly warned Jack and Sarah there were people coming to take them away if they didn't follow their instructions. 'If you don't say Daddy hit Mommy, then they'll take you away, Jack, and you'll never see me again. You'll have no one in this whole world, Jack.'

Sarah remembers Molly writing prompt words on the palm of her left hand as they sat in the Chick-fil-A. Jack argued with Molly over Tracey and David. It wasn't right what Molly and Sharon were saying about them. Their son, Adam, was Jack's favourite cousin.

Heydy Day, the child advocate for Dragonfly House, explained that the children would first talk to her colleague, executive director of Dragonfly House, Brandi Reagan. Reagan was a certified trauma and resilience practitioner, specially trained to conduct investigative interviews with children who were suspected victims of child abuse, or who were suspected of having witnessed domestic violence or abuse.

While Reagan talked to the children individually, Sharon would talk to Dr Amy Suttle about their medical history. After their interviews with Reagan, Dr Suttle would give the children a medical examination.

Sharon was 'insistent' that they interview Jack first, so Day left to consult with the two detectives secreted in the observation room. Detectives Nathan Riggs and Marc Hanna were set up to watch the children's interviews via a live audiovisual feed. They were part of the MDT – a multi-disciplinary team comprising law enforcement, the DSS and Dragonfly House staff. The MDT would work together to formulate a treatment plan for Jack and Sarah if they were indeed victims of abuse.

Riggs had assisted CSI in Meadowlands, measuring the blood spatter. He had taken Sharon's statement, including her revelations about writing an emergency number for Jack and Sarah on the bottom of a Russian doll kept on the guest bedroom nightstand.

Riggs was conscious the children might have been 'coached' prior to Dragonfly. This was a consideration in all such cases. When he learned Sharon was trying to dictate the order of the interviews, with Jack going first, it raised an immediate red flag.

'We decided Sarah should go first,' he said later. 'A lot of the time in investigations we see that kids have been coached. If there was coaching, then we would disturb it.'

Riggs handed Brandi Reagan a list titled: 'Questions for kids'. Until this moment, detectives had been frustrated in their efforts to interview the children. They had erred in giving

Molly custody of the children immediately after the killing, as they had wrongly assumed that Jack and Sarah were her children. Once Molly had taken the children to Monroe, they were outside the jurisdiction. Though detectives wanted to interview the children as soon as possible after the event, they hadn't been able to do so.

Now, four days after the killing, they finally had a chance to question Jack and Sarah, albeit via a proxy interview conducted by Reagan.

Reagan was given specific areas to cover. First, establish if Jack and Sarah were 'afraid of Dad', and if they 'liked or hated Molly'. Reagan was asked to elicit information about the brick, the nightmare that woke Sarah, Jason's relationship with Molly, and if 'Dad ever mentioned a trip to Ireland this month'. Reagan was also instructed to ask about the emergency number written under the Russian doll – who set it up, why and when?

Reagan brought Sarah into an interview room. Two chairs were positioned either side of a small oblong table, with two cameras overlooking from opposite walls. Sarah took a seat.

There was an easel to her left, some crayons, Play-Doh, a box of tissues and anatomically correct dolls. A fan whirred overhead. Sunlight streamed in through the open red curtains either side of a large bay window. Detectives Marc Hanna and Nathan Riggs took up positions in an adjacent room, to watch Reagan's interview with Sarah live through video link. Riggs was the assigned detective, but Hanna, as a highly experienced child abuse investigator, was present to supervise the interviews.

Hanna had personally brought 500 children to Dragonfly House since it had opened in 2010. The facility had expected to help twenty-five suspected child abuse victims annually. In the first year, 277 received help. In the next five years, 1,000 more were assessed.

Brandi Reagan's interview with Sarah began just after 1.30 p.m. Reagan asked Sarah to tell her a little bit about herself.

> **Sarah:** Well I was born, um, I was born in Ireland and I lived a little bit in Ireland and I got older, I like to eat a lot.
> **Reagan:** Like to eat, what kinds of things do you like to eat?
> **Sarah:** My favorite food is Shepherd's Pie that my mum makes me . . . that's my favorite food and then my second favorite food is, well it used to be because it can't be anymore coz I'm allergic to it, um, it was like Lasagna . . . and that's my favorite thing to eat.

Despite living the first four years of her life in Ireland, Sarah's accent and idioms were now American. (Sarah looked as American as she sounded, especially beside Molly. They could be mother and daughter. Most people assumed they were.)

Reagan got Sarah to talk about school. Sarah was really excited to do multiplication in third grade. She liked her second-grade teacher because one day she gave them all blue juice and she called it Jitter Juice, so that was nice. She said she really liked school.

As Sarah spoke, she opened her hands out and gesticulated for emphasis. The video is blurry, but there don't appear to be any words written on the palm of her left hand.

Reagan established that Sarah knew the difference between the truth and a lie. Then, she began the formal interview.

> **Reagan:** Tell me why you're here today.
> **Sarah:** Because my daddy died.

Reagan asked Sarah to think about that day. Sarah described Jason drinking at their neighbour's house. Sarah played Pirates and *Minecraft* with Danny Fritzsche, her 5-year-old neighbour. Molly joined the group. Then, Tom and Sharon arrived. Her dad was not expecting them. (As we've seen, Molly had only informed him approximately ten to fifteen minutes before they arrived.)

Back home Sarah talked with her grandparents, played with their two dogs, then fell asleep on the couch. Someone brought her to bed.

The next thing she remembered was being woken up by the police officer.

'All I found out was that someone got hurt.'

She thought it was Grandpa Tom because he went upstairs to stop Jason and Molly fighting and didn't come back. And then the police came and looked for pants and shoes.

'In the morning time my mum came over and she said my dad died and we were all crying and I went to my uncle's house and that's where we are now.'

Reagan asked Sarah how she knew her parents were fighting if she didn't see it happen. She said her mother told her the following day.

Sarah: She said that um, that um, well my grandma told me that first because she said um, she said like um, she said that um, like um, they were having a fight and then grandpa went upstairs and um, to stop, to try and like um, to try and calm them down and um, and then he didn't come back down.

Reagan: Okay. And then you said later your mum told you that your dad died. What happened when your mum told you that your dad died?

Sarah: Um, we all went into the bed and started crying.

Reagan: And who was there when she told you?

Sarah: My mum, my brother and my grandma and my grandpa. And my grandpa had to take a shower because . . . coz he um, . . . because he shaved his finger on a tree and it wouldn't stop bleeding.

Reagan asked Sarah to tell her about when 'Mom and Dad' were fighting. Sarah said her dad would get mad if someone left a light on. He would scream at Molly. This would happen 'every day or most likely twice a day'.

Sarah: And he would always like call her like every 5 minutes like 17 times and the highest he went on one day was 47 times.

Reagan asked how Sarah knew her dad called her mom forty-seven times one day. Sarah said Molly had told her.

Asked if she had seen her dad hurt Molly, Sarah said: 'No not, not really ever but one time I saw him um, step on her foot, one time I saw him pull her hair and then I thought this might have been an accident, but one time he got mad at her and . . . he rolled over her foot that night.'

Reagan asked how she knew her dad would fight her mum and hurt her when she didn't really see anything. Sarah replied that Molly had been telling her since Sarah was six that 'your dad is not a good dad'.

Asked if she had seen Jason do anything else to Molly, Sarah said no.

Then, when asked if she had ever seen Jason hit Molly, she said yes, Jason had hit Molly in the face, once. She could not remember when this happened. Sarah said Jason would call Molly 'bad names' and say she was 'worthless'.

Reagan next asked Sarah about waking up the night her father died. Sarah contradicted, then corrected, herself. First, she said she had not awoken, but then she said she had.

She discussed the nightmare, how she believed there were spiders and lizards on her bed. She said she thinks her father got really mad when Molly had to come up and change her sheets.

Reagan asked Sarah what would happen if she went downstairs after having a nightmare. She said it was 'not a good thing' to wake her father. 'He just gets really really angry. He says, "Why did you wake me up?"'

Reagan asked Sarah if she liked her dad. Sarah replied, 'Not most of the time but sometimes I did.' She liked how if she was really cold at a party, her father would give her a big hug and keep her warm.

When asked about things she liked about her mum, Sarah spoke effusively about Molly always being there for her and comforting her if she was sick or upset. She 'liked everything about her'. She spoke fondly about craft projects they did together.

Reagan then tried to elicit information about the brick by asking Sarah if they were working on any craft project at the moment. Molly had told Thompson at the sheriff's office that the brick was in the bedroom because she, Jack and Sarah were planning to paint it. Sarah didn't volunteer anything to confirm Molly's claim.

Sarah then revealed their codeword system if there was an emergency. Sarah would call Sharon's number, say 'Peacock,' then hang up. Everybody knew about the codewords except her dad.

Reagan: Do you remember when she [Sharon] came up with that?

Sarah: Erm, the peacock thing? The pe—, well she came up with the practice phone call but in, like this year but then um, but then um, the phone got taken downstairs so now um, then the, like the, like a few weeks before.

Reagan left the interview room to consult with the detectives, then returned. Sarah had now been interviewed for more than seventy minutes.

When asked, Sarah denied to Reagan that she had been coached in what to say by Molly or anyone else. Molly had told her to tell the truth. Sarah then passed a drawing to Reagan which depicted a mother and daughter and love hearts.

Reagan concluded the interview by asking Sarah about what she had heard people talking about in Bobby's house.

> **Sarah:** I heard people talking about my aunt coming to get us, coming to get me and my brother.

After her interview, a nursing assistant walked Sarah across the hall to Dr Amy Suttle's office. Sarah changed out of her party dress, put on a long T-shirt, then followed the nurse over to an examination table.

Next, Brandi Reagan interviewed Jack. She started by asking him why he was here in Dragonfly House to be interviewed.

> **Jack:** Erm . . . my dad died and people are, my aunt and uncle on my dad's side, are trying to take away, take me away from my mom and that, that's why I'm here, my mom's trying to get custody of us.
> **Reagan:** Okay. And who told you about that?
> **Jack:** Erm, my mom, I, I've known this for a while, that my mom didn't have adoption forms. And she's been trying to adopt me ever since my parents got married.

Reagan asked how his dad died.

> **Jack:** He . . . do I have to do it?
> **Reagan:** Yes, I need to know.

Jack: Ok. Well, my sister had a nightmare about insects, she had fairy blankets and insects all over her bed, but that was a nightmare though, and my dad got very mad and he was screaming at my mom and my mom let out a scream and my grandpa came up and started to hit him with a bat, and then my dad grabbed hold of the bat and hit my grandpa with the bat until my mom put, like . . . we were going to clean a brick that was there, like a cinder block – and it hit his temple right here [Jack holds his left hand up to the front left hand side of his head, above his ear] and he died.

The detectives in the observation room were intrigued by Jack's detailed information, given he had not witnessed the killing and Molly had been expressly told on numerous occasions by both Wanda Thompson and DSS social workers that she was not to discuss any detail about what happened with the children.

It is also worth noting here that Jack points to the front left side of the head as being where Molly struck Jason with the brick. There was a laceration that exposed brain tissue at that exact location, whereas the front right side of the head was the only part of the skull to escape injury.

Jack said he knew about Sarah's nightmare because Molly told him. Asked about the brick, Jack said they planned to paint it. They had bought flowers to plant, but it was raining earlier, so the brick was brought inside.

'My mum put it at her desk and that's where it was.'

When Reagan asked about the bat, Jack's answer surprised the detectives.

Jack: It was my baseball bat that I used, well I don't know what exact bat it was . . . but I know it was one of my baseball bats that I'd used previously in my life.

Jack was contradicting Tom's story about it being a bat previously owned by Molly's younger brother, Stewart. But Jack couldn't have seen the bat used, so how could he know it was one of his?

Jack said he was angry and upset that people could be so mean.

Reagan: What do you mean by that?

Jack: How my dad could get so angry, how my grandpa could hit him with the bat, how my mum could hit him with the brick.

Jack told Reagan that he first noticed his parents arguing when he was six, after their wedding. This continued for years. His father would get mad over Molly or the children leaving the lights on, or about bills.

Jack: He would physically and verbally hurt my, physically and verbally hurt my mum.

Reagan: Did you see him physically hurt her?

Jack: Once or twice.

Reagan: What did you see?

Jack: Erm, punching [Jack moves his right hand across his waist in a punching motion], hitting, pushing.

Reagan: I want you to think about a time you saw your dad punch your mum. Tell me about that time.

Jack: Erm, I don't remember what exactly happened before like what it was about but I heard erm, they were out, there was someone, it was late at night and I woke up and then when I, when I went out with, I saw one punch hit my mom right here [he moves his open right hand up to his left shoulder]. And that's all I remember.

Jack reported other incidents where Jason had pushed Molly because he wanted to look at her phone. Molly would scream back sometimes, or she'd just block her ears and curl into a ball. This made Jack 'very sad and angry'. Things had escalated in recent months.

> **Jack:** Getting a lot madder, sometimes he'd just scream, now he's been cussing and screaming a lot more, getting a lot angrier.

Jack told Reagan that his father had talked about moving back to Ireland. Molly wanted to adopt Jack and Sarah, but Jason wouldn't let her. Reagan asked about the codewords, 'peacock' and 'galaxy'. Jack said he was to call his grandparents if things got really bad.

> **Reagan:** And what would really bad mean?
> **Jack:** Um, hitting or cussing that would be going on and on and on without stopping for an hour or two. Maybe more.

Jack said this happened once, maybe the previous October, but he wasn't sure exactly. His father was drunk and his parents had 'a big fight'. Jack denied his father was often drunk.

Reagan left to consult with the detectives. During her 9-minute absence, Jack carefully chose different-coloured crayons and began drawing. Reagan resumed with a question about the Russian doll. Jack continued drawing as he answered.

> **Reagan:** Can you remember when they wrote that number on there?
> **Jack:** No.
> **Reagan:** Is that a recent thing? Like, um, would it have been within the past week?

Jack: No. No.
Reagan: Or like within months?
Jack: Months.

Reagan then asked Jack about Molly. He said he wanted to stay with her.

Reagan: Um, and you said that you were mad.
Jack: No.

Jack stopped drawing at this point and looked up to face Reagan for the remainder of her questions.

Reagan: Or you were angry about how your dad died?
Jack: Yes, and sad.
Reagan: And sad. Thank you. And you said that you're angry and sad about how your dad got angry?

Jack put his elbows on the table and closed his cupped hands over his ears. Reagan continued:

Reagan: About why your grandpa hit him with a bat and why your mom hit him with a brick?
Jack: Yes.
Reagan: Is that right?
Jack: Yes.
Reagan: Um, and just to make sure I understand, how did you find out that your mom hit him with a brick and your grandpa hit him with a bat?
Jack: She told me.

Jack made some final adjustments to his drawing and repositioned the box of crayons as he had found it. The

53-minute interview was over, but its consequences would endure.

Dr Suttle's physical examinations of both children revealed no anatomical signs of abuse, whether physical or sexual. However, the children were deemed, on foot of their revelations to Brandi Reagan, to be victims of domestic abuse, in that they had witnessed domestic abuse in their home.

8. Daydreams

While Jack and Sarah were being photographed and examined like exhibits at Dragonfly House, Tracey met with Sheriff Grice and Lt Thompson.

Thompson felt an immediate empathy with Tracey. Like her, Thompson had grown up the third youngest of eight, with one sister. She could see the pain Tracey was in. But, so far, Jack and Sarah were backing up Molly's story. They had described Jason as an abusive, controlling, angry man.

Tracey's husband, David, siblings Marilyn and Michael, and Jason's best friend, Paul Dillon, were also present at the meeting. Paul got the impression that Thompson was sceptical about the abuse allegations against Jason, but to interrogate the claims she needed as much information about the Martenses as possible.

Given the Martenses' suggestions that Jason's first wife's death was mysterious, Thompson also wanted to hear all about Mags. According to their friends and families, Mags was Jason's 'soulmate'. They met at a party in Limerick in August 1997, introduced by Lynn Shanahan, who had known Jason since he was seven years old.

Lynn and Mags had met when Mags applied for a childcare job where Lynn worked. While waiting to be interviewed, the two women got talking. Within minutes, both were creased over laughing. Lynn told her manager, 'You have to hire her, she's fabulous.'

At the party where they met, Jason told Lynn about his job, the night classes he was taking and his ambitions for a management role at MPS.

Lynn and Mags had big plans, too. The demand for child-care was surging in Ireland's booming Celtic Tiger economy. Lynn and Mags would soon establish and become co-owners of Daydreams, a children's day-care centre in Dooradoyle, Limerick.

When the party continued to Lynn's house, Jason and Mags sat in the living room and talked all night. Lynn watched them leave the following morning. They waited until they were a discreet distance away before their hands touched and joined. They were inseparable afterwards – until life delivered its cruel fate.

Mags and Jason's first official date was on 31 August 1997, the day on which Princess Diana died.

'We won't forget our first date in a hurry,' Mags had said. A besotted Jason observed Mags's beautiful pixie features, the gentleness of her nature, and that laugh, my God. He told all this to his sister, Tracey, adding, 'Mags is the one.' Tracey wrote movingly of Jason's love for Mags in *My Brother Jason*.

Jason would spontaneously send flowers to the childcare facility where Mags worked or turn up unannounced to take her to lunch.

'They were just crazy about each other,' Lynn said. She met her husband, Tim, around the same time, so the two couples would go on double dates and weekend breaks together.

Jason and Mags moved into a riverside apartment in Limerick. After going out together for four years, they got engaged in Barcelona, Spain.

According to Lynn, before the couple's wedding in 2003 in Spanish Point, County Clare, Jason knew he would be apart from Mags for a few nights, so he sent her three letters. 'There was one letter to be opened each night before they met up again for their wedding ceremony,' Lynn recalled. 'They were just beautiful. He was such a romantic and she was the exact same.' Jason and Mags built their dream home in the countryside, a 5-minute drive from Lynn, in Raleighstown, Kilmallock. Mags took photographs during the construction, planning where their furniture would go in each room before the foundations were even laid. She imagined children in those unfinished rooms.

When Jack was born on 13 September 2004 Jason was a besotted father. He taught his toddler to love rugby, a sport for which his native Limerick was famous. Aged two, Jack's party trick was to attempt the Haka – the pre-match ritual dance of the New Zealand All Blacks rugby team. Jack would reduce Jason and Mags to laughter by dancing to the Gnarls Barkley song 'Crazy'.

Mags was entranced by Jack, dutifully filling his 'baby book' with ultrasound scans and all the details only mothers recall – how he was born with dark blue eyes and black hair at 3.43 a.m., weighing 7 pounds 5 ounces, with his first photograph taken three hours later in the arms of his father.

When Sarah was born on 2 September 2006 their family was complete. Jason had his 'little princess'. Mags asked Lynn to be Sarah's godmother. Lynn, pregnant with her first, asked Mags to be godmother to her unborn child.

Less than twelve weeks later, Mags was dead.

At their meeting with Sheriff Grice and Lt Thompson, Tracey, David, Marilyn, Michael and Paul described the events around Mags's death.

Thompson and Grice were told how Mags had suffered with asthma for most of her life.

After 1 a.m. on Tuesday, 21 November 2006, Jason woke Mags's sister, Catherine, who was living with them at the time. Mags was struggling to breathe. Her inhaler didn't help. She tried Jack's nebulizer, too, to no avail.

Mags said to Catherine: 'I'm going to die.' They lived 20 kilometres from the nearest hospital, so Jason frantically called an ambulance and put Mags, still dressed in her pyjamas, in his car. He sped towards the hospital to halve the response time for paramedics. When he stopped at an agreed meeting point – outside the Four Elms pub – Mags slumped forward on to the dashboard.

Jason attempted CPR. When the paramedics arrived, they took over resuscitation in the rear of the ambulance as they raced to Limerick's largest hospital. Jason followed behind.

As soon as Jason arrived at the hospital he was taken into a private room and told that Mags was gone. The doctors declared her dead at 2 a.m. on 21 November. When they took Jason to see her, Jason clung to her body, wept and begged her not to leave him. She looked tiny in her blue-and-white pyjamas, her eyes closed as though she were sleeping.

David and Tracey lived 1 kilometre from the hospital. They arrived in minutes. Jason was pacing with his head in his hands, begging Mags to stay.

Mags's sister Catherine had remained with Jack and Sarah at the house, waiting for news. When the call came, she slumped to the floor in tears. Jason's twin, Wayne, was in Amsterdam when David Lynch called. He got the first flight home.

'Jack was only two at the time,' Wayne recalled. 'I remember him sitting on the stairs in my parents' house, wondering what was going on.'

After her meeting with Jason's relatives and friend Paul, Thompson recorded in her case notes: 'The inquest ruled Mags's death the result of a sudden and severe asthma-related death.'

Family and friends rallied around after Mags's death. Catherine stayed living with Jason, Jack and Sarah, helping them to adjust for the first six months. Sometimes, Tracey would stay at Jason's house for several days, and other times the children would stay with Tracey.

Jason reduced his work hours to a three-day week. However, after a few months, his employers asked him to revert to five days. He would make daily visits to Mags's grave, spending his lunch break reading the newspaper to her headstone.

He tried to fill in Sarah's baby book with as much detail as Mags had managed for Jack. He noted an inoculation at four months, a chest infection at six months, but in the end, there was no replacement for a mother's love and touch. The baby-book page for Sarah's first birthday remained blank.

Paul said Jason cried in his arms many times. 'Every time it was about what the kids lost. He had lost his soulmate, but Jason, as always, never put himself first.'

When Jason decided to recruit an au pair about eight months after Mags's death, Paul helped him register with an agency online. He hired a young Hungarian woman called Florrie. She stayed the standard six months.

'Florrie stayed in touch for a long time after leaving,' Paul recalled. He and Jason even visited Florrie a few months later in Spain.

Jason hired another au pair, this time from the Czech Republic. She was not in Ireland long when a family member died and she had to return home. Jason looked for a third au pair.

'He told me he was speaking with a few and did not know which to go with,' Paul recalled.

One applicant stood out. She had been a foster parent in Tennessee. She had seen Jason's advertisement with the online agency and after an exchange of emails they had several phone calls in February 2008, each impressing Jason more than the last.

It's unclear from the records whose idea it was, but Jason hired Molly privately, not through the agency. As a result,

Molly bypassed the background checks the agency would have undertaken.

Molly arrived at Shannon Airport on 10 March 2008. Immigration police were immediately suspicious of her one-way ticket. She was told to wait in the Departures area for deportation to Boston. She called Jason in a panic.

Jason knew that Lynn was in Shannon Airport that day. He asked her to look out for a 24-year-old blonde woman. Lynn found her sitting at the bar wearing cowboy boots and a fur-lined jacket. She was wearing so much make-up Lynn thought she looked like a pageant queen.

'I immediately thought, she's precisely what Jason does not need,' Lynn recalled later.

Jason arrived at the airport and spoke to Molly in Departures, but he was unable to prevent her deportation. She was put on a flight to Boston, but she returned the next day through Dublin Airport.

Brendan O'Callaghan and his wife, Michelle, friends of Jason's, watched over Jack and Sarah while Jason collected Molly. 'I remember this young American blonde with cowboy boots,' Brendan recalled. 'She made an impression. She was easy on the eye. Southern accent. She was nice. We all tried to be friendly and make things easier for her.'

In her case notes, Lt Thompson wrote:

'Ms. Lynch said her brother told her he started a sexual relationship with Molly Martens on the very first night she arrived in Ireland. She said Jason told her at one point that he had been so lonely and distraught over the loss of Mags that he welcomed Molly Martens into his home and bed to try and fill the void.'

Lynn Shanahan observed Molly's image change in the weeks and months after her arrival in Ireland to look after Sarah and

Jack. The pageant queen disappeared, replaced by a demure Molly dressed in two-piece cardies and pants, her hair tied low at the back.

Gradually, Lynn noticed other, disturbing changes. 'The first day I called to the house,' she remembered, 'Molly was ironing, wearing grey sweats. I was stunned. It was like watching Mags. Molly mimicked Mags's dress sense: jeans and tops going out; and tracksuits around the house.'

Lynn invited Molly to join her, Tracey and Marilyn at Zumba classes. Molly joined, but their conversations were strained.

Over time, however, Molly confided in Lynn that she had come to Ireland to escape her mother. They had fallen out because Molly broke off her engagement to a pastor's son. Sharon wanted a big white wedding, but Molly suspected her fiancé was gay.

Molly told Lynn she had been a foster mum to two children, one of whom was a 12-year-old sexually abused boy. She told Lynn an elaborate story about the boy being 'ripped from her arms' and returned to his mother. Molly said she bonded with this child because she herself had been sexually abused in Florida around the age of twelve.

It would be revealed that Molly had a long history of making personal and dramatic 'confessions' which were, in fact, fabrications.

Unlike most au pairs, Molly was free during the day. Jack and Sarah went to Daydreams, the childcare centre Mags and Lynn had set up together. After Mags's death, Jason had become a co-owner of Daydreams with Lynn.

Lynn cared for Jack and Sarah at Daydreams from 8.30 a.m. to 4.30 p.m. One day, Sarah called Lynn 'mommy'. Lynn told Jason and Molly about it and suggested it was just a passing phase.

Molly kept Sarah out of Daydreams for the next three days. When Sarah returned, she was calling Molly 'Mommy'. Molly said it was because Molly sounded like 'Mommy'.

'That night, I went for dinner at Jason's house,' Lynn recalled later. 'I saw lots of books about Mommy and me. The books included: *Sunny Days with Mommy and Me*, and *Mommy and Me – How I Came to Be*. Jason said Molly bought them and said, "Why should Sarah be the only child without a mommy?" I knew this really hurt Jason.'

Jason's sister, Marilyn, often spent her Saturdays with Sarah. Like Tracey, Marilyn wanted to help fill the maternal void left in Sarah's life. But over time, Marilyn noticed how Molly began to arrive late with Sarah for their Saturday dates. Or Molly would return early to collect Sarah. Eventually, the visits stopped.

According to Jason's family, Molly didn't seem to want the children to be on their own with anyone. She was also determined to come between Jason and his best friend.

'If I tried to speak alone with Jason,' Paul recalled, 'Molly would come and sit on Jason's lap, as if she was a 2-year-old child, to stop the conversation. A lot of the time, Jason was embarrassed. He had to baby her, plámás her, keep her onside.

'He always avoided confrontation with everything in life. I didn't like her. I didn't like how Jason had to be around her. I thought she was a nasty bit of stuff.'

Jason tried to get Molly a job working at Daydreams. However, when Lynn asked to see her credentials, Molly could not produce them.

Lynn was already suspicious of Molly's 'fascinating' life. Molly had claimed variously to have been a Montessori teacher, a foster parent, a referee, a model, a magazine editor and a varsity swimmer who had almost made the US Olympic swimming team. All by the age of twenty-four.

Lynn told Jason that Molly was a Walter Mitty character, inventing lives she never lived.

During their meeting on 6 August 2015 Tracey told Lt Thompson that when she discovered Molly had never been a foster mother in Knoxville she alerted Jason to Molly's lie. He responded by saying Molly was good with Jack and Sarah and he did not want to disrupt a stable home.

Thompson's case notes record that after this conversation with Jason, Tracey didn't revisit the subject of Molly fabricating her experience as a foster mother.

In the summer of 2009, when Jason and Molly had been romantically involved for more than a year, Molly told Jason that he should sell the home he had built with Mags. Molly said she could no longer live with a ghost. All the photographs of Mags unnerved her.

Jason agreed to sell the house. The sale closed on 21 November 2009 – Mags's anniversary. She had been dead for three years.

Tracey wrote in her book that the house sale closing on Mags's anniversary was not lost on Jason. He told Tracey: 'This is a sign I made a mistake.'

Jason proposed to Molly on Valentine's Day 2010, two years after her arrival in Ireland. He seemed embarrassed telling Lynn. 'He was upset that it was so soon after Mags had died,' she recalled, 'but Molly wanted to be validated and not just be the nanny any more.'

Jason, Molly and the children moved into a rented home near Tracey.

When Marilyn arrived unannounced one afternoon she found the curtains drawn and the house in darkness. Molly wouldn't let her in to see the children.

'She went from being so high and jolly, to super low,' Marilyn later observed.

Jack's earliest memory of Molly was in this rented house. He remembers sitting at the kitchen table refusing to eat vegetables. Molly's response was furious. She poured sugar all over his plate, then loaded it up with sweets. She told him to eat that instead.

Paul witnessed Molly's mood plummet. 'We were playing golf one day in Ballybunion,' Paul recalled. 'He [Jason] had sixteen missed calls from her. We came home. I saw her on the living-room floor in the darkness, curled up in the foetal position. I don't know where the children were. I left to give them time on their own.'

Jason later told Paul he had previously found Molly 'lying on the floor pulling her hair out'. Jason said she was bipolar.

Weeks before Jason was to transfer from the MPS factory in Limerick to become manager of MPS's facility in Davidson County, he confided in one of his Limerick colleagues, Morgan Fogarty. Fogarty was close to Jason and was due to take over Jason's old role once he left for America.

Morgan could tell Jason was having second thoughts. He recalled how, when he asked Jason about it, Jason told him about Molly being bipolar.

'He was clearly upset,' Morgan said, 'but he said he "couldn't take another mother away from the kids". I think he felt he was in too deep to pull back.'

Lynn thinks Jason thought he could save Molly. She said: 'He put the children's happiness ahead of his own. Jason thought if Molly was back in America in the sunshine, in a new house where nobody knew she was a nanny and nobody knew about Mags, she would finally be happy and they could have a new life together.'

Wayne went for drinks with his twin the night before Jason left.

'I asked him, "Are you sure you want this?" I think everywhere he turned he saw Mags, and this was his way of escaping that. Not in a bad way. He did care about Molly, but I don't think it was total love. I don't think he ever got over Mags. He was still going up to her grave all the time even before he went to America.

'I never liked Molly,' Wayne added. 'There was always something false about her.'

9. Bleak House

Molly left for America on 10 April 2011, six weeks before Jason. Sharon helped her choose their Meadowlands home. Jason sent $340,000 to pay for it. A week later, he sent $80,000 to furnish the house and purchase a $22,000 Honda for Molly. He sent Tom Martens $49,000 to pay for the lavish wedding which Sharon had planned at Bleak House, a place of historical significance to the pro-slavery confederacy of southern states.*

Jason's finances were in considerably better shape at that time than the Irish state's. Ireland's collapsed economy had to be bailed out the year previously, in 2010, with a 64 billion euro loan required from the European Union and the International Monetary Fund to keep the country afloat.

One in seven Irish workers had lost their jobs in 2010. Jason was an outlier in that he was cash rich. Despite not going to university, he had forged a very successful career for himself at MPS. At this point in his life, he had a 6-figure salary and was also a 50 per cent partner in the successful childcare business which his first wife, Mags, had established with Lynn Shanahan. Jason had inherited Mags's share of the business following her death in 2006.

* Built in 1858, Bleak House was used as a base by confederate generals in a series of civil war skirmishes that became known as the Siege of Knoxville. Knoxville was of strategic importance as its railroad linked the confederacy east and west. Almost 150 years later, racial tensions remained, requiring close monitoring by the FBI Knoxville bureau, where Tom had been supervisor until his retirement three years before the wedding. Molly and Sharon had fallen in love with Bleak House in its modern guise – as a wedding venue.

Jason chose Brendan O'Callaghan as his best man because Paul Dillon did not enjoy public speaking. As regards Molly's bridesmaids, they would later fall out over her 'Bridezilla' behaviour. Brendan experienced it first hand. He rented suits for the groom's party at Tony Connolly's, an upmarket store in Limerick. On the day Brendan was to collect the suits, Molly changed her mind. She booked suits in America, with bright green waistcoats, braces and black patent shoes.

'They were awful,' Brendan recalled.

On their first night in North Carolina Molly treated Brendan and his wife, Michelle, to an excruciating fashion show.

'She was trying on Sarah's clothes, or clothes she had from when she was Sarah's age. She was practically stripping in front of us. The clothes didn't fit her. And we just had to sit there and pay attention,' Brendan said.

The next day was far more disturbing. Paul wanted to find a local pub showing the 2011 Champions League final. Bobby Martens invited them to Charlotte to watch the game in his house. Paul did not want to drive 90 miles to watch the game. Molly became hysterical, crying until Paul relented.

After the match, Molly drove them home.

'Myself and Jason had a few drinks on us,' recalled Paul. 'We were messing around in the car. She just slammed on the brakes and started screaming at Jason. The kids were in the car and she just stopped there. Cars zooming past. This was on a 4-lane motorway, cars travelling at 70 mph, she stopped dead and stayed there for thirty or forty seconds. Jason told her to drive, move, but she was not listening. She was too busy screaming non-stop for thirty seconds. This continued when we got home, her screaming and crying.'

The drama continued in Knoxville. Molly fainted at the wedding rehearsal, but to Jason's twin, Wayne, it seemed performative.

'She fell in stages,' Wayne said. 'It was Academy Award-winning stuff.'

The Martens family had moved from Virginia to Knoxville in 1994, when Molly was eleven years old. In 2002, they upgraded to 12500 Comblain Road, in one of Knoxville's most exclusive neighbourhoods. Their new 5,000-square-foot home cost $525,000, but it would double in value over the years.

At Comblain Road, Molly at last had her own private pool. Previously she'd had to settle for swimming with neighbour-hood kids in a community pool. Her Olympic ambitions floundered. Molly's parents hosted a pre-wedding barbecue in their upmarket Knoxville home. Guests mingled over wine and beers, but Molly was absent. Tracey found her curled into a foetal ball on her bed, crying. Tracey gave her a gift of a necklace and encouraged her to come down, but she refused.

It's likely that Molly was extremely anxious. Her life in Ireland was about to collide with her life in America. Both worlds were riddled with fictions and fantasies. Jason's best man, groomsman and his twin were all out by the pool and herb garden talking to the bridesmaids. They could say anything. They did.

'I remember someone saying about Molly being a swim champion and her bridesmaids looking at us like we'd two heads,' Wayne said. There was a yawning chasm between Molly's ambitions and the reality of her talent. Aged thirteen, she had competed in a Knoxville meet and finished seventh out of sixteen competitors.*

---

* The results of the 1997 Greater Knoxville Area Interclub Swim Association City Swim Meet were published in the *Knoxville News-Sentinel*. Molly finished seventh out of sixteen in the Girls U13–14 50-metre backstroke with a time

The Martenses' barbecue finished, as per the invite, at 9 p.m. sharp. Jason's friends went to a bar with the brides-maids. Molly insisted Jason stay behind with her.

Jenny Walker, one of the bridesmaids, got talking to Brendan. Molly had told Jenny that she had been friends with Jason's first wife for years prior to her death. Brendan was shocked, but he let Jenny continue. According to Jenny, Mags had lived with the Martenses in their Tennessee home when Mags was on a student exchange programme. Then, when Mags was dying of cancer, she begged Molly to raise Jack and Sarah.

As one of Jason's best friends, and as Jack's godfather, Brendan felt compelled to alert Jason's family about what Jenny had told him. They were flabbergasted. It was only twenty-four hours until the wedding. They discussed con-fronting Jason with what Jenny had said. Tracey wrote in *My Brother Jason* that Molly would not let Jason alone with his family and they couldn't isolate him to tell him what Molly had told her bridesmaids.

The next day, Jason, Paul and Brendan went golfing, playing immediately behind Tom and his sons. Given that Brendan and Paul had spoken to Tracey about what Molly's bridesmaid had said, Brendan felt it wasn't his place to raise these concerns with Jason. Paul had long since made his views on Molly known to Jason, and as they played golf he continued to beseech Jason not to go ahead with the marriage.

Furious with Molly's lies, Tracey asked to see Brendan's best-man speech.

'I'd spent two weeks working on it,' Brendan said. 'I came back from golf, and there was one page on the dresser and

---

of 33.80, several seconds slower than the winner. She placed third in the 200-metre individual medley. This appears to have been a career highlight.

about three lines left in it, everything else cut out. Out of five pages, I had about three lines.'

As a wedding venue, Bleak House was magical. Days before the wedding itself, Molly and Sharon had accompanied the photographer to the venue, where Molly was photographed in hundreds of poses.

Molly and Jason were married under a floral horseshoe canopy on the upper tier of the Bleak House gardens, with fairy lights and lanterns illuminating the trees. Molly walked down the 'aisle', with Jack as ring bearer and Sarah as flower girl. Mike Earnest officiated. He had completed the necessary paperwork online to call himself Reverend Earnest.

As Molly approached Paul kept up his pleas to Jason, saying that there was a car outside to whisk him away.

Tracey kept her fury hidden as she lit the marriage unity candle with Sharon. However, when Molly's maid of honour, Susie West, was about to deliver her wedding toast, Tracey set her straight.

Susie, who considered herself one of Molly's best friends, had decided to tell Jason and Molly's story like a fairy tale. There was the tragedy of Mags's dying wish that Molly look after Jack and Sarah, and the true-love story of Molly finding two children and her Irish prince all the way across the Atlantic Ocean.

Just before Susie got to her feet, Tracey told her that it was all a disgusting lie. Molly had never met Mags.

Instead of telling her fairy-tale story, Susie bumbled through an off-the-cuff toast about how she used to feel lucky coming home to Molly when they lived together for a time in Knoxville. Susie said she hoped Jason would come home feeling lucky, too.

The atmosphere was tense as guests sat in the evening sunshine drinking wine – the Martenses did not allow beer or cider at the wedding. Jason's sister Marilyn recalled afterwards that she didn't want to be there. 'Jason asked me would I go for him,' she said. 'It was the most uncomfortable wedding I was ever at.'

Later during the wedding, Jason was dancing with Sarah when suddenly there was a scream. Molly had observed Tracey's 10-year-old son, Adam, drinking from a McDonald's cup. Adam was allergic to eggs and so Susie West had procured him a takeaway.

This ruined the aesthetic of the wedding, according to an enraged Molly, who threw Susie, her maid of honour, out. Marilyn saw this unfold. 'I saw Molly running across the dance floor,' she said, 'like something out of *Gone with the Wind*; she was in slow motion, crying so everyone could see her.'

Molly rushed to Tracey's husband, David, who was sitting with Bobby Martens. Molly screamed that Adam had ruined 'my wedding'. She shouted, 'I paid for this wedding.'

In fact, Jason had paid for everything. Molly stormed off upstairs. Marilyn asked Jason what had happened. According to Marilyn, Jason said, 'It's just one of her dramas, leave her off.'

After twenty minutes, Molly re-emerged from upstairs, still seething. Paul begged Jason to take Jack and Sarah and come home.

'Paul didn't want him to get into the car [with Molly to leave the wedding]. Paul was adamant, it was like a sixth sense,' Brendan recalled.

Paul told Jason he was the unhappiest groom he had ever seen. 'I asked him to just leave her, get on a plane and go home,' he remembered. 'And he said, "I can't."' Jason told him it was too late. He couldn't take another mother from Jack and Sarah.

The remainder of the wedding was tense but short-lived.

The lights went out at 11 p.m. and everybody quietly dispersed.

The more Wanda Thompson learned of Molly during the police investigation in the weeks after Jason's killing, the more worried she was for Jack and Sarah's safety.

Jason knew that Molly had consulted an attorney about divorce and child custody. He knew that if she was allowed to adopt the children, Molly could seek custody following a divorce.

Three months before Jason was killed he talked to Tracey about 'moving home'. Then, two months before the killing, Molly and her parents stepped up the pressure over the adoption issue.

Referring to this time, Thompson's case notes read: 'They became more and more persistent ... telling Jason that allowing Molly to adopt the children would make it easier to get them registered for school.'

Jason had been planning on coming home for his father's eightieth birthday in late August 2015. He had told Tracey that 'helping Molly get the kids registered for school was not going to be an issue because the kids would be in Ireland.'

In text exchanges on 27 July, five days before Jason was killed, he told Paul Dillon that he was bringing Jack and Sarah with him as a birthday surprise for his dad. Asked if Molly was coming, Jason texted: 'She can come or not, either way I'm coming home.'

Thompson noted: 'Mr Dillon said Jason also told him that the real surprise was for Molly. He said Jason told him that when he got to Ireland with the children, he may decide not to come back to the United States.'

Approaching fifty, with bobbed blonde hair and a penchant for ornate neckwear, lawyer Kim Bonuomo resembled a younger version of Diane Lockhart, the fictional attorney in *The Good Wife*.

Two days after Jason's killing, Bonuomo answered a call from the Irish consulate in Charlotte. The call sparked two weeks of 18-hour shifts for Bonuomo's law firm, Allman Spry. After years dealing with bitter divorce disputes, this case reinvigorated Bonuomo with the feeling that she could do 'something good'. She remembered being struck by how well prepared Molly was immediately after Jason's killing.

'She didn't hire the B team,' she said.

Molly's lawyer, Kelley Gondring, was fifteen years younger than Bonuomo. A working mum of two in her early thirties, Gondring cycled or jogged at 5.30 a.m., then home-baked her own croissants before work. Gondring was so ambitious she wrote out a 'goals list' when she was ten years old.

Bonuomo had to deal with a 'flurry of paperwork' filed by Gondring seeking emergency custody, guardianship and adoption. 'Molly acted very quickly after killing Jason to put into place what her goal seemed to be, which was to get the children,' she said.

Even if Bonuomo could establish that Jason's will – which stipulated that in the case of his death Tracey was to become guardian of his children – had legal standing in America, the judge had the discretion to overrule it. Molly would be presented as the only mother the children had ever known, the woman who had raised them lovingly for seven years.

So Bonuomo spent hours talking with Jason's family and friends and gathering statements from others in Ireland – all with a view to exposing the real Molly Martens.

Meanwhile, the investigation into Jason's killing continued.

Detective Smith was briefed by Thompson about Tracey's claims that Molly had once drugged her with lithium. Tracey alleged that Molly had also drugged Tom with lithium on a separate occasion. As several years had passed, neither allegation could be proved, but taken together the allegations raised another question for detectives.

In Tom's case, it was alleged, he asked Molly for an aspirin while at a baseball game, but she gave him lithium. Tom had to be helped from his seat. Later, out of character, he asked to go to McDonald's for ice cream.

The Lynches said this was the punchline of a story told by the Martenses at dinner one night. While the Martenses didn't appear to view it as sinister, Tracey certainly did, especially after Molly allegedly fixed her a margarita in Meadowlands which left her incapacitated for days.

An empty lithium bottle had been recovered along with other prescription medications on the night of Jason's killing. Lots of households have old unused prescription medications stored with everyday items like cough syrups. So finding an empty lithium bottle was not suspicious.

However, given Tracey's allegations, the detectives wondered had Molly drugged Jason before bed? Detective Smith contacted Dr Justin Brower at the medical examiner's office.

'I informed him of the alleged lithium incident. Dr Brower told me the BAC (blood alcohol content) was the only toxicology testing requested by Dr Nelson.'

While Thompson sought further toxicology testing, Smith tried to establish if Jason had left any digital footprints of his intention to leave Molly.

Smith had been contacted by Jason's former employer MPS at local and national level saying that Jason's work laptop was missing. Molly had removed a box of Jason's belongings from MPS. MPS's attorney, Rob Duault, was concerned about confidential business information on the computer. Smith contacted Jones Byrd, Tom's lawyer, to enquire about retrieving this computer.

Next, Smith spoke with Detective Riggs about the children's interviews at Dragonfly House. He heard that Jack and Sarah said Jason physically assaulted Molly; that Jack also backed up Molly's story about the brick in the bedroom; and that Sharon set up the codewords, possibly in recent weeks or months.

Smith followed up on tips from the public. There was one from Sara Neeves, an acquaintance of Molly's whose daughter was a schoolfriend of Sarah's. Sara Neeves would later become one of Molly's ardent supporters.

When Smith called Sara, she said she knew Molly and Jason but was not close to them. However, she recommended Smith talk with Sarah's riding instructor, Tori Adkins, because Molly had confided in her.

Smith's case notes record that Tori Adkins returned a call to him at 11.20 a.m. on Friday, 7 August.

'I was unable to speak with her. She left a voicemail message asking me to return her call.'

Six days after Jason's killing, Tracey finally saw her brother. The dark mahogany coffin was flanked by arrangements of lilies, Mags's favourite flowers. He looked so unrecognizable she wondered if they were in the right room.

When Paul Dillon put his hand behind Jason's head his fingers disappeared into the skull.

'We were looking for marks on his body,' Paul said. 'I felt the hole in the back of his head from what they'd done.'

Tracey asked for some time alone with Jason. She made three promises to him: that she would raise his children; bury him beside Mags; and do everything to ensure Molly and Tom faced justice for what they had done.

That evening, 10-year-old Jack and 8-year-old Sarah were taken to the Martenses' $760,000 beach house in South

Carolina. They would spend the weekend there, accompanied by Molly, Tom and Sharon. The house had panoramic ocean views, and, at the height of the tourist season, could command a weekly rental income of $5,000.

While Jack and Sarah were in Folly Beach, Smith met with Tom's lawyer, Jones Byrd, outside the family home at 160 Panther Creek Court. Byrd handed Smith Jason's work computer.

The police were still searching for Jason's phone, personal laptop and home computer. They had all disappeared from the house after the killing. The Martenses could offer the detective no assistance in that regard. Smith would have to search elsewhere for digital footprints.

Jack and Sarah's tug-of-love story was playing out in Irish and American media and, most virulently, on social media.

Political pressure to charge Tom and Molly was mounting on DA Garry Frank. The Irish foreign minister, Charlie Flanagan, had become personally involved. A Facebook page – Bring Jack and Sarah Home – already had 10,000 likes. More than 1,700 people had signed an online petition to bring the children home.

Paul Dillon's wife, Simone, helped set up a fundraising campaign and a Jason's Journey bank account. The Lynches were facing 6-figure fees to protect Jason's estate, probate Jason's will and fight the guardianship case.

10. Supermom

Eight days after his father's death, Andrea Huckabee took Jack to an interview room at the Center for Child Wellness in High Point.

Between turns on a board game, Huckabee, a licensed clinical social worker specializing in childhood trauma, asked Jack about various scenarios. If something happened at school, for example, would he tell the teacher, a parent, or anyone at all?

This line of questioning was deliberately designed to elicit information from children who had suffered trauma. It was a way of discovering who a child trusted; who they would instinctively turn to for help.

The centre was run by Piedmont Family Services, a charity providing counselling to victims of domestic violence or rape.

Months before Jason's killing, Molly had joined a fund-raising group for Piedmont.* One of Molly's Meadowlands confidantes, Melissa Sams – who'd hosted the birthday party Jack attended on the night of his father's death – was a patron of Piedmont.

It's unclear if Melissa influenced Molly's decision to align herself with a domestic violence charity. However, detectives would later discover that Melissa, an attorney specializing in child custody cases, had advised Molly eight months before Jason's death about an unusual legal avenue which might allow Molly to gain custody of Jack and Sarah.

* Molly joined the Guild of Family Services of High Point, a dedicated group of volunteers who fundraise and raise awareness about Piedmont's services.

After a few turns at the board game at the Center for Child Wellness, Jack told Andrea Huckabee that he didn't want to talk about what happened to his dad. He only knew what 'his mom' had told him. Then, for the first time, he revealed negative feelings about Molly.

Huckabee noted that Jack said to her: 'I don't want to talk about this, I have some angry feelings but I don't want to hurt my mom's feelings.'

Jack expressed mixed feelings about the Lynches, too. Though he cared for them, he wanted to stay with Molly. According to Huckabee, 'He [Jack] said, "I want to be able to stay and see my friends.""*

Huckabee interviewed Sarah, too, then scheduled a second session for nine days later. By then, the children would know if their future lay with Tracey or Molly.

On 13 August 2015, the day before the guardianship hearing, Jason's body was transported to Dublin Airport.† His funeral was postponed until Jack and Sarah could attend.

That same day, social worker Heidi Mathis was dispatched to Bobby's house for one final round of questioning in advance of the guardianship hearing.

Mathis asked Molly about allegations that she had held Jack under running water, causing him to choke and scream.

Jason's sister Marilyn had told Lt Thompson about visiting Meadowlands with Tracey and their father, John, a year after the wedding. It was a hot day and the adults began a playful water fight with the children. When Jack threw water over Molly, she became enraged.

* Molly told social worker Heidi Mathis that she planned to enrol the children in Shiloh Elementary School in Union County. Whatever the guardianship judge decided, Jack was not going back to Meadowlands, so his desire to stay in America to be near his friends was doomed either way.
† An Irish charity, the Kevin Bell Repatriation Trust, paid the $13,000 cost.

'She grabbed Jack, went straight in, turned on the tap and put Jack underneath it,' Marilyn said. 'She was screaming, "Now, how do you like it?"' Marilyn said Jack was crying and choking. Jason tried to stop her. 'It was so upsetting, my dad was crying.'

Tracey recalled Jason crying, too. Later, Marilyn entered Jack's bedroom and found Molly pulling Jack 'up sideways by the arm, and yanking him out of his sleep'. On seeing Marilyn, Molly 'mumbled something about never to tease her'.

Marilyn and Tracey discussed intervening with Jason, but they were worried Molly would punish Jack further.

When questioned by Mathis about Jason's sisters' allegations, Molly denied holding Jack's head under water.*

During the same interview, Mathis told Molly, 'There are concerns regarding your mental health, specifically, bipolar and medications.' Molly said she had been diagnosed with depression when she was fifteen, had been prescribed medications 'off and on' and denied any current mental health concerns.

The day after Mathis's visit to Bobby's house Molly and Tracey came face to face at Davidson County Courthouse.

Molly arrived for the guardianship hearing in a black sleeveless dress. Large sunglasses shielded her eyes. Still wearing her wedding ring, she waved away reporters. Her uncle Mike Earnest spoke to the media on her behalf. 'Molly's really the only mother they have ever known,' he said. 'She is an outstanding mother. I cannot imagine what she is going through.'

David and Tracey were accompanied by Shane Stephens, Consul General of Ireland, who said he was representing

---

* Jack confirmed Molly had held his head underwater, but 'just playfully'. 'It was funny. I knew she was playing with me but my dad didn't like it.' Sarah denied seeing Molly holding Jack's head underwater.

the Department of Foreign Affairs. Unlike the reporters, the Irish government observers were allowed inside the court.

Kim Bonuomo, the lawyer acting on behalf of Tracey and David in their battle to win guardianship of Jack and Sarah, had correctly foreseen the Martenses' strategy. They would downplay Jason's will, which named Tracey and David as Jack and Sarah's guardians, and instead present Molly as a selfless, devoted mother.

Molly had hired three lawyers for the task of securing guardianship. C. Ray Grantham Jnr, a former special forces commander, was chosen to lead the Martenses' case.

Bonuomo wanted to cross-examine Molly about the killing, but Grantham objected, and the judge,* Brian Shipwash, agreed.

'I'm not interested in playing investigator,' Shipwash said, adding that he had prayed for guidance on Jack and Sarah's future all the way down Route 52.

Tracey testified that Molly told her she was diagnosed as bipolar aged seven. Tracey said she witnessed worrying signs prior to the 2011 wedding. 'Molly would stay in bed up until lunchtime. The house would be in darkness all day,' she said. The children, then aged four and six, were sometimes left outside unattended. Tracey detailed the 2012 water fight and her alleged drugging by Molly via a lithium-laced margarita in 2013.

Then she testified about a 2013 incident in Ireland where Jack was endangered while swimming at Spanish Point in Clare. Jack, then eight, had rented an adult-sized surfboard by mistake, but Molly insisted he use it.

---

* Brian Shipwash's title was Clerk of the Davidson County Superior Court, but in guardianship cases the clerk presides and is described as the judge in such proceedings.

'Jason and Molly had a disagreement about it and Jason walked away,' Tracey said. A while later, Tracey spotted Jack in difficulty. Molly was building sandcastles with Sarah, oblivious. Tracey brought Jack to safety, before tackling Molly.

'She said he needed to learn a lesson,' Tracey told the court.

Tracey wrote in *My Brother Jason* about an incident that occurred in Spanish Point later on the day of Jack and the surfboarding incident.

Michelle McCormack and her husband, Damian, who had been best man at Jason's wedding to Mags, were in Spanish Point at that time. According to Tracey, Molly lied to Michelle that she had lost a sister to cancer when she was young. She also claimed her father had testicular cancer and her mother was going blind.*

At the guardianship hearing, Tracey went on to say that also during that 2013 stay in Ireland, she and Molly had clashed over Molly's lithium tablets being left within reach of the children.

Tracey was also convinced Molly was bulimic: 'Molly was vomiting after all of the meals.' And Tracey was alarmed by Molly's alcohol consumption whenever they visited America. 'She would call it her margarita cup. She would drink from that cup while she was driving with the children in the car.'

Tracey said that Molly would spoil Sarah but neglect Jack, and that when Molly and Jack argued it was like two children squabbling. 'There was regular conflict,' she told the hearing. 'Molly was very erratic. She would lose control quite quickly.'

---

* By 2017, Tom had been diagnosed with prostate cancer and Sharon suffered from macular degeneration – similar but different diagnoses to the ones Molly claimed. It is unclear if either parent was unwell in 2013.

Jack would call her Molly and she would get angry and say to call her "mom". He would refuse and get upset.'

While cross-examining Tracey, Grantham Jnr scored two notable concessions. He produced documentation showing Jason had been granted permanent residency in America for himself, Jack and Sarah. If he was planning to leave, why did he apply for Green Cards in March 2014? Tracey conceded she had first learned of this after Jason's death.

She testified that Jason intended to return next on 24 August. However, when asked by Grantham Jnr if she had expected Molly to join Jason, Tracey said yes. This contradicted what she had told Thompson a few days after the killing.

Lynn Shanahan travelled to North Carolina from Ireland to testify at the guardianship hearing.

Lynn told the court that she visited Jason and Molly in 2013, two years after they had married. Lynn, her husband Tim, and sons, Sam, nine, and Jamie, eight, visited the US for two weeks. They spent one week of this holiday sharing a condo in Myrtle Beach with Jason, Molly, Jack and Sarah.

Lynn and Molly drove to Myrtle Beach together with Sarah and Jamie. Jason and Jack drove with Tim and Sam in a second car. The hearing heard from Lynn that Molly had made some startling revelations while they drove to Myrtle Beach.

Molly told Lynn that she had consulted a divorce lawyer, who advised her that if she left Jason she would only gain visitation rights. Lynn told the hearing that Molly was crying as she told her that she was tired of living in Mags's shadow and that she didn't love Jason any more. Molly also revealed to Lynn that she was flirting with an old flame who had contacted her through Facebook. Molly told Lynn that her ex-boyfriend was working at a car dealership near her.

'She told me that we were listening to a CD that he had given her,' Lynn told the court, adding that Molly said she wanted to meet the ex-boyfriend for lunch but she knew Jason would disapprove.

Later that week, in Myrtle Beach, Molly claimed to Lynn that Jason was the one having an affair.

Lynn testified: 'Molly was standing in the kitchen and [she] told me that she had been through Jason's phone and she had seen a private message, and that she thought that he was having an affair.'

Lynn also told the hearing that she saw frequent clashes between Molly and Jack while she was in Myrtle Beach. She stated that one day, Molly said 'she wasn't getting the respect as his [Jack's] mother.'

Jack replied, 'But you're not my real mother.' Molly was livid. She sped out of the car park and straight towards traffic. Lynn screamed. One of her children was in the car. Molly stopped and calmed herself.

Under cross-examination by Grantham Jnr, it was put to Lynn that Molly had told her that Jason had abused Molly, torn her dress and broken her iPad. Lynn denied Molly had said anything about Jason abusing her. Molly had mentioned her iPad being damaged, Lynn told the court, but there was no mention of a torn dress.

Despite Molly's acquaintance Sara Neeves telling Detective Smith that she didn't know Molly well,* Molly's legal team called her as a witness. Sara had first encountered Molly when both were dropping off their daughters for first grade. Wallburg Elementary School expected parents to volunteer, so Sara enquired about becoming a grade parent. The grade

* Sara Neeves refused an interview for this book. She told me she 'barely knew' Molly.

parents organized Halloween, Christmas and end-of-year parties. The teacher pointed to Molly and said the job was already filled. Molly was a grade parent for Jack, too. She also organized school fundraisers.

Even though they barely knew each other, Sara considered Molly an inspiring 'supermom'. Sara, who worked full-time, marvelled at how Molly found time to coach swimming. She told the guardianship hearing: 'I've actually said a couple of times to my husband, I wish I could be the kind of mom that she is. You can tell the kids have very enriched lives with activities. And that's something that I've always wanted to be better at.'

Molly's legal team also called Shannon and Charlie Grubb as witnesses. The Grubbs lived on Red Hawk Lane, diagonal to Molly and Jason's home. The couples had vacationed together.

Years later, it would be revealed that Molly had confided in Shannon ten months before the killing that she was the victim of ongoing domestic abuse. However, Shannon was not allowed to testify about that at the guardianship hearing in 2015. Any testimony that related to allegations of domestic violence, or any speculation about the violent events of 2 August 2015, was not allowed.

For example, when Tracey testified that Molly had told Tracey that she had killed Jason, the judge ordered this comment be struck from the record.

At the hearing, Shannon Grubb took the stand to say that Molly should be the children's guardian. Shannon extolled Molly's virtues as a mother and swim coach. Unlike Sara Neeves, Shannon did socialize with Molly.

Shannon was asked about Tracey's testimony that Molly frequently drank from a margarita cup, including while driving. Shannon said she saw Molly drinking wine at book club or at neighbourhood cook-outs but had never seen her with a margarita cup.

When Molly took the stand, her testimony was laced with the small, intimate details of motherhood. She relayed her various nicknames for Sarah (Sarah Bara, Meatball, Turnip, Sunshine) and Jack (Jackie Foofoo).

Sarah had called her 'mom' within a month of Molly arriving in Ireland. Jack had taken several months, but he also called her 'mom'. By then, Jason was treating Molly as the children's mother.

'My husband had already given me a Mother's Day card from the children and himself,' Molly said.

Molly described her hectic Meadowlands schedule, where weeknights were spent swimming, horse-riding, or going to dance lessons, basketball or baseball games. She permitted television on Friday nights. She detailed how she helped Sarah with her reading difficulties and her 'stress-related physical ailments'.

Demonstrating a remarkable recall, Molly listed what they had done for the children's birthday parties for each of the seven years she had known Jack and Sarah.

Conscious to reject Tracey's claims that she ignored Jack, Molly listed Jack's favourite colour (Duke blue), his favourite food (lasagna) and his dislike of raw broccoli. She gave a long list of his weaknesses, too: Jack was anxious and had a bad dream at least once a month; he was quick to anger and extremely competitive. She didn't repeat what she had told Dr Suttle – that Jack had a tendency 'to lie about minor things'.

Molly denied drinking excessively or driving while impaired, saying she enjoyed a glass of wine with a meal twice a week, and when socializing once or twice a month. She denied being bulimic but admitted she had worried about her weight 'every week since I was fifteen. I'm female.'

Molly told the court that she was diagnosed as bipolar, but when aged fifteen, not seven. She believed she was misdiagnosed as bipolar and was, in fact, depressed: 'The last time I saw someone for bipolar depression was around age seventeen [in 2000]. And probably, the last time I saw someone for depression was eight or nine years ago [2007 or 2006]. I feel that I probably wasn't bipolar. I was given antidepressants and they reacted physiologically with my body. So later on, the diagnosis was changed to depression. It's been over eight years since I've been prescribed anything.'

As we will see, Molly's claim not to have been prescribed anything for bipolar disorder or depression since 2007 is inconsistent with her medical records, which show her being prescribed Seroquel – an antipsychotic drug used to treat schizophrenia and bipolar disorder – between 2009 and 2012.

During her testimony, Molly disputed Lynn Shanahan's testimony that she wanted to leave Jason. 'I told her [Lynn] that I had recently found out that he had been engaging in an affair through social media and I didn't know what to do, but I couldn't imagine leaving my children,' Molly told the court. She denied reconnecting with a former boyfriend but admitted consulting a divorce lawyer about the 'abusive relationship' she was in.

Molly admitted telling one of her bridesmaids that she had known Jason's first wife before her death:* 'I told one of my bridesmaids, who was my friend, before I left for Ireland that I was going to au pair for a family friend and yes, that I had known her [Mags].' Molly conceded this was 'incorrect'.

Bonuomo suggested Molly didn't want her neighbours knowing she had once been the children's nanny. 'Didn't you

* Earlier there had been testimony from Karen Gorey, a manager at the Daydreams crèche and a friend of Jason for twenty years. Gorey told the court that Molly had told her bridesmaids she was pen pals with Mags.

get angry when Jack told the neighbours that you weren't his mother?'

'I don't recall a specific incident,' Molly replied, 'but I was concerned with the kids talking about our relationship . . . without discussing what we collectively wanted them to say to people.'

After seven and a half hours of testimony, Judge Shipwash adjourned proceedings, saying he would have a guardian ad litem – a court-appointed investigator – interview the children, and that he, too, wished to speak to the children before ruling. All parties presumed Jack and Sarah were facing another five or six days in the custody of the Martenses.

Tracey decided to escape Davidson County for the weekend and visit David's sister in Kansas. Her respite would be short-lived.

11. Taken

Brian Shipwash, the judge presiding over the guardianship case, could not get Jack and Sarah out of his head all weekend. Unknown to the wider public, he had met the children in his chambers. They insisted they wanted to stay with Molly. There was something about Molly, however, that unnerved Shipwash. He was worried about leaving the children in her care for the weekend, let alone for the rest of their childhood.

That Sunday, 16 August 2015, the *Irish Mail on Sunday* ran a front-page story revealing how Molly's brother Bobby – in whose house Jack and Sarah were deemed safe – was facing charges of drink-driving with a child in the car. Bobby's mugshot accompanied the story. In Limerick, a public protest march demanding Jack and Sarah's return to Ireland was scheduled for the following Tuesday.

Jason's older brother, John, a health worker, told Ireland's national broadcaster, RTÉ, that he was worried about the psychological impact on Jack and Sarah. 'The kids are staying with people who have been named as suspects by police,' he said. 'That alone is horrifying.'*

Shipwash was acutely aware that the Irish government had its emissaries present in court, and that US and international media outlets were all waiting on his decision. When he'd adjourned the hearing on Friday, he had intended to take up to five days to make his decision, but by Sunday morning

---

* He suggested Molly was motivated to seek custody for two reasons: to help her defence in the event of criminal charges; and to get Jason's money as he had a 'substantial estate'.

his mind was made up. He had decided to uphold Jason's will and declare Tracey and David Lynch as the children's guardians.

Shipwash made an emergency order for the children to be removed from Molly's custody. He informed Molly's lawyers and Tracey's attorney of his decision. However, the attorneys on both sides were bound by a gag order preventing them from informing their clients of Shipwash's ruling until the children were removed from Molly's custody.

'I felt sorry for those children because Molly was the only person that they felt they had a connection to,' Shipwash later told me. 'I knew the children were confused. They were with Molly's brother, Bobby. He had a big house with a pool. Molly was their only connection here. They wanted to go with her, but I knew I was making the right decision.

'It was the first time I had ever dealt with a guardianship hearing that involved a suspected murder. There was no contact between myself and the sheriff's office, but I did liaise with the DSS attorney Chris Watford. He was acting as the middleman between Molly and the Lynches.

'I wanted to know that the children were safe. My main focus was to get them away from Molly and the hell out of the United States. I knew if I got them to Ireland, they would have a good home and upbringing with Tracey, plus that was what Jason had wanted. I was shocked that the DSS placed the children in her [Molly's] custody, to be quite frank.

'I put a gag order on the attorneys on both sides so they couldn't tell their clients anything about my decision until the children were taken from Molly and in our custody. I was worried about what she might do if she found out.'

This was the first time such a gag order had been used in Davidson County. 'I wasn't worried that Molly would physically harm the children,' Shipwash said, 'but the last thing I wanted was Molly freaking out and harming the children [psychologically] before social workers and police could get to Bobby's house.'

Lawyer Kim Bonuomo contacted Tracey in Kansas around midday on that Sunday and told her to return to North Carolina immediately. Convinced something had happened to Jack and Sarah, Tracey begged Bonuomo for details. The attorney said there had been a development but she was legally bound to secrecy.

David drove three and a half hours to St Louis. Tracey made repeated calls to Bonuomo during the drive, and again just before she and David boarded the next available direct flight to Charlotte. On this final call before boarding, Bonuomo told Tracey she couldn't reveal what Judge Shipwash's order said but that Jack and Sarah were safe.

Meanwhile, social workers Shelly Lee and Jon Wilson and two deputy sheriffs from Union County were dispatched to Bobby's house. Mike Earnest was there. Lee asked to speak to Molly. She was in Bobby's pool. Lee handed her Judge Shipwash's emergency order authorizing the DSS to remove the children from Molly, told her to pack a bag of clothes for each child and to say goodbye.

Molly became hysterical, and Mike was enraged. He accused the DSS of planning to take the children from Molly all along. Molly packed a bag each for Jack and Sarah and tried to explain what was happening.

Wilson then unwittingly caused some confusion by telling Lee that they needed to leave as soon as possible 'due to the change in flights'. This was in reference to the Lynches managing to get a flight from St Louis to Charlotte, but Mike misinterpreted it as the children being whisked away on a flight to Ireland from Charlotte that night.

Molly helped to put the children into the back of a black van. Mike recalled afterwards: 'Both children were crying and screaming, over and over, "Don't take me away from my mommy." Unfortunately, neither my wife nor I had the presence of mind to record this event with our phone, but the memory is forever etched in my memory. The children, both of them, dearly loved Molly and she loved them.'

Jack held Sarah's hand in the back of the van. As they drove off, Molly fell to her knees and screamed, before curling into an embryonic ball.

It was only upon landing in Charlotte Airport that the Lynches learned they had been granted guardianship. They drove to the DSS offices in Thomasville, where after an hour-long meeting with social workers Tracey was finally led into a playroom. Jack and Sarah were sitting on separate sides of the room playing with toys. She and David brought the children to their hotel, where they slept for fourteen hours.

Meanwhile, two men presented themselves as federal agents at Charlotte Airport and demanded to see the passenger manifests of all flights to Ireland. A US marshal intervened and stopped them.

In the fourteen frantic days since Jason's killing, David and Tracey had scarcely had time to discuss the practicalities of having two traumatized children to raise. A heartbreaking task awaited them – they could no longer provide a home to the 12-year-old foster girl in their care. This was, and would remain, a lingering source of sorrow for them.

The Lynches were told they could not leave America until Judge April Wood heard Molly's step-parent adoption case, scheduled for Thursday, 20 August, four days away.

Jason's brother John feared Tom's FBI connections were influencing the sheriff's office and others. He told RTÉ: 'I feel that there are sinister behind-the-scenes forces at work in relation to the Martens family's police and judicial contacts.'

Sheriff Grice dismissed John's assertion, stating: 'We are a local police station, but no national agency has any sway here. No one is above the law.'

That Tuesday, 18 August, the contents of Tom's 911 call after Jason's killing were published in the *Irish Daily Mail* under the headline: 'Molly's father told 911, I did it.' Lawyers for Tom and Molly were furious, as the 911 call contents had been sealed by court order on 3 August.

In advance of her step-parent adoption case, Molly's lawyers requested Judge Wood to dismiss Shipwash's ruling and order the Lynches not to leave America. Bonuomo felt this application was almost certain to fail, but given Molly had already engaged five lawyers on civil actions alone, nothing could be taken for granted.

Jason's brother John Corbett wasn't the only one worried about the Martenses' federal contacts. After the attempts to access the flight manifest at Charlotte Airport, the Lynches' lawyers advised them to be extra vigilant about their security and communications. They were told to replace their phones with burner phones – prepaid cellphones that are not linked to an account holder and are typically discarded after a short period, thus making them much harder to tap for surveillance purposes. They were told to carefully safeguard their travel plans home.

Worried the children's passports – which they thought the Martenses had – might be withheld, Tracey asked an Irish consular official how they would get Jack and Sarah home without them. The official smiled and opened his silver briefcase. Inside were duplicate passports for the two children.*

*

---

* These proved unnecessary as the Martenses had been ordered at the beginning of the guardianship case to hand over the children's passports.

Prior to the Martenses' hearing before Judge Wood – at which the judge would decide whether or not to set aside Judge Shipwash's guardianship ruling and order the Lynches not to leave the US with the children until a full step-parent adoption hearing was completed – Molly was granted a 1-hour 'visitation' with the children. Her parents came with her.

Sixteen days after Jason was killed the five people who had been in the house that night gathered for what would be the last time.

Mike Earnest later claimed Molly was unaware that this visitation was in fact a goodbye. But in the video of the meeting it is clear that all the adults knew this was the end of the children's American life.

In it, a crying Molly instructs Sarah to say goodbye to Tom. Sarah hugs her step-grandfather briefly. Tom tells her, 'No matter what, I'm always here.'

Molly is wearing two matching necklaces, each bearing a large silver ring. She gives one to Sarah. Then, she sends Jack to hug Tom. Tom repeats the same line he told Sarah, in a robotic cadence: 'No matter what, I'm always here.'

Jack, wearing a Superman T-shirt and black cargo shorts, returns to sit on Molly's left side, now holding a pristine new baseball.

Then Tom leaves. His sudden departure was not explained, but he had a pressing appointment in Tennessee. One of his colleagues at Oak Ridge was scheduled to interview him as part of his employer's investigation into the killing. Tom had already been suspended on full pay. His employers wanted a full account of his actions on the night, to assess whether his security clearance should be permanently revoked.

Molly had brought photo albums and new toys for the children, including an American Girl doll and a teddy bear. Both Jack and Sarah hug her tight and show genuine love for the woman who had been their mother for more than seven years.

Jack pulls strands of Molly's hair over his head and down his shoulders, seeking to get as close to her as possible. Molly hugs them both, then removes her arm from around Jack's shoulder so she can turn the pages of the photo albums.

Molly and Sharon reference photographs in the album of Sarah at Santa; Sarah at soccer camp; the time they put up a basketball hoop; and the time Jack ate a whole container full of chocolate cake slices, after which his face puffed up because he was allergic to sesame seeds.

Molly asks Sarah: 'They know you're gluten-free, right?' Molly strokes Sarah's hair and squeezes Jack's hand when he places his hand in hers. Her eyes are puffy from crying.

Towards the end of the visitation a woman hands Molly some single-sheaf pages with drawings. As Molly looks at the drawings made by the children while at Dragonfly House, Jack whispers, 'Mom, I need your number, can you write it?'

The visit ended soon after. It's unclear from the video whether Molly provided her number, but in the weeks that followed she added her phone number to her numerous public posts pleading for the children to contact her.

The night before Judge Wood was to hear the Martenses' last-gasp application to prevent the children leaving America, Mike Earnest posted comments on Facebook claiming the children were desperate to stay in the US, and that Jason had told Mike's wife as recently as three weeks previously that he and the children intended to become US citizens.

'It appears we have one last hope with this custodial hearing tomorrow,' Mike wrote. 'Perhaps the most confounding matter is that these two children ages 8 and 10, who could clearly articulate their own desires, have not yet been allowed to speak on their own behalf. We strongly believe these children should be heard.'

The following morning, during the hearing, Judge April Wood said she had never encountered such a case in her thirteen years as a judge. She would set aside emotions and rule solely on the legal issue.

During a half-hour recess in the 2-hour hearing, Molly and Tracey came face to face in the court restrooms. Molly abruptly left. No words were exchanged.

Judge Wood dismissed Molly's application. The children were free to leave.

Before Tracey left the courthouse Wanda Thompson warned her. 'I said, I have no idea if it'll happen or not, but it would not surprise me if they try and get a federal order preventing you from leaving the country, so just be careful about that.'

Molly collapsed outside the courthouse and had to be held up by Bobby as she cried hysterically.

In Ireland, Jason's mother, Rita, told reporters gathered at her home: 'We had to fight to bring Jason home first, and then we had to fight to bring Jason's kids back. Who would put people through that?'

As Thompson had predicted, Molly's lawyers were unbowed. Less than an hour after Judge Wood's decision, they filed a motion to put a stay on her ruling. By then, however, Jack and Sarah were already beginning a circuitous 39-hour journey home that bore all the subterfuge of Tom's espionage world.

The Lynches were advised that in order to put a stay on their leaving, the Martenses would have to physically serve Tracey with court documents. David Lynch and Paul Dillon were advised to protect Tracey from physical approach by anyone unknown to the family.

Irish consular officials, acting on instruction from the Minister for Foreign Affairs, Charlie Flanagan, made shadow flight bookings at separate airports and booked the Lynches into a hotel in Washington DC under fake names.

While at the hotel, Paul was playing with his goddaughter Sarah when he felt something strange in the teddy bear gifted to her by the Martenses. Inside it he found what he believed to be a recording device. Also stuffed inside the bear was a piece of paper with Molly's number written on it.

Instead of flying out of Washington, Jack, Sarah and their new guardians were put in SUVs with Irish diplomatic plates and whisked to New York for a flight to Shannon Airport. Allowed to bypass the regular security checks, they were ushered on board the plane under diplomatic cover.

PART TWO

12. Posts from the Edge

There was a media scrum to get through at Shannon Airport.

It was Saturday, 22 August 2015. Jack and Sarah were scheduled to start school in just over a week's time. Before that, they would be attending their father's funeral. This time the coffin wouldn't be empty.

Jason's death notice, published the day after Jack and Sarah returned to Ireland, described him as the beloved husband of Margaret 'Mags' Fitzpatrick. There was no mention of his second wife.

Molly, determined not to be erased from the children's history, posted on Facebook. 'I miss you with every single heartbeat. Wherever you are, my love will find you.'

Jason was buried beside Mags at Castlemungret cemetery, a 10-minute walk from Jack and Sarah's new home in the Limerick suburb of Raheen. Jack remembers small details from the funeral. It was the first time he saw his grandfather cry. Sarah remembers two white butterflies hovering over the open grave.

Two of the three promises Tracey had made to Jason were now complete – she had returned Jason's body for burial in Ireland, and she was raising Jack and Sarah as her own children. Next, she was determined to fulfil her final promise – getting justice for Jason.

In North Carolina, Davidson County's district attorney, Garry Frank, gave public warnings about a lack of resources delaying his decision on whether to bring charges against the Martenses. The State Crime Laboratory and the medical examiner were under-resourced. Three weeks had passed since Jason's autopsy but, the DA warned, it could be another month before he received the official report.

The Martenses were prepared to spend more than half a million dollars to prove they acted in self-defence.

As an attorney and federal agent, Tom had advised both the FBI and the Drug Enforcement Administration (DEA) on how to prosecute complicated organized-crime cases. Now, he was up against a county DA in Garry Frank, who had been humiliated in the most recent high-profile self-defence case he had prosecuted, the 2010 case in which dentist Dr Kirk Turner was acquitted despite semi-decapitating his wife with a 4-inch pocketknife. On top of this defeat, Frank had lost two experienced assistant DAs to scandals in the past fifteen months.

Even in the sheriff's office there were fears of a mismatch between the Martenses and the DA. Some there regarded Frank as overly cautious; a good manager, but a better politician than he was a district attorney.

Molly's lead attorney, Walter Holton, could smell blood. As a former prosecutor himself, he knew the DA's office was weakened and depleted; and that despite an annual budget of $16 million, the sheriff's office would struggle to fund a complex investigation spread over two states, North Carolina and Tennessee. The sheriff's office was so constrained it had to use seized money from drug dealers to fund some elements of its investigations.

On the first day of the new school term in Davidson County the talk among Wallburg Elementary's 700 students was of the missing Irish children.

Molly took to Facebook: 'I would do anything right now to be brushing out the tangles and making back-to-school gluten-free pancakes, to be packing your lunches with notes of love and hope, and waiting all day to see how it went. I miss you munchkins.'

These emotional touchstones of motherhood garnered support for Molly online. There was no mention, or photograph, of Jason. Molly had recast herself as the victim, a distraught mother missing two children she had loved and raised for more than seven years.

Next, Molly's extended family turned Jason into the accused. Mike Earnest's daughter, Amanda Mui, claimed Molly had survived years of 'abuse from her late husband'. Mike suggested Jason had lived a double life. 'We don't know what goes on behind closed doors.'*

One of Molly's neighbours, Billy June Jacobs, claimed to know exactly what happened at 160 Panther Creek Court. 'You need to understand that everything that happened that night was a result of Jason being a monster to his wife and children,' she wrote on Facebook. 'He was physically violent and verbally and mentally abusive. None of this would be happening now if he had been a good person. I support Molly until the day I die.'

Tracey did her best to shield the children from the increasingly febrile comments on Facebook, but as Molly's lawyer, Walter Holton, would later note, in this case, social media was 'wildfire with gasoline'.† There was no escaping it.

---

* Mike Earnest claimed to have a depth of experience investigating such secretive cases. This seems unlikely given the first eleven years of his career were spent as a naval supply officer. He spent the next twenty-two as a special agent for the Naval Criminal Investigative Service (NCIS). His job in 2015, as a special agent for the office of the Special Inspector General for Afghanistan Reconstruction (SIGAR), was solely concerned with investigating fraud in Afghanistan.
† Walter Holton, 8 June 2017, trial of Molly and Tom Martens on second-degree murder charges.

The Irish-based Jason's Journey Facebook page, set up a month previously, went on to accumulate over 32,000 supporters, some of whom were not shy of going on the attack either.* The failure to immediately arrest the former FBI agent and his daughter brought accusations of a cover-up. The DA's public comments that he was considering several options, one of which was not bringing any charges, fuelled the conspiracy.

But Garry Frank rarely uttered a public word that was not calculated.† He was playing the long game.

Every week, when the Martenses' lawyers called, re-iterating their clients' willingness to answer further queries, Frank let them stew. He knew Tom was desperate to be re-interviewed. The sheriff, Thompson and the DA were privately in agreement that since Tom had already admitted killing Jason a second interview would serve his purposes only.

Publicly, both the sheriff and the DA gave interviews suggesting they could bring the Martenses in for further questioning. This was a deliberate ploy – what Tom's counter-intelligence colleagues might call a tactical briefing.

As Sheriff Grice later told me, referring to Tom Martens' desire to be re-interviewed: 'All they're going to do is fluff up their alibi a little bit. Tom had confessed. What more could he say?'

Molly, meanwhile, refused to accept that she was no

---

* At a pre-trial motion hearing on 8 June 2017 Shannon Grubb told the court that she had been reported to Homeland Security and threatened with the collective power of Jason's Journey supporters on Facebook to 'inflict pain' on her.

† It was not by accident that Frank was quoted warning about a lack of resources causing delays. As a result, Dr Nelson did not take thirty days to produce his autopsy report as feared – he signed off within five days of Frank's loaded comments.

longer involved in the children's lives. Mike Earnest became her proxy, granting interviews with the *Daily Mail*, knowing these would be posted on MailOnline, one of the world's most popular news sites.

The site, which attracts 300 million visits per month, had a disproportionately high female readership, something not lost on Mike, who could match Frank's wiles as a strategist.

Mike extolled Molly's virtues in a strangely puritanical way, listing her attributes as though describing a debutante in a Jane Austen novel.

'She is extremely well read, she's exceedingly polite, she's honest, she's a welcoming host – but all of these attributes pale in comparison to how she has been as a mother with these children. I think Molly really came to be who she always hoped she could be when she came into Jack and Sarah's life. I think she has been, and is, the quintessential mother.'

Molly posted in equally saccharine tones about the children's perfect childhood in Meadowlands: how they chased fireflies after roasting marshmallows, or peeled carrots to feed the baby rabbits on a late-spring evening in the woods at the back of their 'home sweet home'.

Jason was excised entirely from these Hallmark memories.

Molly accused the Lynches of brainwashing the children. 'It is so hard to think that people who love you might be telling you I am not your mother. In such a time of loss, you need more than ever to know your mommy's love for you is unconditional and everlasting.'

As the children started in their new school in Mungret, a suburb of Limerick city, Molly dramatically escalated her campaign. She phoned into an Irish radio show on 2 September 2015. It was Sarah's ninth birthday.

'I am distraught, they are my children,' she said. 'It seems like anyone who has children would understand the pain that I'm in, not having seen or spoken to or held my children in two and a half weeks. These children, that I have raised for eight years, have called me Mom for almost all of that time. I wanted to tell my daughter, my sunshine, that I love you, I love you so much with all my heart.'

The host of the radio show, Niall Boylan, concluded the interview in solidarity. 'Molly, that is probably the most emotional piece of audio I have ever heard,' he said, 'and people would have to have a heart of stone to not believe and understand how you feel about the children who referred to you as their mother for so many years.'

Inviting Molly – officially one of two 'persons of interest' in the killing – to publicly stalk the children live on radio provoked an instant backlash. The irony of the Martenses demanding access, when they had sequestered the bereaved children for fifteen days, was lost on Boylan. He was vilified but unbowed.

The Martenses, too, were undeterred. Mona Earnest, Mike's wife, posted on Facebook: 'The fact that this show has received so much hate mail regarding this loving message sadly confirms a lack of love and compassion in the hearts of too many souls in Limerick. Simply put, Jack and Sarah need a line of communication to their mother no matter what anyone may think of Molly. They love her and need her comfort.'

Mike Earnest continued the campaign on another Irish radio show, *Newstalk Breakfast*, vowing: 'Molly has not lost any faith that her children will one day be returned to her care. And she's prepared to take every legal step available to see that happen.'

The family filed an appeal against the guardianship ruling with the North Carolina Superior Court.

In an extraordinary move, the Martenses tried to hire a plane to fly a banner over the children's school with a birthday message for both children. (Jack's eleventh birthday was just two weeks after Sarah's.) The message was to say: 'Jack and Sarah. Happy Birthday, love Mommy.'*

When an Irish pilot refused the commission, the Martenses tried to publish the birthday wishes in a half-page advertisement in a local newspaper. The *Limerick Leader* refused.

Mike Earnest also made repeated calls to Mags's mother, Marian. 'I had to tell him to stop calling. He would call at all hours. I just hung up whenever he called,' Marian told me. 'Eventually, he stopped calling.'

Molly sent letters to the children, care of their new school, the white envelopes addressed in a red-ink scrawl. Inside, she had written the same three words – I love you – again and again across two pages of yellow paper. She signed off with her cellphone number and Sharon's.

When Molly's attempt to reach Jack and Sarah through their school failed, she sent a Facebook friend request to the girl who sat next to Sarah in school. The Irish police were alerted to this by the Lynches and immediately dispatched officers to the school.

Jack and Sarah were put on an 'at risk' register. In the event of an abduction, an alert system would circulate their photographs to every port and airport in Ireland within minutes.

So long as the Martenses remained uncharged, they were free to travel. The promise of Molly's first Facebook post – wherever you are, my love will find you – was now viewed as a threat.

When Molly moved into Meadowlands and began getting to know the neighbours, she proposed setting up a book club.

---

* Mike Earnest confirmed that he tried to hire the plane: 'The first company we contacted was in Ireland, and the second, a US-based firm that brokers this sort of thing around the world. The Irish firm initially said they could do it, but they backed out. A US firm also thought they would be able to do it, but the pilot they found in Ireland at the eleventh hour backed out.'

Whether discussing a book she had suggested or critiquing someone else's choice, Molly's was always the dominant voice in the room.

At book club she made a lasting impression on Melissa Sams, who, until then, only knew Molly as the glamorous swim coach to her two sons. When Melissa learned that Molly had previously edited a magazine in Ireland and worked for a major publishing house she thought this sassy, funny, articulate woman was wasted as a part-time swim coach.

Melissa was a lawyer specializing in high-conflict child custody cases and worked occasionally as a guardian ad litem, an individual appointed by the court to represent the best interests of a child in legal proceedings. Melissa wanted to employ Molly to write up witness testimonies for her. She sent Molly a text offering her work.

'I needed a writer,' Melissa said later. 'I was offering $13 an hour, working from home with a 90-day turnaround.'

Melissa received no response from Molly for ten days. Molly finally replied by text on 26 January 2015: 'I'm sorry, Melissa. I have been kind of a mess lately.'

Later that week,* Molly phoned Melissa and unloaded on her. She said Jason was physically and verbally abusive and was threatening to take Jack and Sarah away from her.

Melissa was used to acquaintances buttonholing her for free legal advice. But this call, just over six months before the killing, went far beyond that. Molly thought Jason had killed his first wife. 'She didn't believe that Jason's first wife died from an asthma attack,' Melissa said later. 'She thought that he was responsible for her death.'

Molly told Melissa she couldn't leave the children, whom she 'loved as her own'.

---

* Sams was unsure when exactly, but she said Molly called her between 26 and 29 January 2015.

Molly's phrasing made Melissa confused. Molly had spoken in such excruciating detail at the neighbourhood bible-study group about giving birth to Sarah. The bible-study host, Katye Oliver, had listened wide-eyed to Molly's description of the episiotomy she'd endured during Sarah's birth. The procedure involves an incision being made through the area between the vaginal opening and anus.

Katye knew Sarah was not Molly's child, so while Molly's description was anatomically correct and disturbingly well-researched, she was clearly lying.

Melissa asked Molly flat out during their phone call: 'Is Sarah your biological child?'

Molly told her that it was Jason's idea to tell neighbours that she was Sarah's mother. Molly said she begged to adopt the children, but Jason refused. He used the constant threat of returning to Ireland as a means of controlling her.

Melissa advised Molly to consult with Gary Tash, a divorce lawyer based in Winston-Salem. Absent adopting the children, it would be very difficult to gain custody. However, there was one way: Molly could apply for an emergency custody order. To do this, she had to show that Jason was a domestic abuser, or a drunk, and that the children were in danger.

Melissa advised Molly to document the abuse through secret recordings. 'I told her to keep recordings and send the recordings to me,' she said. 'A lot of times, recordings of emotional abuse are helpful in proving what you went through. If, in court, it's a he said/she said situation, and the judge can hear the tone, it's more impactful.'

Melissa and Molly devised a system of codewords in case Jason monitored her phone.

On 29 January, Melissa hosted book club. The next day, Molly sent a WhatsApp message complimenting her on her beautiful home. Molly said she had followed Melissa's book suggestions and was attaching a link for an 'audiobook' recommendation of her own.

Like FBI operatives carrying out an electronic dead drop, the link opened to a secret recording of Jason and Molly arguing. The argument takes place in the bathroom of the master bedroom. Molly is in the shower. Jason opens the door and they argue.

Detectives who later heard the tape said it was a verbal argument only. Though Molly makes reference in the argument to Jason having previously hit her on the head, this event is not captured on tape. The tape contained no direct evidence of any physical abuse.

Having listened to this tape, Melissa replied by WhatsApp: 'If you come across any more good ones, send me a link.'

Over the course of February 2015 Molly sent multiple surreptitious recordings, each described in coded messages as 'audiobooks'. Melissa texted back that she 'loved Molly's audio suggestions' and would add them to her collection.

Years later, in 2023, Melissa would testify in a North Carolina court that she only listened to the first tape, dubbed the 'Shower Tape'. As for the others, she would tell the court in 2023: 'I didn't listen to them. I kept them for safekeeping.'

Melissa may not have been curious in 2015 about the content of the other tapes, but Molly's defence lawyers were.

13. The Hand that Rocks the Cradle

The detectives were several weeks into their investigation when a package arrived from Molly's lawyer, Walter Holton – two secret recordings he described as the Shower Tape and the Pancake Tape.*

Holton knew the tapes might influence a jury, but more importantly, for now, they might persuade the district attorney, Garry Frank, that this was a justifiable homicide; simply a case of a father protecting his daughter from her wife-beating husband. If Tom wasn't guilty, then Molly sure as hell wasn't. The tapes didn't prove that, but they were emotive enough to make you pause and think.

Holton hoped the DA, on hearing the tapes, would have similar cause for pause. DAs were risk-averse and hated to lose. The tapes were an invitation to Frank to drop the case.

'We listen to the recordings,' Lt Thompson told me, 'and we call it in the best light for the defence. We listen to them for the best light of what she was alleging, that there was domestic violence. Do I think that he yelled at her and she didn't like it? Yes. Do I think that she felt demeaned in that relationship? Yeah, she probably did. But does that mean Jason was physically violent? We didn't see any evidence of it.'

---

* Molly had sent more than two recordings to Melissa Sams, but after listening to the Shower Tape, Melissa simply saved the links without opening them. After the killing, Melissa tried to open the other links and found all but one didn't work. Melissa kept notes of her interactions with Molly. One read: 'Received more messages, but did not listen, just dropped them into file. Turns out recordings not attached.'

Melissa Sams had been sent the Shower Tape by Molly on 2 February 2015. She kept contemporaneous notes: 'Alarmed about no response to accusations of hitting on head. She says something like "I'm scared when you hit me in the head." He does not deny it.'

Thompson didn't see it as so clear-cut: 'It [the tape] kind of opens up with her telling him to close the shower door and he's telling her, you know, we need to talk about this, and that goes on, back and forth.' Molly says she's scared of him, and Jason replies that he can't control if she's scared of him.

Molly: If you think the scariness is gonna go away with you hitting me on the head or throwing things at me in the back—

Jason: Yeah, okay, okay, whatever.

The detectives were cognizant of the fact that Molly knew she was recording the conversation, so they had to ask if she was orchestrating it, too.

'She's going to behave all dainty,' Thompson observed. 'She's going to say things on that recording that's going to help her. She's telling Jason that she's afraid of him and he goes, "Why are you afraid? I can't help that you're afraid." There's no evidence. I don't hear anybody getting slapped, anybody getting hit, a door slam, anything that sounds like somebody's getting knocked up against the shower wall, nothing. I mean, the tape just shuts off and they are still in there.'

Next, the detectives listened to the Pancake Tape, a 17-minute recording of the family at the dining table around 7 p.m. Jason has returned from work. It's Shrove Tuesday, 17 February 2015, less than six months before the killing.

In the recording, Jason comes across as aggressive, angry and controlling, losing his temper over not being able to have a family dinner. Molly and the children had eaten earlier, and Molly had not made a meal for Jason. Jason says repeatedly that he had called Molly earlier to tell her that he wanted to have a family meal together.

Molly tells Jason that he said he *didn't* want dinner. He insists he said the complete opposite. She said she didn't get time to make dinner because she was in charge of six children, who she went sledging with because there was snow outside. Molly offers Jason soup.

'I work twelve hours a day and I couldn't have dinner with my family because you ignored me,' Jason says, his voice seething. 'I'm sure I don't have the luxury to choose not to work because I don't have anyone else who is going to provide.'

He asks how her 'job-hunting' is going, if she had filled out her resumé. He says he's been asking her to do it for two weeks. 'You couldn't do it all day? You couldn't do it all last week or two weeks [ago] when I asked you. You just couldn't. I understand. Let's not talk about it.'

Jack says, 'Are we really going to fight right now?'

Jason says, no. Then, Sarah interjects: 'Well, if we're not going to fight, that's good.'

Jason's voice softens and he asks Jack and Sarah about the sledging. Sarah says she went butt-sledging. Jason asks Molly if she sledged, too. She says she did, once.

Jason replies: 'Were all the men over there?'

Sarah quickly interjects: 'Nope. Only women. Well—'

Molly clarifies that Rob came to collect his kids. Jason asks if anyone else was over there. Sarah says she saw Jacob driving. Jack quickly corrects her to say Jacob wasn't with them. This appeared to reinforce the children's claims to social workers that Jason was jealous over Molly being around other men. It's also clear, from Jack and Sarah's interjections, that arguing was not unusual in the home.

Jason gets up to make himself some food. Molly offers to make him something, but he dismisses her, telling her she's obviously too busy. The argument over whether Jason had asked for dinner is reignited and lasts for another seven minutes of back and forth.

After three minutes, Jack leaves the table to go upstairs. Molly tells him to walk faster. Jason tells her not to send the children out of the room when he's talking. He calls Jack back.

Sarah, in a loud, upset voice, says: 'Daddy, you're not talking, you're screaming.'

He is not screaming, but his voice is raised. The argument continues, with Molly and Jason both exasperated, both raising their voices. Jason says she is keeping him from spending time with his children.

'You wonder why I'm considering doing what I'm doing when you think I don't want to spend time with my family?' he says. This appears to be a reference to his threats to return to Ireland.

'Could they just not be here while you scream at me?' Molly says.

Jason replies: 'I'm not screaming at you. I want to know why you keep the kids separate. I wanted to have dinner with my kids.'

Molly tells him to stop screaming. He picks up a kitchen chair, slams it and shouts: 'You have made it very clear you want to separate me from my kids.'

Sarah tries to calm everyone down, but Jason tells her, 'Shut up, Sarah.' Sarah asks them both to 'please stop. It's very upsetting.'

Then, Jason angrily asks to see Molly's phone to check that she called a doctor about Sarah's blood tests because the doctor had left a message three days prior. His voice rising, Jason says: 'Show me where you called on the cellphone.'

This appeared to reinforce claims made by the children that Jason would check Molly's phone.

Wanda Thompson knew Holton would present these tapes as evidence of an angry, abusive and controlling husband who was frightening his wife and children.

Detective Brandon Smith noted that Molly had been making recordings since at least the end of January 2015 – based on what Melissa had told them. Were these two tapes the best evidence she had gathered in the six months leading up to Jason's death? There was certainly shouting, but no evidence of violence.

Thompson agreed with Smith. She later told me: 'The day they make couples arguing and yelling and saying mean, hateful things to each other illegal, I'm going to be throwing everybody in jail. It's not against the law, is it? Does that equate to domestic violence? No. He didn't put his hands on you, he didn't do anything, there's no weapons, there's no nothing, so that tape doesn't mean shit to me.'

While the detectives considered the two tapes sent to them by Molly's lawyers as lacking any evidentiary value, they also recognized that should the case come to trial, the tapes could be emotive enough to influence a jury. They were also wary of selective edits being leaked to the media. Listened to in isolation, and without context, selective edits would undoubtedly influence public opinion.

Holton's hope that the tapes would make the DA drop the case was forlorn for now. The DA was determined to proceed with preparing indictments for a grand jury.

However, years later, the tapes would prove significant as Tom and Molly battled to convince a court and the public that their killing of Jason Corbett was justified.

*

One month after returning to Ireland, Jack and Sarah began counselling. They had told three separate social workers, a grief counsellor and the guardianship judge that they loved Molly and wanted to stay with her. They were conflicted and needed time to grieve, not just for their father but for Molly and their lost American lives.

An 11-year-old boy could not be shielded from the internet. His friends shared with Jack Molly's repeated pleas on Facebook.

One night in September 2015, several weeks after returning from America, Jack asked that David bring him to his father's grave. It was after 8.30 p.m. and dark outside. David left Jack alone by the graveside while he watched from a discreet distance.

Jack was angry when he returned. He asked David, 'Are the Martenses locked up yet?'

David explained it was a slow process. On the way home in the car, Jack said he had lied in the interviews he gave in America. He said he needed to 'fix it'.

Molly had told Sarah she needed to eat gluten-free food. But once in Ireland, all Sarah's digestive issues, which Molly had diagnosed, disappeared.

One day, when Tracey brought Sarah shopping, Sarah stole some items. Tracey returned them immediately. Sarah told her she didn't realize it was wrong, that Molly had taught her to shoplift and they had done it many times.

On another occasion, Tracey discovered Sarah attempting to make herself sick after a meal. Molly had taught her to vomit as a way of keeping thin.

Jason's personal laptop had disappeared from the house on the night of the killing, but Tracey was able to access his gmail exchanges with Molly. Detectives also got access to the emails on foot of a search warrant they issued to Google. The emails revealed a relationship fraught and volatile from the outset.

Detectives already knew that Molly slept with Jason the night she arrived in Ireland. Their emails revealed a whirlwind romance. Within weeks, Jason was telling Molly that he loved her. Five months later, Molly was pushing Jason to propose.

But then, according to the email thread, Jason wanted to slow things down.

When Molly's visa expired she returned to Tennessee for a few weeks. Jason used the break to suggest she get a job au pairing for another family when she returned. That way, they could have a normal dating relationship, instead of living like husband and wife.

In the email exchange with Molly, Jason said that he didn't want Jack and Sarah (who were only four and two years old at the time), to get too attached to Molly, and then lose her, like they lost Mags. The exchange continues:

Molly: I wish you wouldn't think of me as such a weapon for the kids. Shut up. It feels horrible. And even if I was with you, it would be eating me up and tearing me to pieces knowing you weren't sure you wanted me. Sorry. I said more than I meant. I just want to be loved. Not even as much as I love you. I just want to be loved back. What I am saying is that neither of us should live life with so much doubt. It hurts to carry doubt. And it hurts more to know that someone you love doubts you.

Jason: I'm not made of stone. I'm sick of fighting. I feel bad. I'm as upset as you are. It hurts me, too, you know. I just want a normal boy girl relationship. You were right that this does put pressure on us to sink or swim. That is pressure after five months we should not be under. We should be having fun getting to know each other. Going on dates. Not husband and wife.

Molly: You want to stay together even though you know you won't marry me. I know you don't want to lose me, but I'm not sure you want to keep me either. I wish you were as sure about me as I am about you. I'll be missing and mourning you and the kids for a long time to come.

Jason: Please know that I miss you and I love you so much. But I'm scared. Scared to let go in case I lose someone again. Or the kids lose someone again. I couldn't live through it. I really want to work through this, Molly. It may take time, but I want to try. Lots of love, and please don't cry.

Jason: You were the closest person to me and the last person on earth I would want to hurt. My concern is for Jack and Sarah. They've had enough tragedy in their short lives, and while I know they are resilient, I am nervous about putting them through anything further. I am really scared, Molly. I don't want to lose you. But more so, I don't want to risk Jack and Sarah losing another mother if we don't work out.

Molly returned from Knoxville, and they continued as before. Eighteen months later, on Valentine's Day 2010, Jason proposed marriage.

When Molly travelled ahead to organize the wedding and their new home, her email exchanges with Jason renewed. They were not typical of a couple in love. Molly was terse, volatile and demanding. Jason was clearly unsure, but he couldn't stomach the thought of Jack and Sarah losing another mother.

Back in the US, Detective Brandon Smith uncovered two valuable pieces of information through interviewing the women who attended Meadowlands book club.

One of the Meadowlands neighbours, Karen Davis, told detectives about a party in Molly's neighbour's house on the Friday night before the killing. Molly was openly taunting Jason at the party, calling him 'fat' and 'meatloaf'. After this happened several times in full view of numerous neighbours, Jason became upset and left.

Karen said this was not the type of behaviour you would expect from someone claiming to be a victim of domestic violence. She also told Detective Smith that she'd been spooked by two books which Molly had recommended at book club just weeks before the killing. They were *Gone Girl* by Gillian Flynn and *The Hand that Rocks the Cradle* by Robert Tine.

'I'd heard of the books,' Thompson told me, 'but I'd never read either one of them. Just so happens, that night, *Gone Girl* was on the television. So I watched the movie. I was like, holy crap! The whole movie is about the wife setting the husband up.'

The Hand that Rocks the Cradle was made into a 1992 movie of the same name. It's about a deranged woman who infiltrates a family by pretending to be a nanny.

14. Blind Date on Berlin Drive

Molly Martens' teenage years were difficult for her and her family. She missed two semesters at Farragut High School when diagnosed, aged fifteen, with bipolar disorder. She had physical problems, too – a malformation on her right foot where a cluster of veins caused regular discomfort. This required occasional surgeries; but Molly's mental anxieties were far more serious than her physical ailments.

At first, Tom and Sharon deluded themselves that Molly could overcome her teenage struggles. They decided she was intelligent enough to study at Clemson University in South Carolina, even if her grades didn't quite match their ambition. Clemson cost $7,200 per semester. Tom signed a cheque.

In 2003, Molly moved to South Carolina. She wore the Clemson University branded sweat tops but regularly missed classes. She earned a reputation as a party girl, but after the burn there was often a crash. Classmates found her to be either morose or manic.

When Molly was manic, her roommate, Jessica Thompson, would have to bunk in with other students because Molly liked to stay up all night making collages that she pinned to the wall. When morose, she would fixate on a framed photograph she kept by her bed. She told Jessica it was a photograph of her baby sister, who had died of cancer.

One classmate spent a weekend in Molly's home in Knoxville and noticed that there were no photos of this deceased sister anywhere in the house on Comblain Road. Back at Clemson, Jessica took a closer look at the framed picture beside Molly's bed. She shared her suspicions that the 'deceased sister' had never existed with Gundi Simmons, a male student who lived across the hallway from Molly. Gundi already suspected that Molly was a compulsive liar.

When Molly was discovered sitting fully clothed in a shower, water cascading over her as she consumed 'soup and chips', Tom and Sharon were summoned. They pulled Molly out of Clemson before the first semester was over. In Molly's telling, she dropped out due to mononucleosis.*

Molly moved back home with Mom and Dad. To soften the blow of dropping out of college, she got a $7,000 5-year-old Nissan Altima.

Molly told some friends at Clemson that she had transferred to the University of Tennessee. She was already on the cheerleading team there, and things were going well. Most of her former Clemson friends knew she was lying. Some were compassionate, others quietly belittled her, asking about her cheerleading adventures, knowing she would embellish her story with every telling.

In truth, after leaving Clemson, 19-year-old Molly got work as a receptionist in Monty Howard's Visage hair studio in downtown Knoxville. It was here that she met Susie West. They shared an apartment and became close friends. Molly would later choose Susie as her maid of honour when marrying Jason.

Sharon wanted Molly to study psychology or mass communications at Pellissippi Community College. But Molly was not going back to her old life, with her mother and father controlling her every move. She knew exactly what to do. She was going to fall in love with Jeremy Taylor, a colleague at Visage.

Molly must have known that Jeremy's shoulder-length hair, copious tattoos and elaborate jewellery would irk her father. Jeremy liked to wear his tight shirts unbuttoned to

* In an interview with *Elle* magazine in 2021.

the midriff so that people could see the tattoo on his sparrow chest declaring: 'The Lord is the strength of my life, of whom will I be afraid?' He was a wannabe musician and graffiti artist, smoked marijuana regularly and longed to live a carefree life on the road.

Despite being the polar opposite of a company FBI man, Jeremy was welcomed into the Martenses' home and enjoyed a good relationship with Sharon, in particular.

Sharon often suffered from 'low moods' and had her own mental health challenges over the years. But she could be good fun. Jeremy liked to dance with her. Sharon wasn't quite as good a dancer as Molly – who boasted to Jeremy of her childhood proficiency as a ballerina – but on family occasions, such as Bobby's wedding in Puerto Rico, Jeremy found Sharon, then aged fifty-four, playful, especially when imbued with a few drinks.

Jeremy and Molly moved into an apartment together in Oak Ridge. Molly had to occasionally take time off work because of pain in her foot, or for 'girl's reasons', as Jeremy put it. But otherwise, all was well. Jeremy did not notice Molly suffering from any psychological difficulties.

In the end, it was Molly's developing interest in religion that caused Jeremy to fall out with Tom and Sharon. Jeremy's mother was a preacher with a zest for the King James Bible. Over time, Molly began parroting some of Jeremy's religious phraseology. Tom took Jeremy aside and issued a sermon of his own. He told Jeremy he didn't appreciate Molly being brainwashed.

'Her father was working for the FBI at the time,' Jeremy said later. 'I am very involved in my faith, my mother is a preacher, and I talked about this a lot with Molly. She was starting to share the same views and her parents were not happy and made that clear.'*

* Interview in the *Irish Daily Mail* on Sunday, 17 July 2017.

Soon afterwards, Jeremy decided to pursue a life on the road, and his relationship with Molly came to an end. After travelling to Miami, he went on to star in a reality-television show called *The Dukes of 2Square*. The show followed Jeremy and a friend living out of a van, scratching a living as guerilla-style graffiti artists.

Though Molly and Jeremy's parting was amicable, they never spoke again. Molly did write to his family, though. She told them: 'Unfortunately for me, I am in love with a man who never wants to grow up. Jeremy Pan.'

With Jeremy out of the picture, Molly was persuaded to get her life in order. She left the Visage hair studio on good terms. The staff even had a whip-round and gave Molly a cash gift.

In autumn 2004, Molly took a psychology course at Pellissippi Community College, where Sharon taught mathematics. As part of the course, Molly studied stress, states of consciousness, memory and psychological disorders. In the spring of 2005 she took a course in mass communications and submitted her essay, 'Molly's Inferno'. This fictional re-working of Dante's *Inferno* saw Molly recast as the central character, chaperoned through purgatory by her 'dead baby sister'.

Also in 2005, Molly opened an account on the social media site Myspace. She used an alias and pretended to be a primary-school teacher struggling to impress her 8-year-old stepdaughter. At the time, Molly was actually twenty-one, a student and single.

However, on Myspace she wrote: 'I have a beautiful stepdaughter whom I deeply love and cherish. I understand her standoffishness (forgive the fake word) because she's only spent one summer and a few holidays with me in her life. She spends the school year with her mother and stepfather 10 hours away. But she'll be here for her birthday and I want to get her something perfect. She will be eight.

'I don't want to have to ask her mother [for gift suggestions] for a variety of reasons,' Molly's post continued, 'and as her innocent voice reminds me, "dad is clueless." I know she's a Disney kid, high school musical, cheetah girls, etc., but I really want to get her something special. I love kids, I get them, don't get me wrong. I'm actually a primary school teacher myself. I'm just looking for a little extra help this time. Any ideas?'

In other Myspace posts, when offering advice about the virtues of a university education, Molly claimed to be a privileged graduate of the prestigious universities Clemson and Emory.

Years later, in 2023, when psychiatrist Dr Scott Hampton assessed Molly, he found that she believed in manifestation – dreaming of something, then planning and acting to conjure it into existence. A second psychiatrist, Dr David Adams, concluded that Molly had a deliberate plan, dating from before she married Jason, to marry him, divorce him and then take his children.

In the fictional online life she created from her early twenties there were lots of clues as to what Molly imagined her dream life to be. After losing Jeremy Pan, she set about manifesting her future family.

In 2005, like millions of others, Molly dumped Myspace for the latest craze, Facebook. By 2015, that platform would become her sole means of communicating with Jack and Sarah, the two children she 'manifested' – through executing a deliberate plan to marry Jason Corbett and take his children from him.

But that was still ten years away. In the meantime, Molly discovered online dating and set up an account on Yahoo Personal. This was how she came to meet the next man in her life, Keith Maginn. At the time she was working as a childminder to two children.

Had Keith seen Molly in a bar, he would have shot himself down before she could. Though he was attractive and intelligent, Keith lacked self-confidence and was still dealing with the end of a previous 6-year relationship. He was also suffering from a range of other problems: a debilitating arthritic disease, narcolepsy, anxiety and depression.

Keith later admitted in *Turning This Thing Around* – a self-help memoir he wrote about this period in his life – that at the time he considered Molly, to whom he ascribed a pseudonym, way out of his league. But she had liked his profile on the online dating site, and they had established a connection, through several marathon phone calls, prior to meeting for the first time.

Their first date was great: white wine in Molly's two-bed condo on Berlin Drive, her cat circling their ankles as they talked effortlessly for hours, then a late-night meal at Pelanchos Mexican Grill in downtown Knoxville. But, as Keith accompanied Molly back to her condo, he was not expecting her to ask him to move in.

The west Knoxville condo was the only one whose front balcony was still bedecked in Christmas lights. It was February. Molly said she was going to keep the lights on all year round and ride the hell out of 2007. She just loved Christmas. Keith liked how quirky and energetic she was.

Giving herself and the condo the hard sell, Molly urged Keith that if he moved in they could split the rent, split groceries and save on bills. So why not? The condo was part of the Palisades Community, so she had access to a community clubhouse, a saltwater swimming pool and tennis courts.

'The whole night seemed magical, surreal,'* Keith recalled afterwards.

A month later, he moved in.

* Maginn, interviewed by Catherine Fegan for the *Irish Daily Mail*, April 2016.

'We fell in love fast and hard,' Keith said. 'She was happy, fun, beautiful. Molly had a zest for life I hadn't encountered before. She was unique, special.'

Tom and Sharon had bought the $70,000 Knoxville condo that Keith and Molly were now sharing as an investment property* two years previously, adding it to their $525,000 home in Knoxville and their $760,000 beach house in South Carolina.

Tom wasn't too impressed by Keith when he first met him when he came to collect the rent.

From the westside suburbs of Cincinnati, Keith had moved to Knoxville in September 2001, a few days after the attack on the Twin Towers in New York. While Tom was working all hours at the FBI offices in Knoxville, fighting the 'war on terror', Keith went to work for Habitat for Humanity, a charity that builds affordable homes for the poor.

Tom had worked as the FBI supervisor in Cincinnati between 1986 and 1991, but he found little else in common with Keith, who he dismissed as having no financial future.

For the first couple of months of their relationship, Keith found Molly free-spirited, if a little hyper. She told him she had been diagnosed with bipolar disorder in her teens, but the medication helped. Keith didn't really know what a bipolar diagnosis meant. However, he had suffered bouts of depression and anxiety. Maybe he and Molly would be kindred spirits, their broken wings healing together?

At the start of their relationship, Molly had boundless energy, so much she couldn't sleep. Sometimes, she went for long runs in the middle of the night, or she read a book from start to finish in a single sitting. On other days, incapacitating migraines left her unable to get her head off the pillow.

---

* The property was purchased in June 2005 with Sharon Martens listed as the registered owner.

Within months, however, Keith witnessed the hyper, jolly Molly disappear. 'It was like someone flipped a light-switch,' he recalled. Molly was missing work, harming herself. Keith was paying all the bills. At one point, he asked Tom Martens to cut him some slack because it was hard, on his salary, trying to pay for everything. Tom told him the rent was due and Keith needed to sort it out, one way or another.

Some days, Keith returned from work to find Molly in the bath, drinking wine. They had 'explosive' arguments. Keith said Molly was never physically violent but she would become hysterical and prevent him from leaving: 'She felt that if I left, I was never coming back. It was exhausting because I would need to get away and she wouldn't let me. There was no escape.'

What Keith didn't know was that Molly went through highs and lows all the time. Six weeks before meeting him she made diary entries describing herself as a failure, a horrible daughter and sister who kept blowing every opportunity given to her. She bemoaned how she sabotaged her relationships. She complained about gaining weight and all the medications she was on.

In diary entries from late December 2006 Molly wrote about Tom being depressed because he was due to retire from the FBI: 'I think after 30 years it seems somewhat anti-climactic like no one really cares. Mom is honestly thinking of leaving him because she is selfish and thinks it will be bothersome to have him around all the time. I have nightmares about it.

'Overall, I'm mostly just sad. I would like to sleep continuously. I am a continual disappointment to myself, my mother and pretty much the world at large. I want to be in love. I want children. Maybe I don't want these things right now but even the hope for their existence in my future is starting to fade.'

Just as she later would with Jason, five months into her relationship with Keith, Molly pressured him to propose. He bought a 'for now' ring online for $150 and they celebrated their engagement with a dinner at Pelanchos.

Molly briefly rallied in September 2007 but was soon back to being morose and volatile.

Then, to Keith's horror, Molly announced she was pregnant. The birth control they had been using must have failed. Molly was taking sixteen different medications for her bipolar disorder. She told Keith she had a nightmare about a miscarriage. It came true. Keith rushed to the hospital to find Molly's parents already there.

'I was honestly counting my blessings that it did not work out,' he said later, 'for that poor kid's sake, and for our sake.'*

Molly plunged deeper into depression. The once hyper, joyous young woman Keith had fallen in love with was gone. Molly told Keith that her mother was bipolar, too. Sharon had always been controlling, Molly said, ever since Molly's 'baby sister died . . .'

Molly told Keith that she had reached the end. She was going to kill herself. Keith got the Martenses to help. On 6 February 2008 they had Keith drive Molly to what they were calling a rehab centre in Atlanta, Georgia. In fact, it was a secure psychiatric unit within Emory University Hospital.

Molly was hyper the whole way down in the car. She'd gone out jogging during the middle of the night, and now she was talking non-stop. Keith accompanied her into the unit in Emory. She begged Keith for Coca-Cola and muscle relaxants, anything to take the edge off as she prepared to be weaned from the sixteen daily medications she was on, plus the ten she took 'as required'. Keith refused and she lost her temper, shouting at him to leave.

* Interview with Pat Kenny on Newstalk radio.

Keith returned to his 'shithole motel' in Atlanta and wondered how that bubbly, beautiful young woman in Pelanchos restaurant had come to this.

Molly's detox was brutal and lasted for three days. She was discharged on 9 February. On 10 March 2008, Molly left the US to travel abroad for a job minding two children. She told Keith, who was still her fiancé at the time, that she would only be gone for a few weeks.

'I thought it was another of her far-fetched fairy tales that wasn't going to really come to fruition,' Keith recalled, 'but then she did actually follow through with it, which surprised me. She wasn't well enough to do the groceries, so I was thinking, how is she going to look after children? When she left, I never saw her again.'

Four weeks after leaving a psychiatric unit, Molly presented her passport to immigration officials at Shannon Airport. They asked her if there was anyone she would like to call before they deported her.

Molly called the new man in her life: Jason Corbett.

15. Neighbourhood Watch

It was just after 1 a.m. on 12 October 2014 when Charlie Grubb's wife, Shannon, woke him. The bedroom was in darkness but for the blue light emitting from Shannon's phone. Charlie could hear shouting. He recognized the man's voice. Then, screaming. The caller's name was lit up: Molly.

The Grubbs lived on Red Hawk Lane around the corner from the horseshoe close at Panther Creek. Their daughter, Ashlyn, befriended the new Irish girl in first grade and swam with Sarah at Meadowlands swim and tennis club, where Molly was a part-time coach.

Shannon and Molly would chat at length at Ashlyn and Sarah's gymnastics classes. They socialized at Baptist bible-study groups and, from late 2014, at the book club Molly established for six women in Meadowlands.

Jason and Charlie Grubb hit it off, too. Charlie ran casino parties.* He had twenty-five employees and a Virginia lake house. At neighbourhood cook-outs, Jason was usually to be found with Charlie and another neighbour, Tony Turner. Jason and Tony were tribal opposites – an Irishman and an Englishman, a Liverpool fan and a Manchester United fan – but they shared a similar sense of humour.

Charlie didn't always get the irony at the heart of Jason's jokes, but he liked his big Irish neighbour. They got on so well Shannon talked about Jason, Molly and the kids joining them at their lake house.

---

* Gambling was illegal in North Carolina except on Indian reservations or at a licensed casino party. Charlie held one of the much-coveted licences.

Tony Turner's wife, Jennifer, was one of the first neighbours to question the happiness of Jason and Molly's marriage. Jason would draw Molly into his embrace when they were out, but Jennifer sensed something.

Then one day, when Jennifer told Molly that she looked pretty, Molly coldly replied that Jason had just told her that she 'looked like a whore'.

Shannon Grubb considered herself to be Molly's closest friend. Yet she was one of the last to discover Molly's marital secrets. Billy June Jacobs was the first.

Billy June described herself on Facebook as a 'Domestic Engineer at Home Sweet Home'. Her daughter, Ellen, was best friends with Sarah and Ashlyn, Shannon's daughter. Billy June and Molly alternated school pick-ups and walked together most evenings in Meadowlands or around Union Cross Park.

In spring 2014 Molly told Billy June that things 'weren't good at home'. 'She told me there was physical, mental and emotional abuse,' Billy June said later.

While they were out walking, Jason would harass Molly. According to Billy June: 'We couldn't get more than a few steps before Jason was calling or texting. After numerous texts and calls, she [Molly] would answer. A lot of the time he would be yelling. I could hear at times because she would have it on speaker.'

Jason would demand to know where she was. 'He left voicemails,' Billy June said, 'always just screaming at her: where are you, what are you doing? He would call her names. He was always angry. I was very scared. I was wondering what would happen when she got home.'

Molly often cancelled their walks, telling Billy June the malformation of veins on her foot was too sore from Jason stepping on it. Billy June came to view Jason as a 'monster'.

She urged Molly to leave. Molly refused. 'She said, I'm not going to leave the kids behind,' Billy June recalled. 'I'm going to wait until Sarah is old enough to make her own decisions about adoption.'

Molly told Billy June that she had been advised by a lawyer about a provision in North Carolina law which allowed children who had not been adopted to choose which parent they wanted to live with in the event of marital breakdown. The children had to be at least thirteen, however, which meant Molly faced six more years under Jason's control.*

'I was fearful that someone was going to get hurt really bad at her house,' said Billy June. 'It was getting worse all the time.'

She and Molly discussed a plan. 'We talked about putting cameras in the house and recordings on cellphones.'

Six months later, at 1.01 a.m. on 12 October 2014, Molly put through her frantic call for help – but it was to Shannon Grubb, not Billy June.

Shannon answered her phone to heavy breathing. In the background, there was arguing and screaming. She woke Charlie and put the call on speaker.

'Jason was very angry,' Shannon said, 'and Molly was screaming, "Please don't do this to us."'†

Shannon thought about calling 911. She thought it was Jack or Sarah who had dialled her number, but when she called Jack and Sarah's names, nobody answered. She and Charlie listened for four minutes, then hung up.

The next day, Molly seemed initially unaware of the call,

---

* Children could express a preference at age thirteen, but the judge was under no obligation to grant the child's wishes. The judge's decision had to be 'in the best interests of the child'.

† Testimony Shannon Grubb gave to a sentencing hearing in November 2023.

then embarrassed. Shannon told her to get help, but Molly said she would not leave Jack and Sarah.

Tensions escalated through the winter of 2014. Shannon witnessed Jason's jealousy when a group of neighbours hired a limousine to attend a charity gala event.

When Molly got out of the limo, according to Shannon Jason 'grabbed her and yanked her to the side and there was a disagreement about something'. Molly told Shannon that Jason was angry because she exited the car at the side where all the men were.

One school morning, Molly called Shannon from a local park and asked her to bring shoes for Sarah. Molly said she'd had a fight with Jason and didn't want to bring Sarah back to get her school shoes. 'When I met her [Molly] in the park to give her the shoes,' Shannon recalled, 'Sarah was hysterical, crying. She didn't want Molly to go back home without her.'

Weeks after the 1 a.m. phone call, Molly arrived for a gathering at the McDonells' house looking distressed. Shannon Grubb saw her take a blood-soaked tissue from under her hat and replace it with a new, clean one. 'She said that they fought before they got here,' recalled Shannon. 'I thought this can't continue. She's going to get hurt worse.'

In an undated event around this time Molly called in person to Jennifer Turner's house one evening, saying she had been in a really bad fight. 'She was crying and saying she couldn't leave because she loved the kids,' Jennifer stated.

Jennifer was not surprised by this escalation as she, too, had heard aggressive voicemails which Jason had left on Molly's phone. She was out shopping with Molly one day when the calls started. 'He called eight or nine times,' Jennifer said. 'She was scared to go home.'

One week after Jason's killing, Lieutenant Wanda Thompson requested further toxicology testing to check if Molly had drugged Jason with lithium – as she had allegedly drugged Tom and Tracey in the past – or trazodone.

Frankie Young, the CSI chief, had found an empty lithium bottle at the house. He'd also found trazodone, an antidepressant widely prescribed as a sedative. The trazodone had been prescribed to Molly two days before the killing, after Molly requested a 'sleep aid'.

Molly's records at Kernersville Medical Center raised further red flags. For three years, from 2009 to 2012, Molly was taking Seroquel – an antipsychotic drug used for treating schizophrenia and bipolar disorder. This contradicted claims Molly had made under oath at the guardianship hearing that it had been at least eight years since she was prescribed any psychoactive medications.*

One year after marrying Jason, the Seroquel prescription was discontinued. Had Molly gone off her meds and spiralled? At the time of the killing, Molly was taking Imitrex, ibuprofen and aspirin for migraines and headaches – common Seroquel withdrawal symptoms, along with insomnia.

Molly's Kernersville records contained a further interesting note. Apparently Molly had a younger sister who died as a baby . . .

The detectives' working theory was that Jason might have been drugged via the jug of mojitos† which Molly had made on the night of the killing.

* Molly had testified: 'The last time I saw someone for bipolar depression was around age seventeen [2000]. And probably, the last time I saw someone for depression was eight or nine years ago [2007 or 2006]. I feel that I probably wasn't bipolar. I was given antidepressants and they reacted physiologically with my body. So later on, the diagnosis was changed to depression. It's been over eight years since I've been prescribed anything.'
† Detectives photographed used glasses, a blender, a bottle of seltzer water and a bottle of Bacardí – a flavoured rum often used in mojitos – in the

Detectives also wondered why Sarah thought the ballerinas on her sheets were lizards and spiders. Was she hallucinating? Had Molly drugged Jason and the children before they went to bed?

There was another glaring red flag in the medical files. Once the defence attorneys, David Freedman and Walter Holton, got hold of it, it would undermine the prosecution.

On 16 July 2015, two weeks before the killing, Jason complained to his doctor about feeling faint and dizzy. These spells had started six months previously but were now occurring once a week. He was 'more stressed and angry lately for no reason'.

Jason's doctor noted that this might be related to Jason not taking his thyroid medication for six to seven weeks. Suddenly stopping thyroid medication could cause blood pressure changes, fatigue, joint pain and depression.

The district attorney knew the defence would feast on Jason's 'anger issues' weeks before the killing. Multiple women were claiming to have heard him shouting and screaming at Molly. She was telling others that he was hitting her. Shannon Grubb saw her bleeding. The children had told social workers that they had seen their father hit and punch Molly. There was a pretty good case that Jason *was* abusing Molly.

Even if there was domestic violence, the DA still had to decide if Jason's killing was a justified homicide or not.

In the detectives' first meeting with the DA's office there were plenty of sympathetic voices for Tom, or any father, taking a bat to someone choking his daughter. But the crime scene, the medical examiner's report and the blows to the back of the head all pointed to one thing: Jason wasn't running towards Tom and Molly, he was running away.

---

kitchen sink. However, the blender and glasses were not preserved and could no longer be tested for the presence of sedatives.

Even if Jason was the aggressor, even if he had been abusing Molly, the threat was over as soon as he backed out of the fight or was no longer the aggressor. That was the law in North Carolina.

So far, all these women in the neighbourhood had been painting a pretty bleak picture. In the best light for the defence, Molly was the victim of domestic violence. But Wanda Thompson still had some nagging doubts. What did these women in Meadowlands actually see?

Some of the Meadowlands husbands – Tony Turner, Tom Maddock, Chip McDonell and David Fritzsche – discussed telling Jason about the domestic violence rumours swirling among the wives at book club and bible-study group. In the end, they didn't get time to.

Tom Maddock's wife, Jerusha, had initially found Molly friendly but soon noticed her propensity for exaggeration. It became a 'running joke' among some of the wives.

Molly often boasted about her education at Clemson University. Marketing flyers circulated by Meadowlands swim and tennis club stated that head coach, Molly Martens, had been on the Clemson swim team.* Around this time, through sheer serendipity, Jerusha's husband, Tom, bumped into an old friend who had attended Clemson. Molly came up in conversation.

Tom's friend Gundi Simmons started laughing. He had

---

* In fact, Molly's Clemson career was another illusion – she left after the first semester and had never represented the swim team. She was a better than average swimmer – clocking five minutes and forty-five seconds for the 500-metre freestyle, a time that saw her place fifth when competing in Knoxville at the age of fifteen. However, she was barely good enough to be a peripheral figure for Farragut High School swim team in 2001, and nowhere near good enough to represent Clemson in 2003, never mind challenge for a place on the United States Olympic swim team, which was another of her claims.

lived across the hall from Molly at Clemson, where Molly was a notorious liar. She left after one semester* and subsequently claimed she had relocated to the University of Tennessee, where she was on the cheerleading team. Or so she had said.†

When Molly asked Jerusha to store her fertility drugs and then spoke about buying 'black market sperm' on Craigslist, Jerusha cut off contact with her.

By January 2015 Molly was telling Melissa Sams that Jerusha had betrayed her when she went to her for help over Jason's abuse. Jerusha avoided social situations where Molly might be present and took her child to another swim club. When Molly showed up at the new club, Jerusha didn't believe it was a coincidence. Molly's mother, Sharon, even called Jerusha to complain about how she was treating Molly.

Katye Oliver had hosted bible study and book club in her home and witnessed Molly lying about her episiotomy. Katye told detectives that Molly couldn't remember which lies she had told or to whom. She was like the movie character Forrest Gump, inserting herself into all kinds of false memories or momentous achievements.

Though Katye's daughter occasionally babysat for Jack and Sarah, Katye kept a reserved distance from Molly, about whom she'd had reservations since 2012. She was disgusted that Molly would seek to erase Mags and deny her existence as Sarah's mother.

Michele and David Fritzsche were already wary of their

---

* Molly is photographed in the Clemson yearbook for 2003.

† Jessica Thompson was one of the people who knew Molly at Clemson. After Jason was killed, Jessica posted a comment under a photograph of Molly wearing a Clemson University sweatshirt: 'I wonder if she is still a cheerleader at the University of Tennessee . . . remember that? The night when we were checking the roster and the weather reports . . . ha, ha, ha.'

next-door neighbour and, after learning about the episiotomy story, were convinced Molly was a 'compulsive liar'.

Even Charlie Grubb, whose wife, Shannon, was Molly's closest friend in the neighbourhood, wasn't sure who to believe. Charlie supported his wife – that 1 a.m. call sounded bad. But screaming matches were not unheard of in marriages. And there were all these strange stories circulating about Molly, too.

The Grubbs were hosting a cornhole party in their house on 31 July 2015, two nights before Jason would end up dead. They had to invite both Molly and Jason.

Many of the Meadowlands couples gathered for the party in the Grubbs' house. Things were changing in Meadowlands. Tony and Jennifer Turner had split up. From the way Molly was acting at the party, it looked like she and Jason could be next.

At the party, in front of numerous neighbours, Molly repeatedly insulted Jason about his weight, saying he must have taken all of the nutrition from his twin because he looked like he had eaten for two.

Jason became upset and left. He posted a quotation on Facebook at 11.15 p.m. – less than twenty-eight hours before his killing. 'People will question all the good things they hear about you but believe all the bad without a second thought.'

Wanda Thompson wondered later if this was the tipping point. Was Molly off her meds and experiencing another mental health crisis? Did Jason decide, that's it, I'm taking the children and leaving? Or had Molly decided she wasn't going to be a victim any more? That she was going to tell the whole neighbourhood who Jason really was?

Whatever happened that Friday night, or the following morning, Tom Martens was spurred into cancelling his Saturday-night dinner plans with his boss and instead embarked on the 4-hour drive to Meadowlands with Sharon.

Tom was Mr Calm and Controlled. He didn't make impromptu 4-hour drives. Molly must have summoned him.

A search warrant had been issued for Tom's, Sharon's, Molly's and Jason's phone and internet contacts on the days around the killing. Until they got the data from various phone companies, Google and Facebook, Detectives Hurd and Smith were told to keep digging.

The crime scene indicated chaos. But after Jason's killing Molly had been so organized, filing emergency custody, guardianship and step-parent adoption applications within three days. Had neighbour Melissa Sams unwittingly inspired Molly with the faint hope that she could make recordings of Jason being abusive and thereby take the children without adopting them?

Melissa told detectives that she texted Molly when she learned Jason was dead, on the Sunday, around 5 p.m. Molly called her back that evening and said Jason had been choking or strangling her. Melissa couldn't remember which word Molly had used. But she remembered what Molly said next.

'It was him or me.'

16. Keep Fighting

The pressure mounted on DA Garry Frank to bring charges against the Martenses. ABC, CBS and CNN were all circling the story. The Irish media was obsessively reporting on Molly's regular Facebook posts, in which she pleaded for the children to never forget how much she loved them, even if they were now living another life in another country.

The Martenses' supporters were adamant: Molly was the real victim – a mother ripped from her children for the crime of defending herself from a drunken Irish wife-beater. Tom was a hero who had served his country and saved his daughter.

Meanwhile, Jason's supporters believed the domestic violence allegations were fabricated and that the Martenses were walking free because of Tom's FBI connections, wealth and privilege.

Two months into the investigation, prosecutors and detectives had a case conference examining two questions: was there domestic violence, and were Tom and Molly justified in their actions?

In the best light for the defence, multiple witnesses were told of domestic abuse. Their stories were consistent. Yes, their source was Molly, and they had not actually seen anything,* but two witnesses had heard Jason shouting and screaming over the phone.

---

* Two of the women saw Jason become irritated with Molly over 'car trouble' at bible study. They feared what would happen to Molly when she and Jason went home after that incident, but their fears and suppositions were not evidence.

Billy June Jacobs witnessed Jason stalking Molly's movements on their walks. Shannon Grubb saw Molly remove a bloodied tissue from under her hat. She only had Molly's word for what caused that injury, if indeed it was real. However, together these witnesses were persuasive, especially when paired with the Pancake Tape.

Jack and Sarah had told three social workers they saw Jason hit, punch and slap Molly. Jack had told Brandi Reagan that a bad fight might last an hour or more, and when asked, he thought the last big fight had been in October 2014. Was this what the Grubbs heard on that 12 October call?

The crime-scene photos of bedsheets* strewn on Sarah's bedroom floor corroborated Molly and Sarah's story about her nightmare. Jack corroborated why the brick was in the bedroom. All these pieces formed a mosaic of truth.

Detectives countered that Molly might have been recording for up to eighteen months. Billy June Jacobs said she and Molly discussed recording Jason in spring 2014. They knew from Melissa Sams that Molly was definitely recording from January 2015. She had failed to record a single instance of physical violence.

And what if the 1 a.m. phone call was an edited recording? Shannon Grubb assumed it was Jack and Sarah who had called, but the children's bedrooms were upstairs. Had they come downstairs and called standing close enough for Shannon to hear their heavy breathing and a loud argument unfolding a few feet away? How did they access Molly's cellphone? Molly kept her cellphone on the nightstand beside her bed. Sarah insists that neither she nor Jack called Shannon Grubb.

Billy June Jacobs said she had been able to hear Jason

---

* Bedsheets matching those described by Sarah are visible on the floor in State's Exhibit 62, a photograph of Sarah's bedroom.

shouting during her walks with Molly, because he was so loud or because the phone was on speaker. What if Molly was orchestrating these situations, gaslighting and provoking Jason into shouting, so that she could edit and use those recordings to her advantage?

Molly was known to leave the house without explanation, leaving the lights on and the doors open. This exasperated Jason so much he had made a recording, too – a video of himself coming home to this exact situation. The April 2015 recording was found by Tracey after Jason's death.

Tracey believes Jason made this video to prove to himself that he wasn't going mad: that lights were being left on and the doors left open by Molly, who would then gaslight him by saying he was imagining things, or that he was the one responsible for not locking doors.

Molly was also known to leave Jack and Sarah unattended, both in Ireland and in Meadowlands.

Had Jason come home from work to find his children alone in an unlocked house? Had Molly recorded his furious calls to her wondering where she was? Had she then used these recordings to convince Shannon and Billy June that Jason was abusive?

At their meeting, the prosecutors and detectives discussed how the jury wouldn't buy all this conspiracy. They would think the simple explanation was true – that multiple witnesses heard Jason being aggressive, controlling and scary.

Sarah had told a social worker that 'Dad was always calling her [Molly] – called her forty-seven times one day.' Jason slammed a chair on the Pancake Tape. He comes across as aggressive, angry and controlling, losing his temper over his dinner not being on the table. Domestic violence was a sensitive subject and Jason's own children were damning him.

Wanda Thompson agreed. However, she said, there was no evidence of anything physical. Sharon lied to Tracey about the sheriff's office being called to the house six times to deal with domestic violence reports. There wasn't a mark on Molly after Jason's killing, and no one had seen her with injuries in the four years they'd lived in Meadowlands.

Molly refused to provide any dates or details of any medical treatments she had. She wouldn't sign a Health Insurance Portability and Accountability Act (HIPAA) waiver – a legal document that would allow detectives access to her health information. It's understandable that she might have wanted to keep treatment for abuse injuries private at the time, but it didn't make sense for Molly to do that now – not when she was facing twenty years in jail and proving domestic violence would go a long way to proving self-defence.

The detectives and prosecutors knew Molly was a liar. She had lied about Mags begging her from her deathbed to raise Jack and Sarah. Where would she draw the line? She taunted Jason in front of his work colleagues and humiliated him in front of neighbours at the Grubbs' house. This was not behaviour typical of someone being domestically abused.

'At the swim club, Molly walked around in a string bikini that barely covered what she had,' Thompson said. 'If she had bruises or if he had beaten her, people would have seen it. And nobody ever saw it.'

The attorneys said it wasn't in Molly's interests to kill Jason when she knew his will granted guardianship to Tracey, and when Melissa Sams had advised her of her limited rights. She did stand to gain financially though, the detectives countered. The insurance policy was reputedly worth $600,000 and Tracey had information that the policy had been changed online not long before Jason's death to make Molly the sole beneficiary.

Had Molly changed Jason's life insurance policy, drugged

him with trazodone or lithium, then attacked him? Had she found out that he was leaving with the kids, so she summoned her parents to talk him down, but all the while her plan was to kill him and claim self-defence? If the lab results came back positive for trazodone in Jason's blood, and if the insurance change stacked up, then they might have premeditation.

All the search warrants were issued as part of a 'first-degree-murder' investigation, but the DA and his assistants remained sceptical about premeditation. Surely a former FBI agent trained in the use of all kinds of firearms,* a lawyer and counter-intelligence expert, could come up with a better plan than turning up out of the blue with a child's baseball bat? Assistant DA Greg Brown pointed out that Tom had been very careful to stick to his story when he was interviewed by Commie Byrum, his counterintelligence colleague at the Department of Energy, on 20 August 2015, eighteen days after the killing. But in that interview, Tom did add one new detail.

He told his employers that he had brought two gifts that night, not one. In addition to the baseball bat, he brought a tennis racket. Brown believed Tom, a fellow lawyer, recognized there was a hole in his original story: what grandfather would visit with a gift for their grandson but nothing for their granddaughter?

The detectives suspected the bat was already in the house and the whole story of Tom bringing a gift or gifts was fabricated. If Tom had brought the baseball bat, then why didn't he just give it to Jack when he met him that night?

The feeling in the room at the prosecutors' case conference was that premeditation remained a possibility, but only for Molly. As they headed into the third month of the investigation, everyone agreed that Tom hadn't planned this, he

---

* According to Tom's counsel, David Freedman, addressing the jury during the criminal trial on 8 August 2017.

had just stepped in to save Molly. But not from Jason – from herself.

The detectives believed there was a confrontation, Molly flipped, grabbed the brick and hit Jason. Then, Tom came in. It spiralled from there.

Jason's passport was on the dresser in the bedroom on the night of the killing. He had told his friend Paul Dillon that he was coming home without Molly. Wanda Thompson said Tracey had been searching Jason's emails and she'd found one from Expedia encouraging Jason to complete his search for flights. The attorneys pointed out what the detectives already knew – the Expedia email was of no value as it hadn't detailed what the flight search query was.

The prosecutors and the detectives agreed that even if there was domestic violence, the Martenses would still have to justify their response.

'Ultimately,' Thompson pointed out, 'the crime scene just does not match the story that Tom and Molly are telling.'

Even if Jason was the aggressor, the Martenses' response was not reasonable. The medical examiner's findings – at least twelve blows to the head, some of them post-mortem, most of them to the back of the head – were stark. Jason was moving away from the Martenses when hit, and eight of the blows to the head were individually enough to render him unconscious.

In the words of the North Carolina legislation on self-defence, Jason had withdrawn from the fight. Molly and Tom continued to beat him to a pulp. Yet neither of them had a mark on them. They had faked CPR. Everybody with any expertise in CPR knew it as soon as they walked in that room, Thompson asserted. The body was cold.

The attorneys countered that the medical examiner put no store whatsoever in the body being cold. He said time of death could not be determined based on body temperature because there were too many variables.

Thompson said the scene was still hugely suspicious. If the back of a man's skull had been bashed in, how could you lift his head, turn his 262-pound body over, then pump his bloodied chest for ten minutes and have scarcely any blood on you? How could you claim to have been in a 'fight for your life' and not have a single injury?

DA Garry Frank knew that a blood-pattern analysis would be key. He commissioned the world-renowned blood-spatter expert Stuart James.*

After they were back in Ireland, Jack and Sarah began to remember things. Jack remembered Tom giving him a present of a black Louisville Slugger baseball bat with red markings, exactly like the weapon used to kill his father.

Tom gave it to him in the summer of 2014, a year before the killing. If Jack was right, then Tom's whole story fell down – it meant he had diverted to the garage to get the bat, rather than just impulsively grabbing the bat in the basement. It meant he had fabricated the whole story about bringing a baseball bat and tennis racket as presents that night.

Detectives noted that Jack had also made an interesting comment in his Dragonfly interview when asked about the bat: 'It was my baseball bat that I used, well I don't know what exact bat it was . . . but I know it was one of my baseball bats that I'd used previously in my life.'

Thompson got a warrant to search the garage of 160 Panther Creek Court – where Jack had kept that bat in a black sports bag since the summer of 2014.

It was November 2015 when the warrant was executed. Molly had been in control of the house for months. This

* I later learned that the DA's budget was so constrained Garry Frank had to ask Sheriff David Grice to put up money seized from drug dealers to pay the $5,000 necessary to commission Stuart James.

search seemed a fruitless exercise – if Jack was right and Tom had taken the bat from the garage, then the black sports bag would be empty, because that bat was the one used in the killing and was therefore already in a police evidence bag. They had executed a search warrant to look for something they hoped wasn't there.

As expected, the bat was not there. Jack believed there were photographs of him using the bat, so the search warrant allowed detectives to search the whole house. Molly had removed most items of a personal or sentimental nature. They seized two digital photo albums but found no pictures of Jack with the bat.

Facing her first Christmas without Jack and Sarah, Molly publicly pined for them on Facebook.

Describing Jack and Sarah as 'my babies', she wrote about the lifeline they shared, and how there were a billion strands to this lifeline, each strand a memory of simple things like brushing their teeth or singing 'Twinkle, Twinkle, Little Star'. She wrote about all the fun they had baking cakes and cookies, painting, colouring, playing memory games. 'No one can take those things away from us or say they never happened,' she said.

Molly expressed no empathy for Jack and Sarah facing their first Christmas without their father. She pined only for the Christmas she would be missing. She shared on Facebook how she, Jack and Sarah should be making Santa lists. Instead, the courts had ripped them apart.

Then, three days before a US court was to rule on Molly's appeal – her final chance to regain custody – she posted a picture of Jack and the message: 'I hope both of you are being nice to one another and that you know how much you are loved and missed. I love you. Mum.'

Molly's appeal was dismissed. She took aim online.

'It's not about the best interest of the child,' she wrote. 'It's about the law. Our loves do not matter in the eyes of the law. A will made when you were infants and before I came into your lives is what matters. It does not matter that clear decisions were made after this short document – moving across the ocean to another country, a marriage . . .

'It does not matter,' she continued, 'that I took you to every doctor or dentist appointment. It does not matter that I signed every parent form you ever had at school from age four up. It does not matter what you wanted. It does not matter that I kissed you goodnight and tucked you in every night. It does not matter that I held you as you got your vaccinations or helped you with your homework or read you stories. It does not matter that you have given me Mother's Day cards every year.'

Molly garnered support online by depicting the court's ruling as an attack on stepmothers.

'She is not even a real parent,' Molly wrote, describing how she felt the law viewed her. 'What matters, in the eyes of the law, is that I do not share your blood and I am not listed as your guardian on a document created before I met you. I am heartbroken, and devastatingly sorry. Our lives together may not have mattered in the eyes of the law, but they are what matters most to me. Jack and Sarah . . . I love you and will always be your mommy.'

Each social media post prompted fresh tug-of-love stories in the media, which in turn prompted further commentary on Facebook.

Stuart James's blood-spatter analysis was a game changer.

James was able to show a descending pattern of blows, evident from the blood spatter on the south wall – the wall to the right as you entered the bedroom. One blood spatter was approximately 4 to 5 feet above the floor. The next blow hit

Jason's head when he was 2 feet from the floor. Thick transfer stains and hairs on the south wall indicate his head was bleeding heavily when it hit the wall.

The 'descending succession of impacts' continued, with the last impact site just 5 to 16 inches from the floor. One blow may have been delivered to the back of the head when Jason was inches from the ground and facing the wall.

James said stains found on the inside left leg of a pair of boxer shorts worn by Tom had to have 'travelled up from below to be on the inside'. These stains indicated that Tom was standing over Jason when the blows were struck. A pair of pyjama bottoms worn by Molly also had stains on the lower legs, which showed Jason's head was 'close to the floor' when struck.

James also concluded that a vacuum cleaner in the bedroom had been moved after blood had impacted it. Pictures taken at the scene showed it to be standing upright behind Jason's head. He said the blood spatter on the vacuum was 'going sideways', and this indicated that the vacuum was on its side when blood was deposited on it. 'This shows alteration of the scene,' James reported.

James said the brick had blood on multiple sides, consistent with it hitting Jason's head more than once. Bloodstains close to the bedroom door handle could have been from fingers. Neither Molly nor Tom had much, if any, blood on their hands. So were these partial fingerprints Jason's? Was he trying to escape?

With this information from the blood-spatter analysis, DA Frank was convinced that, even if there was domestic violence here – and that was in dispute – Jason had left the fight and was beaten to death long after he had ceased to pose any threat.

Thompson told me that this was the bottom line. 'Even if he's the one that's starting the fight,' she said, 'he's stopped. As soon as that happens, you have to stop. And if you don't, you can be criminally charged. You now become the aggressor.'

Those two words – the aggressor – would prove of enormous significance in years to come.

Thompson continued. 'Even if we give them [Tom and Molly] the benefit of the doubt over all these little flags, worst-case scenario, they still went over and above what they needed to do to defend themselves. He was completely and totally defenceless, not an aggressor at all when he's on his hands and knees on the floor, and you're still beating him. He is no longer coming after you. He's no longer assaulting your daughter. He's no longer a threat to either one of you, and you continue to beat him. That's the deciding factor for us.'*

The medical examiner returned with a positive finding in Jason's system for trazodone – the antidepressant sedative prescribed to Molly two days before the killing.

Then, eleven days before going to the grand jury, the State Crime Laboratory returned its analysis on two hairs found on the bat and twenty-five hairs found on the brick.

The lab had isolated one hair on the brick which was not Jason's or Tom's. It had both 'similarities and differences' to Molly's. Whose hair was this? It wasn't Tom's, so the only other person in the house with genetic similarities to Molly was Sharon.

Detectives didn't believe the story Sharon had told them. They felt that her statement to Detective Riggs three and a half hours after the 911 call was not consistent with what a mother or grandmother would normally do.

In Sharon's statement, she'd said she was awoken by their dogs barking. The dogs' barks were followed by screaming. Sharon told Riggs: 'I could hear Molly screaming upstairs

* Interview with author in North Carolina, October 2024.

and some thumping. My husband said he was going up to get them to calm down or he was going to call the police. He told me to stay there. I heard more screams and more thumpings. Then it got quiet and the dogs settled down. I figured that he got them calmed down.

'I pictured that he had taken Molly to the living room and was talking to her, and I thought it wouldn't be good if I went up there all emotional after he had calmed things down. I guess I had fallen back to sleep because the next thing I knew, I was woken up by a strange voice calling "Sharon". It was an officer who asked me to stay down here with the kids.'

Also in her statement, Sharon said: 'Jason and Molly have fought since they were married. Molly always told me it was only verbal but I suspected it was physical. Molly knew I would be hysterical if I knew he was hurting her.'*

The prosecutors were all asking themselves the same question: what mother goes back to sleep when her daughter and husband are in a violent dispute upstairs? They all had their suspicions about Sharon, but they did not intend to prosecute her. It would be hard enough getting a conviction for Tom and Molly. To add a third defendant to the indictment would spread resources too thinly.

Also, too much could be made of that mystery hair on the brick. It was probably Sharon's, but so what? She was such a frequent, and recent, visitor, her hair could have got embedded into that bloody brick in innocent ways.

Hair or no mystery hair, Sharon was going to get a pass.

On 25 December 2015, 11-year-old Jack and 9-year-old Sarah sat down to their first Christmas meal without their father. It was also their first Christmas in seven years without Molly.

---

* Detective Nathan Riggs took this statement from Sharon Martens at 6.34 a.m. on 2 August 2015.

On the other side of the Atlantic, Molly was clearly finding this first Christmas without 'her children' traumatic. Via Facebook, she pleaded to Tracey on Christmas Day, begging for someone, anyone, in her [Molly's] family to be allowed to speak with Jack and Sarah: 'For you, Jack and Sarah. Not for me. Could someone consider, please, the possibility that it would be a gift for you to enjoy such a call? Please. On Christmas.'

The Lynches were acutely aware that Molly had been Jack and Sarah's mom for the majority of their short lives. They knew Jack and Sarah missed her. But in her posts, Molly never mentioned one word of remorse. She presented herself as the wronged loving mother. The posts were essentially a form of emotional blackmail.

The Lynches decided it was not in Jack and Sarah's best interests for them to have any contact with Molly or her family.

On New Year's Eve in a Facebook post, Molly accused David and Tracey of teaching Jack and Sarah to hate her. Molly said her love was unconditional. She would love them even 'if you believe somehow that I was a bad person or a bad mother. Even if someone has taught you to hate me, I will love you. I will love you like I did the day you wrote me this letter. I will always love you.'

The 'letter' she posted for the world to see was deeply personal to Jack and Sarah. They had written short notes to Molly the last time they saw her. The DSS forwarded the notes to Molly.

Jack had written: 'Dear Mom, I love you so much times 999 billion. We will never leave you. You are the greatest mom anyone could have. Thank you for being a super mom. I love you past the universe and back. Love Jack.'

Sarah wrote: 'Dear Mom, I love you so much. I hope this makes you smile. Love Sarah.'

*

Molly might have felt the whole world was against her that Christmas, but there was worse to come. On 18 December 2015, a grand jury had returned indictments charging both Tom and Molly with second-degree murder and voluntary manslaughter.

Usually, following a grand jury indictment, the murder suspect is immediately arrested. In the Martenses' case, this did not happen. A decision was taken to keep the indictments sealed and allow the Martenses to spend Christmas and New Year at home.

On 3 January 2016, Molly was with her parents and younger brother, Connor, in Alexandria, at the home of Mike and Mona Earnest, when Tom's lawyer, David Freedman, called. He informed Tom and Molly of the grand jury indictments and told them to present themselves for arrest in Davidson County on 5 January.

Molly was 'crushed' to learn of the murder charges. Lt Thompson had told her on 2 August 2015 that Jason's killing sounded like self-defence. Molly had assumed there would be no charges, at least against her.

On 5 January, the day Molly and Tom had to present themselves for arrest, Molly took to Facebook again, writing: 'I have loved, nurtured and protected you to the best of my ability in the environment we found ourselves [in]. I do not know what you will remember about our lives but I know some of the things you are being told. I pray one day you are able to remember with truth and clarity some of the events of our lives. You are my heart and soul, my sunshine and my happy, and I will always love you.'

That day, Molly was cuffed by Thompson outside the Davidson County Courthouse in Lexington. She and her father were each released on $200,000 bail. Facing charges of second-degree murder and voluntary manslaughter, they were told to surrender their passports and agree to cease contact with Jason's immediate family, and specifically with his two children.

Producers on CNN's *Nancy Grace Show** lined up DA Garry Frank and the Martenses' attorneys, Freedman and Holton, for interviews live on air. Frank was his usual taciturn self – he wouldn't even confirm outright that Jack and Sarah were not Molly's biological children. He said that was 'his understanding'.

Freedman and Holton were less reserved – they said there was no evidence that Jason was leaving Molly.

Days later, at school, Jack borrowed a friend's phone during a break between classes. He called Molly nine times. He left a voicemail.

'Hi Mom, this is Jack. This cannot go public. I miss you and I love you. Keep fighting really hard. I want to know how you are. I love you so much. Next time I get this phone – it's my friend's – I will call you back. And get this as soon as you can and call me – if it's not in the next hour – break's finished.'

Three minutes later Jack sent Molly a text. 'Hi Mom, this cannot go public. I miss you and still love u. Cannot call on this number. Call you when I can. Keep fighting.'

---

* *Nancy Grace Show*, 18 January 2016.

17. In Limbo with Grace

Molly and Tom launched a GoGetFunding page with a target of $300,000.

Tom would have found shaking a begging bowl on the internet mortifying, but lawyers were gorging themselves on his retirement funds. At this rate, he would have to sell his beloved house at Folly Beach. The publicity around the charges cost Molly her job at Chico's, a women's clothing store in Knoxville. Unperturbed, she racked up more bills by refusing to hand over Mags's engagement ring and two eternity rings, which Jason had 'gifted' to Sarah. Jason's estate had to sue Molly to recover them.*

Molly was also refusing to return hand and foot casts which Mags had made of the children soon after their births. Though Molly gave no outward signs of missing Jason, she insisted on keeping his name, calling herself Molly Martens Corbett.

Detectives interviewed Keith Maginn about Molly's stay at the psychiatric unit. Without Molly's approval, the detectives were unable at this time to access records about her stay there.

However, when Detective Michael Hurd interviewed Jessica Thompson, Molly's former roommate at Clemson, he got a shocking insight into the depth of Molly's psychological problems. The roommate told him that Molly had invented a

---

* The Lynches said in a court motion that Molly was refusing to return the items unless she received direct acknowledgement of receipt from Jack and Sarah. The court sided with the Lynches.

dead baby sister. The treasured photo frame of Molly's dead sister, which Molly had kept by her bed throughout her few months at Clemson, was just a ruse.

Jessica told Hurd that the girl in the frame was actually just a model, the photo a stock shot used for illustrative purposes. When Molly's roommate had looked closely, the frame dimensions were printed on the photo.

Molly had told Lynn, Tracey, Jason, her bridesmaids, doctors and others about her baby sister dying. Depending on the telling, her sister was called Grace and she died either as a baby, aged five, or aged seven. Grace had also featured in 'Molly's Inferno', the essay for which Molly received an A at community college.

An addendum to the essay explained that some of the characters were based on real people encountered by Molly through her work saving child-abuse victims. Two characters were the parents of a foster girl, Alysha, whom Molly had saved from abuse, only for the child to be taken from her.* Molly told her lecturer that Alysha had committed suicide and that she left a letter asking for Molly to speak at her memorial service.

A second set of parents in 'Molly's Inferno' were also real, Molly claimed. Molly had tried to save their sons from abuse. The parents disappeared with the children, she said, before social services could react to Molly's alert.

In each case, Molly was the hero, the maternal would-be saviour of children who had been tragically ignored. Molly's guide through hell was her baby sister, Grace, who died of leukaemia aged five. Grace was a 'child of hope,

---

* Molly also told a version of this story to Lynn Shanahan, but in this story the foster child was a boy – not Alysha – and the boy had been 'ripped from her arms' and returned to his mother. When Jack and Sarah were later taken from Molly, she used the same phraseology, saying they had been 'ripped from her'.

faith and wisdom', Molly wrote, and she lived forever in Limbo.

Defence attorneys David Freedman and Walter Holton agreed it didn't look good that Molly had been released from a psychiatric unit just weeks before going to Ireland, or that Tom knew about this and allowed her to go.

But really, what had any of that to do with Jason's killing? DA Garry Frank would never get this information before a jury. It was not a crime to suffer mental illness.

The crime Molly and Tom were charged with was second-degree murder, and for that the DA had to prove they acted with malice. The autopsy findings and the blood-spatter analysis would paint a damning portrait of malice delivered through a descending pattern of blows to the back of Jason's head. Freedman and Holton had to counter that by showing Tom and Molly's fear was real, a visceral terror which overcame them.

Establishing Molly's fear was easy – the children and the Meadowlands confidantes would do that. Tom was terrified, too, not simply because he was in 'a fight for his life' against a man half his age and twice his size.

Tom had laid out their defence in the first few words he volunteered to Detectives Smith and Hurd in the hours after the killing.

'Perhaps it would be helpful,' Tom had said, 'if I just kind of launched into a story . . . 'cause it will contribute to my state of mind. He's an Irish citizen. He was married in Ireland. He had those two children and his first wife died in mysterious circumstances.'

The defence attorneys would argue Tom and Molly were truly terrified that Jason had killed his first wife, and Molly was next.

*

Between January and March 2016 the DA's office released 5,000 pages of documentation to the defence under discovery.

In March and April of that year several of Molly's confidantes demanded to make new statements, saying their original ones were inaccurate. Of the fifty statements taken in Meadowlands, only Molly's confidantes complained of inaccuracies.

In Shannon Grubb's second statement, she mentioned two new things: Jason would get angry if Molly got up at night to comfort Sarah. 'Jason would say he didn't want her going up and I think the word he used was "coddle",' she said. 'He didn't want her coddling the kids. They would fight about it.'

Shannon also offered some corroboration of Molly's statement about how the brick came to be in the bedroom. She said Molly and the children would sometimes paint bricks and stepping stones.

Billy June Jacobs told detectives a similar story: her kids would sometimes get together with Jack and Sarah and 'paint rocks with crayon'.

Sharon initially had no explanation when asked in the basement by Detective Nathan Riggs why Molly would have a brick in her bedroom. However, she later clarified that she remembered Molly mentioning something about painting bricks with the children, an idea Molly had seen on Pinterest.

Like Shannon Grubb, Billy June Jacobs had also asked to change her original statement. 'There were general inconsistencies,' she said. 'It made it sound like there was no abuse; that I had been walking along in Meadowlands one day and she [Molly] told me. It's so not what I told her [Wanda Thompson]. It [Molly confiding in Billy June] happened over time, building a relationship and building a trust in each other, so that she [Molly] could be able to confide in me. I felt terrible when I saw the statement. I said, it's not accurate.'

Billy June's new statement added a startling revelation. 'During sex,' she stated, 'he put a pillow over her face and would strangle her to "blacking out". Molly was afraid that this was what happened to Mags and that was what was going to happen to her.'

Billy June said that Molly had sought her advice about medical treatment. 'She said they had an altercation where he [Jason] had hit her head on something. The next morning, her head was just throbbing but she didn't want to go to her own GP because they would put it into the records. I suggested she go to the health centre in Kernersville. I think that's where she went.'

Thompson tried to investigate this claim. During Molly's voluntary police interview, she claimed she had sought medical attention 'somewhere in Kernersville'. 'It struck me at the time as odd,' Thompson recalled, 'that she was so vague about where she went and what her injuries were. If your husband injures you such that you need medical treatment, that's the kind of thing you remember.'

Because Molly wouldn't sign a waiver of her privacy rights, afforded to her under the HIPAA, she was able to prevent the release of her health records.

'They [Molly's lawyers] put up all kinds of privacy arguments,' said Thompson. 'So we were never able to establish any record of Molly definitively getting treatment in that psychiatric unit, for example.'*

In March 2016 a new witness came forward[†] – Helen McCormac, a nurse who lived next door to Bobby Martens. Helen told

* Confirmation that Molly was in the psychiatric unit between 6 and 9 February 2008 came years later, via a single line in a psychiatric evaluation of Molly which was referenced in sentencing documents.
† Detectives Smith and Hurd travelled to the Union County Sheriff's Office on 31 March 2016 to take a video-recorded statement from McCormac.

detectives she wanted her statement video-recorded because she had heard other statements had not been taken accurately.

Prior to moving to Ireland to be a nanny for Jack and Sarah, Molly spent the week at Bobby's house. Helen McCormac, oblivious to Molly's recent stay at a psychiatric unit, remembered Molly showing her photographs of Jack and Sarah and painting such a vivid picture it seemed as if Molly had known them for years.

Since then Helen had met Jason at various events in Bobby's house over the years. 'He was always watching her [Molly] and who she was talking to and what she was wearing,' she said. 'He didn't let her stay long in small groups, especially if a guy was in the conversation. He would come up behind her and put his hand on the nape of her neck and guide her away from the conversation.'

According to Helen, Jason controlled what clothes Molly wore: 'He'd come whisper in her ear, suggest she go upstairs and she would come down wearing a different outfit. One time she was wearing cut-off shorts and a tank top and she came back down wearing a bikini with a cover-up.'

Helen felt that things seemed to have taken a sinister turn in August or September of 2013 when Molly arrived at Dewdrop Court, the horseshoe-shaped cul-de-sac in Monroe where Bobby lived. Helen met Molly as she got out of her car. Molly was a 90-minute drive from home.

'I thought it was a bit odd,' Helen said. 'She looked like she had been upset and crying. Her phone kept ringing and she was ignoring it. I said, "Do you need to get it?" She put it on speaker and Jason was screaming at her, calling her a bitch.

'He told her that she should have never left the kids [then aged eight and six], that she was going to pay for it, for leaving. She fumbled and turned off the speaker. I asked, how long has this been going on? She said, "A while."'

*

Molly's attorney, Walter Holton, was confident of beating the charges being brought against Molly and Tom.

Jack and Sarah would be the star witnesses. Their Dragonfly statements would condemn Jason. Then Shannon Grubb, Billy June Jacobs, Jennifer Turner, Melissa Sams and Helen McCormac would be the supporting cast.

Holton couldn't risk Molly or Sharon* on the stand. Putting Molly on the stand would expose her to cross-examination about the various lies she had told. Likewise, Holton did not want Sharon's credibility questioned, which it surely would be once she told the jury that her response to the violent altercation taking place in the bedroom above her was to go back to sleep.

Holton was confident he could get the Russian doll and the system of codewords into evidence via the crime-scene photos. The Russian doll with Sharon's number written underneath would be a powerful exhibit, showing there was such ongoing concern among Molly, Sharon, Jack and Sarah about Jason's anger issues, and his regular arguments with Molly, that they instituted this alarm system, enabling the children to call Sharon for help the next time there was a domestic dispute.

The Martenses' defence lawyers were feeling cautiously

---

* Sharon's statement on the night was strong. She claimed there had been ongoing abuse, which required her to set up the system of codewords with Jack and Sarah. 'Jason and Molly have fought since they were married. Molly always told me it was only verbal but I suspected it was physical,' Sharon told Detective Riggs. 'Molly knew I would be hysterical if I knew he was hurting her. But Jack and Sarah have told me about when Jason would grab Molly or push her into the wall and hit her. I would ask Molly about it and she would say they were just exaggerating. After the kids told me about the fighting, I asked them to write my phone number on the bottom of something near the upstairs house phone. They were afraid of their dad. They made practice calls to me. We had a codeword that they would be able to just say and I would know it was them and I would call the police so they wouldn't have to. Molly would tell me "Mom, everybody fights except you and Dad,"' Sharon said.

confident – until it transpired that Molly's confidantes weren't the only ones who had something new to say.

A month after Shannon and Billy June made new statements, and five months after urging Molly to 'keep fighting', Jack recanted his accusations against Jason.* In a Skype interview with assistant DA Ina Stanton, Jack said he and Sarah were told to lie about their father being abusive.

While en route to Dragonfly House, Molly, according to Jack, 'started making up little stories about my dad, saying that he was abusive. And then she started crying, and she said if you don't tell the truth, we'll never, ever see you again. If you don't tell this, we'll never see you again.'

When Stanton asked why he was 'telling the truth today' after lying previously, Jack replied: 'Because I just want the truth. And I found out what happened to my dad, and I want justice to be served.'

Jack added: 'I didn't tell the truth at Dragonfly. I didn't tell the truth again when a woman came over and interviewed me at Bobby's house. And I didn't tell the truth when she took me to another different doctor in High Point.'

Jack said he did this because he was scared 'of her [Molly] and her whole family'.

The children's suppressed memories had been surfacing as part of the diary-keeping they'd been doing since 2016, under advice from their counsellor.

In March 2017 Jack asked Tracey to read his diary entries. Sarah wanted her diaries sent over to detectives, too. They were entered into evidence as Exhibit 68.†

---

* Skype interview with Jack, conducted by assistant district attorney Ina Stanton on 27 May 2016.
† Exhibit 068 – two diary books, and a handwritten note saying diaries of Jack and Sarah Corbett, from David Lynch – received 27/3/17.

The children confirmed domestic violence, but Molly was the perpetrator, not Jason. A year after urging Molly to keep fighting, Jack, now aged twelve, wrote in his diary:* 'All those things that the Martens [*sic*] told me to say at those first three interviews is [*sic*] a bunch of lies. Molly and Sharon Martens told my sister and I to tell the DA that my dad abused Molly Martens. I've never seen him hurt anyone. I was scared of the Martens [family], especially Molly. She abused me so much. She beat me up if I didn't do a chore right or I told a small lie. She would mentally abuse me, too.'

Jack wrote that Molly coached him and Sarah before each of their interviews with social workers: 'Molly told me and Sarah before each interview to tell the person that my dad beat her up and cursed at her. She had brainwashed us both and manipulated us. She had told us so many stories about my dad beating her up. I never saw any of it. She told us these things at Bobby Martens' house and in her car.'

On 12 January 2017, Jack's diary entry reads: 'Molly your [*sic*] a child abuser, murderer, liar, manipulator, sociopath and coward. Everyone is going to know about you Molly and now they are really going to see all the Martens [*sic*] true colors.'

Jack had remembered the brick paving stone. 'Molly told me to put one in her room, so I did. I didn't know why but I did.'

Jack's diary had one last extraordinary revelation. 'You told me my dad murdered my mom by stuffing her head in a pillow while she was having an asthma attack.'

* Diary entry, 12 January 2017.

18. Voir Dire: To Speak the Truth

Weeks before jury selection began, Tom's attorney, David Freedman, filed a 'statement of intent'. It was the legalese equivalent of shots fired: Tom believed Jason killed his first wife. He would testify that he met Mags's father at Molly's wedding. And Mags's father told him that 'he believed Jason caused the death of his daughter.'

In the two years between the killing and the trial, social media commentary had raised and spread the possibility that Jason was a violent, controlling and jealous husband. Now Freedman's legal filing allowed mainstream media to publish Tom's theory that Mags's death was mysterious. Before the jury had even been empanelled, the victim had been transformed into an abusive husband and possible wife-killer.

Even though Jack and Sarah had now recanted the allegations they made at Dragonfly House, Freedman intended to argue that they were only doing this now because they had been brainwashed by their Irish guardians, David and Tracey Lynch. Freedman was confident that once the jury saw the Dragonfly interviews with the children, they would see that they were telling the truth then, and not now.

Jack and Sarah couldn't be compelled to testify, and they would not be summoned from Ireland. So, in Freedman's analysis, the Dragonfly tapes would be all the more powerful in their absence.

The tapes were CCTV of their grief. The jury would be presented with an 8-year-old girl and a 10-year-old boy as exhibits. Their daddy had died four days previously. They were orphans at the centre of an international custody battle.

And all they wanted in that moment was their mommy. Freedman believed there was a visceral truth to the Dragonfly interviews that would outweigh any subsequent recantation delivered via Skype.

The DA filed a motion* to prevent the Dragonfly tapes being played for the jury. The motion said the children would not be testifying, had recanted their allegations and, as such, their Dragonfly statements constituted 'inadmissible hearsay'.

Judge Lee reserved judgement on the Dragonfly tapes. In the meantime, he proceeded with jury selection.

On Sunday, 16 July 2017, the day before the trial started, Jason's siblings Tracey, Wayne and Marilyn, and his friends Brendan O'Callaghan, Paul Dillon and Tracey's husband, David Lynch, were brought to a room in the DA's office.

They were shown autopsy and crime-scene photographs to prepare them. They saw the clumps of hair and scalp in the bathroom hallway, the blood saturating the carpet, spattered up the walls and smeared in fingerprints on the door. Marilyn vomited.

When the case got under way, others would, too.

On the first day in court, Molly's demeanour stiffened with defiance as assistant district attorney Alan Martin began his opening statement.

'At the time of that killing there were three people in that bedroom,' said Martin. 'Two of those people walked out with almost not a mark on them. Jason left that room on a board with a head that had been so badly crushed pieces of his skull fell out. You are going to see pictures of his skull

---

* The motion was filed on 12 May 2017, a month before pre-trial hearings were due to commence.

that look like a hard-boiled egg got dropped on the counter. That's how Jason Corbett left that room.'

Martin's projector was set up directly in front of Brendan O'Callaghan, best man at Jason and Molly's wedding. 'I was seeing these horrific pictures before they went on the screen,' he recalled. He saw photos of Jason's hair embedded in a brick which was saturated on all sides with blood; and pictures of Jason's head, which had been hit in ten different places.

Brendan tried to shield his wife, Michelle, from the photographs. Martin detailed the repeated blows to the head and how they were delivered in a descending pattern. One of the last blows hit Jason's head less than 2 feet from the floor.

'I never hated anyone in my life,' Brendan told me later. 'But pure hatred kicks in. I wanted to go over and strangle her.'

Martin said he would tell the jury the who, what, when, where and how of Jason's death. 'That leaves why? Why didn't they stop?'

When it was Freedman's turn, he set about humanizing Tom. He told the jury of nine women and three men how Tom was a dedicated family man who had served his country in the FBI for thirty years.

Tom decided on the morning of Saturday, 2 August 2015 that they didn't have much going on, so why not drive four hours to North Carolina to see Molly and the children. Tom brought two gifts, a baseball bat and a tennis racket. He decided not to give Jack the bat because it was so late. He went to bed with Sharon in the basement.

'All he's thinking about,' Freedman told the court, 'is what he's doing tomorrow – playing golf and seeing his grandchildren. That's the only reason he's come up to Wallburg, North

Carolina, on his weekend off, to see his family, because he's been a dedicated family man his entire life.'

Freedman outlined how Tom awoke to loud noises above him, grabbed the bat and rushed upstairs, thinking there might be an intruder. Tom found Jason choking his daughter, threatening to kill her, so he intervened to save 'his little girl'.

Freedman urged the jury to keep an open mind when they heard evidence from the medical examiner and the blood-spatter expert, because Tom's story matched every photo taken from the scene. There was one exceptional photograph, however, which Freedman urged the jurors to concentrate on.

This photograph was of a long, single strand of blonde hair found between the bloodied fingers of Jason's right hand.

'You will be able to see the picture of Jason's right hand even in death still clutching Molly Corbett, still not letting her go.'

From the off, it was evident this case could stand or fall on the outcome of discussions held in voir dire – a legal term for proceedings in a trial which are held in the absence of the jury, to consider things such as the admissibility of evidence.

The defence scored major voir dire victories that the jury was totally unaware of.

For example, during voir dire questioning – a cross-examination of witnesses which is recorded before the judge as part of the official court transcript – 911 operator Karen Capps was forthright in her belief, described in Chapter 6, that Tom and Molly faked CPR. She described in detail why she felt that Tom and Molly's CPR attempts were performative, not real. But she was not allowed to say this when she took the stand in front of the jury.

During Capps' voir dire questioning, in the absence of the jury, assistant DA Ina Stanton asks Capps how Molly came across over the phone during the supposed CPR.

'She was very tearful,' Capps says. 'A little excited . . . She counted. But she counted like she was yelling. She wanted to make sure that I heard her counting.'

What the jury actually heard from Capps, in court testimony as opposed to in voir dire, was a vastly diluted version of her experience, stripped of any opinion or insight.

After Capps had testified before the jury the 911 tape was played for them. The DA just had to hope the jury heard what Capps had heard – CPR being staged.

Before Corporal Clayton Dagenhardt, the first police officer on the scene, could take the stand, he was examined in voir dire, in the absence of the jury.

Dagenhardt described seeing pooled, congealing blood around the body. This was important evidence because it went to the heart of whether the Martenses delayed calling 911 and thus whether their CPR attempts were staged.

Byrd interrupted Dagenhardt's voir dire testimony with an objection. He told the judge that he did not want the jury to hear Dagenhardt's view that the blood was not fresh. Dagenhardt was not an expert in blood flow.

Stanton countered that Dagenhardt had been to more than 200 scenes where blood had been spilled. 'He should be allowed to state his conclusions and opinions as to the blood that night,' she said.

But Judge Lee sided with Byrd. Dagenhardt could not say anything in front of the jury about the blood being fresh or not fresh.

The prosecution made some progress with their next witness, but she would also help the defence.

Kate Wingate-Scott, a nurse at Kernersville Medical Center, confirmed that both Jason and Molly were patients there between 2012 and 2015.

Molly was prescribed trazodone in 50 mg doses on 30 July 2015, two days before Jason's killing. As we know, toxicology reports revealed traces of trazodone in Jason's blood. Wingate-Scott's testimony left the jury wondering how a sedative prescribed to Molly ended up in Jason's bloodstream on the night of the killing.

But Wingate-Scott's testimony was a double-edged sword. As Wanda Thompson had predicted, the defence would feast on other information in Jason's medical records.

The jury heard from Wingate-Scott what readers will remember from Chapter 15 – that Jason was found in 2013 and 2014 to be either moderately or mildly depressed. Just seventeen days before his death, Jason told doctors he had been feeling 'faint and dizzy'. This started six months prior to the killing and was occurring 'at least once a week' by July. Jason said he had been 'more stressed and angry lately for no reason'.

The defence attorneys would later state, during closing arguments, that Wingate-Scott's testimony proved Jason had caused his own dizzy spells and anger problems by stopping his thyroid medication for six weeks prior to his last GP visit, and that these 'anger issues', noted two weeks prior to the killing in Wingate-Scott's records, corroborated Molly's claims about Jason losing his temper and choking her on the night of the killing.

These were questions the defence and the prosecution would return to. First, the jurors were talked through the autopsy findings of the associate chief medical examiner, Dr Craig Nelson, who had given expert testimony in nearly fifty cases.

'The autopsy documented multiple blunt-force injuries,'

Dr Nelson told the court. 'These included ten different areas of impact on the head, at least two of which had features suggesting repeated blows indicating a minimum of twelve different blows to the head.'

Martin was talking Dr Nelson through some gruesome photographs of Jason's ruptured skull when suddenly, Nancy Perez, one of the jurors, lurched forward and vomited into a small trash can in the jury box. Freedman and Holton both wanted her removed from the jury. The judge allowed Perez to stay.

The physical evidence did not get any less gruesome. Dr Nelson said there were multiple impacts to the exposed sites at the back left and back right of the head.

'I cannot, however, tell you exactly how many impacts there were,' he added, 'because with repeated blows there may be additional injury and further crushing of already injured tissue.

'On the left side you can see there's almost a triangular area where there's a portion of skull missing. On the right side we see an irregular area where there's a portion of skull missing. The portion of skull is missing because when the scalp was pulled back, those pieces of bone had fractures all the way around so they fell out of place. The degree of skull fractures in this case are the types of injuries that we may see in falls from great heights.'

Dr Nelson confirmed that Jason's blood alcohol was 0.02 per cent – one quarter of the legal limit for driving. Despite drinking all afternoon, Jason was not drunk.

Toxicology testing found low levels of trazodone* in Jason's blood. This level was 'not a therapeutic dose'. It was possible Jason had ingested it an hour or so before dying,

* Testing for trazodone yielded a blood plasma concentration of 0.308 milligrams per litre.

and the drug had not been sufficiently ingested to infuse his bloodstream with a therapeutic dose. Another possibility was that he had only taken a partial dose.

The court heard how on the Saturday afternoon before he was killed, Jason had shared some beers with his neighbour, David Fritzsche, on David's driveway. Molly and David's wife, Michele, had joined them. At 8.30 p.m., Tom and Sharon Martens arrived in their car.

David saw Jason help Tom with his luggage. The next time David saw any of the Corbetts was when Molly arrived with a police officer at his door around five thirty the next morning.

'She was upset. I did not notice any injuries,' David told the court.

Lt Frankie Young didn't notice any injuries on Molly that morning either. As chief of Crime Scene Investigations, Lt Young took 695 photos at the crime scene. He photographed Molly at the scene, and later again at the sheriff's office.

The jurors were shown close-ups of blood on Molly's face, forehead and cheeks. Young said he saw dried blood but he didn't see any injuries. He described how Molly 'continually tugged and pulled on her neck with her hand'. Young had to ask her to stop.

'After several requests, she did,' he said.

Jurors were shown the 28-inch, 17-ounce aluminium baseball bat with which Tom hit Jason. The black volcanic ash used to test for fingerprints was still visible. The brick was put into a transparent container and passed along the jury box, so each juror could examine it from above and below. It was hard to believe this brick was originally grey. Now, it was a dark rust red, soaked in blood on all sides.

Forensic scientist Melanie Carson had found twenty-five hairs on the brick. All but one of them were Jason's. The outlier was a pale yellow, almost colourless hair. DNA testing had shown this hair was not Tom's or Molly's but that it bore genetic similarities to Molly's. The criminal trial did not explore further whether this hair was Sharon's – the only other person in the house with genetic links to Molly. However, this mystery hair would feature prominently when a wrongful death claim brought by Jason's estate was eventually settled in December 2018, more than a year after the criminal trial. We will return to that later.

At the 2017 criminal trial, the jury was shown Lt Young's photos of the hairs – including the mystery colourless one – embedded in the brick. Then the jury was shown Young's photos of the brick and baseball bat as they were found at the scene, and photographs from the hallway connecting the master bedroom to the bathroom. This was State's Exhibit 107 – not for the squeamish, it featured what Young described as 'two clumps of hair with scalp attached'.

The who, what, where, when and how of this killing were all there in the crime-scene video shot by Young. State's Exhibit 135 showed the crime's aftermath in full horrific colour: the fallen lamp and broken wedding picture; the pools of congealed blood on the carpet; red impact splashes and spatter descending the south wall where Jason died from twelve blows to the head.

The brick had been lifted and moved. It left behind a red stain in the cream carpet. In the way that memories can sometimes be more evocative than the real events that inspired them, the brick-shaped stain tie-dyed deep in the woollen fibres seemed somehow more ominous than the brick itself.

Assistant DA Alan Martin hoped the jury would be left with just one question: why? He thought he knew the answer: Molly wanted everything Jason gave her – the house, the lifestyle, the income, but most importantly, his two children. Molly wanted everything but Jason. He was the one thing standing in her way. Molly had manifested this version of herself, the obsession she'd had since childhood of one day being a mother.

Because Molly had blocked detectives from accessing her private health information, prosecutors were unable to confirm Molly's stay at a psychiatric unit back in 2008. The prosecution, as a result, could not fully elaborate what they believed had happened – that Molly had been spiralling out of control for at least two years before Jason's death, mimicking previous breakdowns in 1998, when she was fifteen, and 2008, when, aged twenty-five, she was admitted to the psychiatric unit.

Thus, in the courtroom, for now, Martin didn't explore the why of Jason's killing. He hoped the jury would be focused on figuring that out for themselves.

Stuart James, the blood-spatter expert, testified that blood found on the sheets and the box springs showed that an 'impact incident' took place on the south side of the bed.

'It may well be where bloodshed first occurred,' he told the court. Some jurors misinterpreted this evidence, believing James had said the first blow was while Jason was in bed.

As we saw in Chapter 16, analysis of the south wall, against and beneath which Jason suffered his lethal blows, showed a descending succession of impacts, beginning with Jason's head hitting the south wall, at a point just to the right of the bathroom hallway, 4 to 5 feet from the floor.

A second area of spatter was 'consistent with impact to the head of Mr Corbett' as he was descending. His head was 'impacting the wall as well as an object striking him'.

A third impact site was 24 to 28 inches above the floor. In this stain there were hair fragments, which would indicate an injury to the head. The fourth and final impact site was just 5 to 16 inches from the floor.

James, co-author of the definitive book on bloodstain analysis,* was present to delineate cold, scientific facts and his expert extrapolations. He was not there to provide a simple narrative. The jury members would likely have wondered, however, about those four blows to the head, delivered while Jason was falling. They also would likely have taken note that one of those four blows was to the back of the head.

If Molly was telling the truth and she had only tried to hit Jason once with the brick, and that was earlier in the fray, then Tom alone would have delivered those four descending blows. It would take remarkable stamina, agility and hand–eye coordination for a 65-year-old to hit a 262-lb man's head four times as his body slumped down that wall.

If Molly wasn't also swinging the brick and hitting Jason as he descended the south wall, then how did she get Jason's blood and tissue on the lowest parts of her pyjama bottoms? James said these stains showed Jason's head was 'close to the floor' when struck.

Using a Celestron digital microscope, James was also able to identify Jason's blood, skin and tissue embedded in the fabric of Molly's pyjama top.

'This led me to conclude that the wearer was in proximity to Jason Corbett when blows were struck to his head,' he said.

Molly only admitted to having tried to hit Jason with the brick, once. James said he found hair fragments, transfer and spatter stains on the brick. 'The presence of transfer stains on all surfaces of the brick is not consistent with a single impact,' he said.

As we know, stains were also found on the inside left hem of Tom's boxer shorts. According to James, this blood had

---

* As the co-author of *Principles of Bloodstain Pattern Analysis*, James was described as a world-renowned expert in his field.

to have 'travelled up from below to be on the inside'. He told the court: 'The source of the impact spatters is most likely the head of Jason Corbett while it was close to the floor in the bedroom.'

Under cross-examination by Tom's second attorney, Jones Byrd, James admitted he had not tested the stains underneath the hem of the left leg of the boxer shorts to confirm they were bloodstains. James said it was not practical to test every single stain.

The blood-spatter analysis questioned Tom's story of what happened in the bathroom. Tom said he had managed to strike Jason in there. In the bathroom James found blood transfer stains on the wall and light switch, an oval dent on the wall, and blood droplets on the floor tiles, but no evidence of impact spatter. Jason was already bleeding when he entered the bathroom, but he was not struck in there.

James's testimony had conjured the lasting image of Tom and Molly standing over Jason and beating him. However, it was his testimony about bloodstains on the master bedroom door that hit home most with many present. James said blood on the door handle could have been from fingers. Jason was the only one with blood on his hands – literally, if not metaphorically.

This would indicate that Jason was trying to escape that room.

Tracey was glad she had scheduled her daily Skype calls with Jack and Sarah for the mornings before court. After a day listening to such harrowing testimony, she couldn't hide how weary and drained she felt. In the mornings, at least, everyone could put on a brave face and start again.

Back home, Jack and Sarah were holidaying in Spanish Point with their new siblings, David and Tracey's children,

Dean and Adam. They were being protected from news reports and took their updates directly from Tracey.

Mid-afternoon of 3 August 2017, Tracey took the stand. It was two years and one day since her brother had been killed.

It was not like the movies. This wasn't one of those cinematic, cathartic moments where Tracey finally got to have her say. Instead, there were rules about what she could and could not say. The judge wanted to listen to what she proposed to say, and then he would decide if the jury should hear it or not.

This voir dire proceeding concerned Tracey's belief that Jason intended to return permanently to Ireland with Jack and Sarah. Tom and Molly's attorneys did not want the jury hearing that. So, Tracey outlined in the absence of the jury how she had spoken to Jason about coming home for good a full year before his death.

'We had discussed his planned move back to Ireland initially in August of 2014. He was very homesick and lonely. He had good friends and missed them and he planned to move back to Ireland before Jack was to start secondary school.'

Tracey added she was 'aware of attempts he made to book flights'.

However, it was conceded under voir dire questioning from Tom and Molly's attorneys that Jason had not booked flights and that Jack and Sarah were both enrolled in school in Wallburg for the fall of 2015.

The defence attorneys said Tracey now wanted to give evidence that Jason was coming home without Molly, but this contradicted what Tracey had said under oath in the guardianship hearing. At that hearing, Tracey had said that Molly was coming to Ireland with Jason and the children for her father's eightieth birthday on 2 September 2015.

In another victory for the defence on voir dire, Judge

Lee said: 'It may be premature at this time to allow the testimony . . . about the alleged victim feeling homesick and lonely, planning to move back at this time.'

The defence had one more victory before the court adjourned that day.

The prosecution had wanted to put up Travis Rose, a co-worker who had a conversation with Jason two weeks prior to his killing where the Limerickman said he was unsure of his future at their company, MPS, and was considering moving home.

Jason had told Travis that relations between him and Molly were strained. The defence objected to Travis speaking in court. Judge Lee agreed, and would not allow Travis to testify.

The state rested its case.

Before Judge Lee concluded proceedings for the day he heard arguments on whether the jury should hear Tom's claims about Jason killing his first wife.

In a remarkable admission – especially in light of developments years later – Tom's lawyer, David Freedman, said they were not intending to argue that Jason had actually killed his first wife, just that Tom believed he did, and this influenced the actions he took which led to Jason's death on 2 August 2015.

Similar to Tom in the hours straight after the killing, Freedman wanted to launch into a story not because it was directly relevant to Jason's killing but because it would help establish Tom's state of mind.

This was another pivot point in the trial. If the jury got to hear that Jason might have killed his first wife, and the defendant, a former FBI agent, believed Jason had killed before, then it could swing the whole trial.

Tom's attorneys wanted the jurors asking themselves what they would have done in those circumstances, if it was their daughter being choked by a man they suspected of killing his first wife.

The judge said he would need to think about it overnight. He would let all sides know his decision the following morning, prior to Tom Martens taking the stand.

19. Tom Takes the Stand

By the time of their trial, the Martenses' GoGetFunding campaign had raised less than a tenth of its target. Facing legal bills approaching half a million dollars, Tom and Sharon would be forced to sell their Folly Beach property.

Days before the criminal trial started, Jason's estate had lodged a wrongful death suit, naming Sharon as a defendant alongside Tom and Molly. The DA might have decided to give Sharon a pass, but Jason's family had not.

The trial resumed on 4 August 2017 to hear the first witnesses for the defence.

The day started badly for the Martenses. Judge Lee refused to allow the jury to hear Tom's 'self-serving' story about Mags's father, Mike Fitzpatrick.

As described in Chapter 18, Tom had claimed in a 'statement of intent' document filed with the court that Mike Fitzpatrick told him that he believed Jason had caused his daughter Mags's death. Tom claimed that Mike told him this at Molly's wedding. Unfortunately for Tom, Mags's father was not at Molly's wedding, and he signed a legal document denying he had ever said this about Jason.*

Tom's lead lawyer, David Freedman, would need all his skills to get Tom off now. The severity of Jason's wounds and

---

* Detectives did not believe the story. Even if Fitzpatrick had been at the wedding, they would have asked what kind of man, let alone someone who had spent thirty years in the FBI, learns on his only daughter's wedding day that she is marrying a man who killed his first wife – and does nothing about it.

the descending pattern of blows screamed malice. Freedman had intended to justify the violence by amplifying the fear Tom felt, arguing he was driven by primal survival instincts and that he stopped assaulting Jason once the threat was over.

Now, however, the helpful story about meeting Mags's father was left on the cutting-room floor. The jury would not hear Tom's theory about Jason killing his first wife.

According to assistant DA Greg Brown, it was hate that drove Tom, not fear. Detectives Brandon Smith and Michael Hurd had unearthed a witness to this hate among the 13-person counterintelligence unit at Oak Ridge, where Tom worked.

Tom's colleague JoAnn Lowry remembered sitting alongside Tom at terminals in a room dedicated to classified work. It was the beginning of June 2011. Tom had just hosted Jason's family for a pre-wedding party at his home.

JoAnn told the court that Tom told her that Jason's family were 'rude and crude. They smoked, drank beer, and cursed.' Tom frequently denigrated Jason, JoAnn said in court. Everyone in their unit knew Tom disliked Jason

Two months before the killing, Tom told JoAnn: 'That son-in-law, I hate him.'

Tom admitted under oath: 'He wasn't my favourite person. I didn't like him. I'm sure I said disparaging things about him.'

He and Jason 'made nice' when he arrived in Meadowlands on 1 August 2015, Jason's last night alive.

'We were superficially friendly,' Tom said.

Tom described waking in the early hours of 2 August.

'I heard thumping,' he said, 'like loud falls on the floor above me, and I heard a scream and loud voices. There was an obvious disturbance going on above me somewhere in the house. It sounded bad. It sounds like a matter of urgency.

I reacted instinctively and jumped out of bed and grabbed the baseball bat and went upstairs.'

He opened Jason and Molly's bedroom door.

'Seven or eight feet in front of me,' Tom said, 'Jason had his hands around Molly's neck.' Tom closed the door behind him – a strange move for a 65-year-old confronted by a naked man half his age, twice his size, choking his daughter. Why close off the only avenue of escape?

Tom instructed Jason to, 'Let her go.'

According to Tom, Jason replied: 'I'm going to kill her.' They both repeated themselves several times, engaging in what Tom bizarrely labelled as 'silly dialogue'.

'I don't know how many times that happened,' Tom said, starting to cry. His tears were interrupted when he suddenly realized he had forgotten part of his story. 'But I left something out. When I entered, he had his hands up around her neck, and as soon as I entered, he reversed himself so that he had her neck in the crook of his right arm.'

'She was in front of him, between me and him. He was really angry. And I was really scared.' Seeing Jason step towards the hallway to the bathroom, Tom had to act.

'I was afraid that he would get to the bathroom and close the door and that would be the end of that.'

Crying again, Tom continued: 'I took a step to my right and I hit him in the head, the back of the head with the baseball bat. That seemed like the most effective place to hit him. I didn't want to hit Molly.'

The blow was ineffectual and merely enraged Jason, Tom said. Undeterred, he followed Jason down the hallway, attempting to swing a 28-inch-long bat in a 3-foot-wide space.

'Molly was no longer wiggling. She was just weight, being dragged back into the hallway. So I tried to hit him. I don't know how effective those hits were because I didn't have room to manoeuvre – but I tried.'

In the bathroom, Tom could swing. He landed a blow to Jason's head. 'So I know of two times that I hit him in the back of the head,' he said, 'and whatever happened in the hallway.'

Tom's testimony appeared to contradict the analysis of the blood-spatter expert, Stuart James, who had found no impact spatter in the bathroom. If Tom didn't connect in the hallway, who did? Someone was responsible for the two clumps of hair and scalp lying on the hallway floor.

In Tom's telling, Jason rushed him. They ended up back in the bedroom. Tom swung for Jason's head. 'He puts up his left hand and catches the bat perfectly right in his palm as I swing the bat at the back of his head.'

Having caught the bat so cleanly, Jason should surely have left some trace. But the crime lab found no fingerprints, not even Tom's, on the bat.

As Jason caught the bat – according to Tom – Molly wriggled free. Tom and Jason struggled. Jason pushed Tom across the width of the bed.

'I'm on the floor with my back to him and face down on the carpet,' said Tom. 'I'm thinking, the next thing is going to be a bat in the back of the head. I'm on the ground. I hear Molly scream, "Don't hurt my dad."'

Assistant DA Greg Brown objected, and the judge instructed the jury to disregard Tom's last comment. Tom said he lost his glasses when shoved by Jason. When he got back to his feet he saw Jason standing a few feet from Molly, between her and the bedroom door.

'She can't get past him,' is how Tom described the scene in court.

Given that it was approximately 3 a.m. in a bedroom with no lights on, Tom was remarkably observant for a man who'd lost his glasses.

In court he said: 'He's [Jason] got the bat. He's in a good

athletic position. He has his weight down on the balls of his feet. He's kind of looking between me and Molly. And so I decided to rush him and try to get a hold of the bat.'

They struggle, four hands on the bat. 'This is not good for me. He's bigger and stronger and younger . . . I get control of the bat. He loses his grip. And I hit him. I hit him until he goes down. And then, I step away.'

Tom said he didn't know how many times he hit Jason.

'He said he was going to kill Molly. I certainly felt he would kill me. I felt both of our lives were in danger. I did the best I could.'

Tom left out one part, at least. He'd told his employers that after Jason reclaimed the bat, Molly struck him with a brick.* This statement went further than Molly's police statement, where she admitted only to 'trying' to hit Jason with the brick.

Molly chose not to take the witness stand in her own defence, so the jury never got to hear her version of what she did with the brick, or why it was in the bedroom to begin with.

Brown began Tom's cross-examination. He knew to play on Tom's pride. That was his weakness.

Brown talked Tom through his training in self-defence, firearms and deadly force at the FBI Academy in Quantico. Tom trained using revolvers, pistols, shotguns and rifles. Through wrestling and boxing sessions, he learned how to defend himself.

---

* In Tom's interview with the Department of Energy on 20 August 2015, he said: 'I grab at the bat, and I'm able to wrestle it away from him. And I didn't know this at the time, and I'm told this by my daughter, but I'm not witness to this, that while I'm down on the ground she grabs a brick that she and Sarah were going to decorate and put out by their mailbox. And she hit him with the brick.'

Brown put a slight curve on his next question. FBI agents were also trained, were they not, in how to bring someone down by hitting them across the ankles or knees? So why had Tom deliberately aimed for Jason's head multiple times? The head was the only part he could hit without injuring his daughter, Tom said.

Brown asked about the 911 call next, and how long Tom waited before calling. Tom said he'd gathered his thoughts for a couple of minutes.

Next, Brown asked why he didn't call a lawyer for himself. Tom couldn't resist. 'I don't want to sound, you know, any smarter than I am, but I thought, I did what I did and I'd be happy to give them a statement and tell them what I did.'

Brown talked Tom through his illustrious FBI career. Then he asked Tom about his conversation with Detective Hurd in the sheriff's office after the killing.

Tom had said he enjoyed 'pitting his wits' against multimillion-dollar foreign intelligence agencies. Tom denied Brown's suggestion that he was also attempting to pit his wits against the detectives of Davidson County.

'Isn't it correct,' Brown asserted, 'you interrupted their questioning and took charge of the interview by saying "and perhaps it would be helpful if I just kind of launched into a story because it would contribute to my state of mind"?'

Tom, a little testily, replied: 'I don't remember verbatim what I said, but I will accept your reading of the transcript as what I said.'

Brown countered: 'You were using your legal knowledge and FBI experience to attempt to extricate yourself from Jason's murder based on self-defence, isn't that correct?'

Brown asked Tom about $400,000 which Jason transferred to the United States so Molly could buy and furnish the Meadowlands house. This was an extraordinary sum of money for most people, but not, seemingly, to Tom.

'I can't testify with specificity to the amount,' he said.

Tom could recall the $49,000 transferred by Jason to pay for the wedding. Asked if he approved of this transfer, Tom merely replied 'sure'.

This blasé attitude did not endear him to the average blue-collar juror. When Brown described Meadowlands as an 'upscale' neighbourhood, Tom bizarrely took issue with this description.

'It was a nice neighbourhood, yes. Upscale is your word.'

Sensing an opportunity, Brown asked Tom about a work colleague at Oak Ridge, Jonathan Underwood, who, a couple of weeks before Jason's killing, had asked Tom if he was going to join Molly, Jason and the children on their upcoming trip to Washington.

To his colleague's question, Tom had replied: 'Why would I want to go on vacation with that asshole?'

Tom said he had no recollection of saying this. 'I can't recall with specificity, but I'm sure I called him rude. I'm sure that I called him disrespectful. I'm sure that I said I didn't like the way that he treated my daughter.'

Jason had reneged on a wedding promise to allow Molly to adopt the children, but Tom denied that his ill will developed into hatred. 'He didn't measure up to what I thought my daughter's standards should be.'

Tom admitted he had never witnessed physical violence between Jason and Molly. He claimed to have seen bruises on her but didn't know what had caused them. He said he suggested a divorce, but Molly didn't take his advice.

Brown suggested Molly was motivated by money. He said $600,000 had been paid out on Jason's life insurance, with the money held by the court pending a civil action for wrongful death. The outcome of that civil action would depend largely on the outcome of the criminal trial.

'In this particular case, we have 600,000 pieces of motive why malice is present,' said Brown.

Walter Holton, Molly's attorney, denied that the beneficiary of the life insurance policy had been changed – as alleged by Wanda Thompson when she spoke with representatives from Unum, the insurance company. Thompson was acting on information from Tracey that shortly before the killing Jack and Sarah had been written out of the policy so that Molly would be the 100 per cent beneficiary.

'There was never a change of beneficiary,' Holton insisted to the jury. 'This was absolutely false.' The prosecution did not raise the insurance issue again.

Tom gave different answers in his police interview, in the interview with his employers, and in the witness box, when asked what time he woke up on the night of the killing.

In court he guessed 2.30 a.m., whereas he had told his employers it was possibly 2 a.m. If this was the case, then why did he wait so long – until 3.02 a.m. – to call 911? Tom denied stalling for time and couldn't remember if he and Molly had both washed their hands and bodies before calling 911.

Tom said that, under instruction from the 911 operator, he had tilted Jason's head and reached under the neck. Asked by Brown how he could have done this without getting blood on himself, Tom replied: 'I can't testify to that. I don't know.'

Tom was asked about stains on his boxer shorts and if these were there before the incident. Tom tried to make a joke of it: 'I hope not.'

Brown asked: 'Is this funny?'

For some jury members, this added to their sense that Tom was arrogant.

Asked about the brick, Tom said: 'I have no knowledge of the brick.'

Brown: Mr Martens, you and your daughter murdered a naked, unarmed man, who was down on the floor incapacitated . . .

Freedman: Objection, your Honor.

Brown: . . . in his bedroom by bludgeoning him to death. Isn't that the truth?

Freedman: Objection.

The Court: Overruled.

Tom: That is not the truth.

Brown: No further questions.

Tom stepped down from the witness box. Any relief he felt to have the ordeal over with must have been short-lived. Judge Lee issued a ruling which cut the legs from under the defence. He would not allow Jack and Sarah's Dragonfly statements to go to the jury.

Despite all the pre-trial publicity, and two years of smearing Jason's character on social media, domestic violence would barely feature in the trial. Apart from the alleged choking incident on the night, and Tom's claim to have seen unexplained bruises on Molly, the jury members were scarcely aware that domestic violence was even an issue.

20. Verdict

Two days of closing arguments began on Monday, 7 August 2017, and assistant district attorney Greg Brown pulled no punches. Tom and Molly bludgeoned Jason to death, delayed calling 911, staged the crime scene and faked CPR.

'The story about CPR was fake CPR, staging for the story,' Brown told the court.

Jason's body was cool, and the blood was congealed like Jell-O, when the emergency medical services (EMS) teams arrived.

Brown painted a visceral picture of the EMS sergeant Barry Alphin putting his hand inside Jason's skull and feeling his 'mushy brain'. Yet Tom had supposedly put his hands on the back of Jason's head and emerged with no blood on his hands.

'Recall the 911 instructions that Miss Capps gave to Mr Martens? "Mr Martens, tilt his head back, clear the airway." I examined Mr Martens about that fact. He said, "Oh, yes, that's what I did." His hands were spotless. He did not do that.'

Brown said the vacuum cleaner was moved.

'The blood has dried running horizontal, side to side, indicating that that vacuum was not in that position when that blood was put on there. We know it had to dry in that position or the stains would be up and down. Again, that goes to show that there had been quite a bit of time passed before 911 was called. The defendants basically forget the laws of nature.'

Brown then went through Jason's injuries – ten different impact sites, some of them overlapping. This was excessive force. At least one injury was post-mortem.

'Malice and overkill. Let's talk about it,' Brown said, picking up the bat as he paced before the jury box. 'This bat, State's Exhibit 150. One blow to the head with a bat or brick, two blows to the head with a bat or brick, three blows to the head with a bat or brick. How about four blows, five blows, six blows, seven blows, eight, nine, ten? Is that excessive force? Is that malice? Why didn't they stop? Malice? Yes. Hatred? Yes. Excessive force? Yes. Overkill? Yes.'

Brown said Jason was naked and unarmed in the middle of the night, with his two young children upstairs in bed. He was not the aggressor. The wounds to the back of Jason's head showed that 'Jason was retreating, not coming forward.'

Tom concocted a story to fit the scene. 'That story was made up while Jason's body was cooling and the blood from his body was congealing,' said Brown.

Molly had no bruises or abrasions. No torn or stretched clothing. 'Even the plastic clip in the back of her hair is still in place. Is that consistent with being choked? Is that consistent with being in the crux of someone's arm fighting for her life? It is not.'

And what about Sharon? 'She never came upstairs. She never called 911. She never called the police. Is that reasonable? Is that believable?'

The truth, Brown said, was that the crime scene was staged, CPR was faked.

'In fact, Jason was left to die before 911 was even called so as to allow the FBI agent, the lawyer, to develop the story that he was going to tell you and to attempt to match wits with you.'

Finally, Brown showed the jury a photograph of the door. 'We have finger marks. The only person that had a bloody hand was Jason. How low was Jason at this point in time to have his fingers in this particular location on the lower half below the handle?'

Brown showed the jury how the blinds on the opposite side of the bedroom had spatter stains. He asked the jury to consider the amount of force needed to strike Jason's head on one side of the room and for the spatter to carry all the way across the bedroom. Brown produced the brick. It had blood on the left side, the right, front, back, top and bottom.

'And not only did it have blood, it had hair, tissue,' he said.

Brown referenced the descending pattern of blows, and the impact spatters on the inside hem of Tom's boxer shorts and up and down each leg of Molly's pyjamas.

'The presence of transfer stains on all surfaces of the brick is not consistent with a single impact to his head. Malice, excessive force, overkill . . . Both defendants are in the thick of the excessive assault when Jason is down near the floor. Both are acting in concert. Malice, overkill, excessive force. Why didn't they stop?

'We will never know whether Jason tried to cry out,' Brown said; 'whether he begged for his life, or was he thinking of his two children, Jack and Sarah, during this heinous, atrocious and cruel murder?'

The jurors were left to ponder the prospect that Jason's last thoughts were of his children being left in his killers' care.

In his closing speech defending Molly, Walter Holton asked why the jury had not been shown the video recording of Molly's interview, just her brief written statement.*

'That alone should be a showstopper,' said Holton. 'Right there you should say, hold on, something is not right.' Holton was not allowed to tell the jury that Wanda Thompson had

---

* Later, when the jury was considering its verdict, they asked the judge to see transcripts of Molly and Tom's interviews at the sheriff's office. This was denied, as these were not entered into evidence.

expressly told Molly at the end of the recorded interview that it 'sounds like self-defence'.

Holton continued this theme of evidence being withheld. He said a long blonde hair had been photographed by the CSI chief, Lt Frankie Young. The hair was trapped between the bloodied fingers of Jason's right hand. However, that hair was not preserved or tested.

Jason's fingernails hadn't been tested. The mark on Molly's neck – dismissed by the prosecution as dried blood – was also not tested.

'How did it get there?' Holton asked. He said paramedics David Bent and Sgt Barry Alphin noted redness on Molly's neck when they examined her in Meadowlands. Molly had difficulty swallowing, another sign she was choked. The paramedics should have checked under Molly's eyelids for signs of petechial haemorrhaging, but they didn't.

'If you want to prove beyond a reasonable doubt that she was not strangled, then you need to answer these questions.'

Molly had nothing to gain by Jason being killed. 'She's not in the will. She did not adopt the children. Children are gone. They are in Ireland. She has no home. Lives with her parents. She has no assets, according to her father. Don't you think if Molly got one nickel out of this situation, this tragedy, that you would have seen it blown up the size of that wall? What did Molly gain? Nothing.'

The blame lay with Jason. He was responsible because he didn't take his medication and this may have caused him to lose his temper.

'Molly and Tom have no fear of your decision,' said Holton. 'They have waited two years for this. Enough is enough. This is a tragedy. I'm sorry Mr Corbett didn't take his thyroid medicine. I'm sorry he drank seven or eight beers . . . Tom and Molly didn't make those choices. He made those choices.'

*

Tom's lead attorney, David Freedman, used his closing argument to lay out Tom's service to America, his thirty-five years with a top-level security clearance.

'Who of Tom or Jason was the more likely to have snapped on the night – a 65-year-old grandfather who had spent his life protecting us from drug dealers and foreign intelligence, making us safe, or a man who had stopped taking his thyroid medication, was feeling dizzy and getting angry for no reason?

'We know he had depression issues. We know he had sleep issues. We know two weeks before he had his hands around Molly Martens' throat that he felt stressed and angry for no reason.'

Freedman said Jason was a 'ticking time bomb'. When Tom walked into that room, he acted on two of our most primal instincts – survival and protection of our young. He found himself on his knees, thrown across the room.

'Tom knows there's only one way to live,' Freedman said. 'That's to rush Jason.' Tom was in a fight for his life.

'All he wants is Jason to stop. Jason hasn't stopped. The other hits have not stopped Jason. Tom has no choice at that point. It's Tom or Jason. And he continues to hit until the threat goes away, until Jason goes down.'

Every blow was necessary because, 'Any time Jason could have left the situation.'

Freedman did not offer any explanation for the partial fingerprints found on the inside of the bedroom door handle, which to many observers were the perfect rebuttal to the idea that Jason was free to leave.

Because Tom had opted to take the stand in his own defence, this gave the state the right to give the final argument to the jury.

Alan Martin got to his feet and delivered an eviscerating

90-minute closing statement. Stepping into the well of the court, he carried two large photos in his hand.

'This is Jason Corbett,' he said, raising one photo showing the handsome business executive smiling. He paused and raised the second photo, showing Jason disfigured. 'This is what became of Jason Corbett.'

Martin walked slowly along the length of the jury box. 'This was Jason Corbett and they killed him.' He pointed at Tom and Molly in succession: 'He killed him with the bat. She killed him with that brick.' Molly lowered her head and her cheeks flushed. Martin pointed at the brick and paused. 'They literally crushed his skull.'

Martin kept using the word 'beat'. How they beat him in the bedroom, and down the hall, and in the bathroom and back again.

'He's down here 24 to 28 inches from the floor when his head hits the wall. They beat him in the head. The blood spatter tells you that he hit him when he was down. They beat him in the back of the head after he was down.'

Pointing between exhibits of Jason's injuries and photos of the Martenses uninjured, Martin said: 'This is what they did to him. They destroyed his head. And this is what he did to them – nothing.'

Martin said there were ten impact sites on the head. He knocked on the jury box ten times. 'He's hit at least four times after he's unconscious.'

Holding the bat, Martin returned to the prosecution bench and asked the jury how much force it takes to cause a laceration. Then he struck the table in front of him with the bat.

'How much does it take to split the flesh all the way to the skull?' He hit the table, harder and louder this time. 'Have you ever tried to rip all of the flesh off of a T-bone? How hard is that? Not with a knife, but with a ball bat. How much force does it require to rip flesh from the bone?'

Martin hit the bat off the table four more times, harder each time. 'It takes a lot of force.'

Martin showed them Jason's crushed skull. 'How much force does that take?' he asked, again striking the table. 'It takes "I hate you" force,' he said, hitting the table so hard the sound echoed through the silent courtroom and, in its wake, left a vacuum for imaginations to fill.

Martin had Greg Brown lie on the floor of the court in front of the jury so he could demonstrate how close Tom and Molly had to have been for Jason's blood and tissue to embed in the fabric of Tom's boxer shorts and Molly's pyjamas.

There was tissue embedded in the brick. 'Not stuck to it, not laying on top of it, embedded in the brick. Embedded means something that happens with force.

'You know what malice feels like when it comes from the brick that Molly had?' Martin picked up the brick. 'It feels like "I hate him. I want those kids."'

Martin struck the table twice with the brick. He then suggested that Molly might have started it and Tom had to finish it.

'Malice might sound like "Oh, God, I've hit him with a brick and he's hurt and he's going to leave me and he's going to take those kids and I can't stop him. And he might have me arrested ... My life is over. Now, I have to kill him." Murder to cover up an assault by either one of these two people is malice.'

Martin said counterintelligence was about deception and lies. 'In this case the enemies are not the Russians,' he said, 'the Chinese or North Koreans. If you smashed your son-in-law's skull in and you are trying to get away with it, the enemy is justice.'

Right from the outset, Tom attempted to deceive: 'This master spy stuff started right away.' Martin said you end up with some ridiculous statements from Tom, such as him having no knowledge of the brick.

'First order of business, protect Molly. So somebody has to take responsibility and he is the wit-matcher. He understands crime scenes and he understands the crime-scene evidence. Between Molly and me, I will take the witness stand and see if I can get the jury to excuse me because I'm an FBI agent and I tell the tale of self-defence.'

Martin said Tom adapted his story to fit the scene, but he made mistakes – such as closing the door.

'Oh my God, she's being strangled, but hold on, don't do anything. I have got to close the door. What? That makes no sense at all. There's no reason for anybody in that situation to do anything other than stand in the door and turn the light on. He doesn't do either one.'

He added the detail about closing the door because he knew the blood spatter was going to show the door was closed. 'He has to figure out what covers Molly, what's consistent, what's reasonable with the consistent evidence . . . If he can't get by with ambiguity, his memory fails. All you get is, "I don't recall with specificity."'

Tom deliberately kept Sharon out of the story. Martin didn't raise the issue of that one unidentified hair on the brick. Instead, he asked the jury to consider why Tom was insistent that Sharon slept through the whole affair.

'Did you call her? No. Did you wake her up? No. Did you scream for her to call 911? No. Did she show up? No. It is like she vanished from the face of the earth in Tom Martens' testimony. Why is that?'

Then, with his natural dramatic flair, Martin answered his own question.

'One person keeping a story straight that ain't true is awfully hard. And the special agent who was in charge of the crime scene that night, if anyone knows that, knows that.

Two people keeping a story straight is exponentially harder and three people keeping a story straight is darn near impossible. To go from three to two, we have to get Sharon out of the picture.'

Martin said Tom delayed calling 911 so he could get his story straight. He had to think about all this pounding, smashing, screaming and yelling, skulls being crushed, flesh being ripped from the bone, and why and how Sharon could have slept through it all and not come upstairs.

That's why the blood was dried and the body was cool – because Tom was staging the crime scene and getting his story straight.

Martin painted the picture, from Sharon's perspective, of two police officers arriving in the basement at 3.30 a.m. with your grandchildren, saying they are conducting an investigation upstairs; yet Sharon is totally calm, and merely asks: 'Is everything okay?'

This was not credible, Martin said. 'Do any of you all know a grandmother on the planet that would respond in that situation in that way?'

It was unbelievable, Martin said, that this loud exchange between Tom and Jason – with Tom shouting, 'Let her go' and Jason responding, 'I'm going to kill her' – could have happened without Sharon waking, or the children coming down from upstairs.

Martin could not explicitly state the prosecution's suspicions here: that the children might have been sedated prior to going to bed. He relied on the jury asking themselves the question: how could Jack and Sarah have slept through all that violence?

Martin gave the jury a flavour of just how loud all this violence must have been as he unequivocally told the jury that Sharon's story just did not add up.

'All of this pounding, all of this smashing, screaming, all

the yelling, skulls being crushed, flesh being ripped from the bone, thumping – all of this great ruckus upstairs, she [Sharon] doesn't either wake up or come upstairs.'

It was also unbelievable, Martin said, that an FBI agent with Tom's training would risk crushing his own daughter's skull by swinging the bat at Jason's head. He could have hit Jason on the ankles or knees.

Martin said there was a 'void' in Tom's testimony. Tom claimed Molly did nothing but go limp and scream, yet she said she tried to hit Jason with the brick and the pieces of scalp on the brick show she was successful.

Tom had explained how there was a shouting match, a back and forth between him and Jason. Yet, in her written statement, Molly said: 'My father came in the room and I can't remember if he said something or just hit Jason.'

Martin said these accounts were contradictory and unbelievable. If Jason was screaming that he was going to kill her, that's the kind of thing she ought to remember.

There was malice, Martin said, because Jason wasn't good enough for Tom or Molly.

'He's not good enough for her. He's not good enough for my family. He's beneath me and beneath my family. I hate him. That's what malice sounds like.'

Martin said Molly was never strangled. There were no marks. In Tom's evidence he heard voices before he entered the room, not gurgling. 'If the air is being cut off here,' said Martin, 'you are not talking.'

Molly had to be asked to stop rubbing her neck. She was trying to create a redness. 'The only evidence she was strangled is that Molly said her throat hurt. I'm having a hard time swallowing even though there's not a mark on me. My throat hurts. Well, in some houses that might get a first grader out of school. In this case, it ought not get Molly out of murder.'

Martin finished with the awful prospect of what really happened.

'The evidence with the bloody handprint on the back of the door is that he tried to escape . . . Jason Corbett did not have to die. He did not have to die in his own bedroom. He did not have to die with his children at the top of the steps. Jack and Sarah did not have to become orphans.'

Martin walked over to stand in front of Molly. 'He did not have to die that brutal, vicious and savage death at the hands of the woman that he came to America for. He did not have to die at the hands of her father.'

Martin walked back over to the jury box and concluded. 'You have a duty to return a verdict that speaks for the conscience of Davidson County. You have a duty to return a verdict that speaks the truth. You have a duty to return a verdict that will deliver justice for Jason.'

At 1.05 p.m. on 8 August 2017 the jury was dispatched to deliberate. Molly draped a blanket around herself and sat outside Courtroom C eating grapes. Both sides settled in for a long wait.

They were shocked when, the following day at 11.27 a.m., there was a knock on the jury door. A unanimous verdict was in. Tracey and David were summonsed. Reporters from US television networks ABC, CBS and NBC, and from multiple Irish media organizations, ran inside, many expecting a not-guilty verdict as the jury had returned after less than four hours of deliberation. After seventeen days of court proceedings, the end came in haste.

The number of bailiffs in court doubled, and they were now fanned around the well of the court. Judge Lee warned that any outburst would be met with up to thirty days in Lexington jail.

Tom and Molly stood as the judge asked the jury foreman,

Tom Aamland, to read the verdicts. Both were found guilty of second-degree murder.

Almost all the Corbett family and Jason's friends wept with relief, but no one uttered a word.

Across the aisle, the Martenses were devastated. Molly wailed. But Tom displayed no emotion. He turned to his wife, who was sobbing in the arms of her brother. Armed bailiffs moved forward and stood behind Tom and Molly. After thirty years in the FBI, Tom knew what was coming next. He stood and put both hands behind his back.

As Sheriff Grice cuffed Tom, Connor Martens sobbed loudly before burying his face in his hands.

Molly had to be instructed to stand. Weeping uncontrollably, she broke from the comforting embrace of one of her lawyers, Cheryl Andrews, and turned to face her mother and brothers in the public gallery.

Before a female officer could put the cuffs on her, Molly shouted: 'I'm really sorry, Mom, I wish he'd just killed me.' For her supporters, this anguished cry encapsulated the tragedy – a wife who, in defending herself against domestic violence, killed her husband, lost 'her children' and caused her own father to be sent to jail for at least twenty years.

After a 15-minute recess, arguments about sentencing were put forward.

Alan Martin told the judge there had been repeated attempts by Molly to contact Jack and Sarah. A maximum sentence of twenty to twenty-five years was required to protect them from any such interference.

Tracey read out a victim impact statement on behalf of the family.

'We ask ourselves, was he in pain? Did he cry? How long did he live before he took his last breath? Jason's murder took everything from his children. It took their innocence. It took their security. It made them orphans and it fundamentally changed the course of their lives forever. They sometimes have trouble finding joy in the simple pleasures of life. Being happy doesn't seem right any more.'

There was another grieving mother in this story – Jason's. Rita Corbett described the cruelty of never hearing a single word of remorse or condolence from the Martenses, of being prevented from speaking to Jack and Sarah at the most tragic time of their lives. She described the pain of the daily dawning, that: 'I will never see him again.'

Martin broke into tears as he read a letter from 12-year-old Jack into the record. Jack said his father had been his biggest supporter, but now, 'he will miss everything I do in life.' Jack spoke for Sarah, too.

'She knows her daddy won't be there to walk her down the aisle. She will never have a father-daughter dance, and Sarah and my dad had been planning that for ages.'

Jack's letter said Molly Martens was 'so many bad things, but one thing she is not is part of my family'. He said she would be remembered as a 'murderer'.

Tom was invited by the judge to speak, but he declined. Molly had refused to take the stand, but she opted to speak before sentencing.

'I did not murder my husband. My father did not murder my husband. The incidents of August 2nd happened in a way that they happened on a somewhat regular basis – the difference is that my father was there.'

Crying, she continued: 'I am sorry that I screamed. And I am sorry that he saved my life because if I had just died, then my children would have lost just one more parent and not two. And the jury did not hear all of the evidence—'

Here Molly's lead attorney Walter Holton quickly intervened to shut her down, fearful her comments would be deemed a contempt of court.

'It's okay,' he said. 'Your Honor, that's all. I'm sure the court recognizes it's obviously very emotional for everyone involved.'

Judge Lee imposed a 20- to 25-year sentence with the recommendation that Molly receive 'such psychiatric and/or psychological counselling and treatment as may be available to her in the Department of Corrections'.

Immediately, David Freedman and Walter Holton gave notice of their intention to appeal on behalf of Tom and Molly respectively.

Sheriff Grice got Tom and Molly ready for jail.

Tom asked Grice if they could spend a little time with the family.

'They were allowed to hug in a private room,' Grice recalled. 'Molly kept repeating, "I'm not a murderer."'

After an hour with their family members, during which time Grice remembers 'there was not much talk out of them at all,' Molly and Tom were placed in handcuffs and ankle chains and marched to a prison van. They put Molly sitting in a cage at the front right and Tom sitting on one of the benches in the back. There were two guards with them.

Barring a successful appeal, this was possibly the last time Molly would see her 67-year-old father. Not a single word passed between them on the 112-mile journey.

There was no embrace when, one and a half hours into the journey, Molly was dropped at the North Carolina Correctional Institute for Women outside Raleigh. Tom carried on for Central Prison, Raleigh, alone with his thoughts.

PART THREE

21. Retrial by Media

Two days after the verdict, and one day before Tracey and David Lynch had even returned to Ireland, ABC's *20/20* investigative programme broadcast explosive allegations about Jason. Other networks had chased Molly for months, but she and Tom had sat down for exclusive interviews with ABC, recorded in Knoxville in May 2017, before the trial.

The show could draw 4 million viewers for its character-driven true-crime specials. Molly guaranteed eyeballs on screen and online. The public was fascinated by female killers, and the telegenic Tennessee woman was almost the perfect media construct – a chameleon who completely divided opinion.

Some saw a mother who defended herself from a toxic man; others saw a manipulative liar who killed her husband to get his children. Either way, people would tune in, comment, post and share. This was good news for ABC, but also for Tom and Molly's defence. The Martenses planned to piggyback the publicity by launching another online fundraiser to help with their appeals.

Molly's interview was set up so the viewer saw all the lighting and the camera equipment as Molly walked into shot towards an empty seat, as though she were the accused finally taking the stand. She had refused to testify in court but she was happy to set the record straight here, on TV.

Molly had a makeover for the occasion. Luminescent under the 320-watt lights, she wore a sober blue top beneath a tailored, tan-coloured trouser suit. Sitting cross-legged, she looked like a glamorous executive PA.

Her styled blonde tresses fell in long loose swirls over her right shoulder as she spoke in sombre, demure tones, pressing the palm of her right hand into her left, as though she had to compress each thought into words.

Not subjected to the rigorous cross-examination she would have faced under oath, Molly set about slowly assassinating her former husband's character.

Asked if she had ever been in love with Jason, she closed her eyes and paused before whispering, Princess Diana-like, 'I was.' She alternated between looking at the ground and up, off to her left, even when discussing seemingly benign things like how, in high school, she had planned to become a doctor.

At their trial, Tom and Molly denied acting in concert to kill Jason with malice. In their ABC interviews, they were very much a team. Their stories dovetailed neatly.

Tom, dressed in his customary suit and tie, was unrepentant. 'It's horrible,' he said. 'A man died. But a man also attacked my daughter. And a man tried to protect his daughter.'

Tom was here to set the record straight, though some of his claims were as fanciful as Molly's aspirations to become a doctor. The man who had spent thirty years in the FBI and had trained FBI and DEA agents had totally missed the second murder weapon in the room: the bloody brick sitting on the cream woollen carpet. He still could not recall anything about the brick. He couldn't even be sure if Molly had hit Jason, so he refused to speculate.

This was strange, given that Tom knew Molly had struck Jason with the brick. He knew because she had told him. Tom was recorded saying this to his employers eighteen days after Jason's killing.

Unlike Tom, Molly was happy to speculate. Though she had told Lt Wanda Thompson that she could scarcely remember anything after her father first hit Jason, now Molly recalled things with a specificity Tom would surely have admired.

She remembered when the 'last hit' was. 'The last hit he [Jason] was still standing up. I'd like to think there's science to prove that.' Her eyes went up and to the left as she added: 'The truth is the truth.'

Had Stuart James been watching down in Florida, he would have been shouting at the screen. There *was* science to prove when Jason was last hit – it was when his head was less than 2 feet from the ground.

Molly's depression and anxiety were mentioned during the ABC interview, but her stay in a psychiatric unit four weeks before she travelled to Ireland was omitted. Instead, over footage of Molly jogging through the Tennessee woods in pink shorts, she described going to Ireland to 'just figure myself out for a while'.

Molly denied sleeping with Jason that first night but admitted they had got together quickly. She appeared to suggest that this was a mistake, that she had entered into a romantic relationship with Jason too soon and felt trapped. 'I didn't want to call up my parents and say I'm uncomfortable with this, and I'm coming home, I've failed again,' Molly told the interviewer.

As we've seen, email correspondence between Molly and Jason, which dates from five months after her arrival, shows Molly pushing Jason to commit to a long-term future with her. In it, Molly doesn't appear to be a woman who feels trapped in the relationship.

Molly told her ABC interviewer that despite being uncomfortable, she stayed, and the children 'filled a void' in her life. 'I felt like I was worth something,' she said.

When they all moved to North Carolina, life was magical. Jason loved America and the children found Meadowlands to be 'a wonderland'. Jason got on well with neighbours, who saw him as a 'gentle Irish giant'. But soon frictions emerged in the marriage, over Jason's refusal to allow Molly to adopt Jack and Sarah.

Molly became emotional as she detailed the dark secrets of her marriage. Jason became increasingly controlling and domineering over time, she said. At first she thought, 'Oh it's just because he loves me so much.' But darker forces were at play.

He was paranoid, jealous, and would dictate what she could and couldn't buy. He saw nothing wrong with spending $500 on golf clubs but would lose his temper if she bought raspberries for the children. This was a side of Jason hidden from the world, Molly said. He would smile at neighbourhood gatherings, and everyone liked him, but behind closed doors there was another Jason Corbett.

In his interview with ABC, Tom said Jason would dictate everything, from what clothes Molly wore to when she could leave the house. Tom said that Jason enforced this control by texting and calling Molly all the time, or by monitoring her phone and internet history.

ABC then played clips from the Dragonfly interviews, the ones which the trial judge would not allow the jury to see. Viewers saw Jack accuse his father of hitting and punching Molly.

ABC had also been leaked the Pancake Tape – the recording from February 2015, six months before the killing, of the family arguing around the dinner table – which added an authenticity to Jason's secret persona behind closed doors.

Her voice quivering, Molly said she stayed for Jack and Sarah. 'I never would have left the children. Maybe I was being selfish and they'd have a better life, but I didn't want them to lose a second mother.'

As the interview progressed, Molly's allegations about

Jason became more extreme. He would choke her during sex; so forcefully she had passed out on several occasions. 'It did always make me think of Mags,' she said, 'his first wife, and wonder, is this what happened to her?'

Tom then parlayed his Mike Fitzpatrick story: he had asked Mags's father what he thought about Jason. 'His response was, "I think he killed my daughter." And I go, "Woah," I'm not really expecting that kind of thing.'

Molly joined the dots of Tom's suspicion: 'The twentieth time you are suffocated or strangled or someone holds their hand over your mouth or a pillow over your face and you can't breathe for an extended period of time, you think, "Oh, his first wife died at three in the morning, maybe that's going to happen to me."'

In her police interview, Molly had neglected to mention these twenty occasions where she had been strangled or suffocated.

During the TV interview Tom said he regretted Jason's death, but he also said he felt 'righteous' about it. 'I'm going to do everything that I have to do to save her life. And if I die trying, well . . . she's my daughter. I'm not going to live with not trying.'

In a clear, steady voice, Tom reinforced this point with a sentence so perfectly crafted it sounded almost pre-prepared. 'I tried to do the right thing. And I'd rather live with what I did than live with what I didn't. Better to die in jail than to have my daughter die before my eyes.'

The audience's verdict on *20/20*'s Martens investigation was far from unanimous. Some believed Molly's story. Others were unsympathetic, suggesting that her interview was as performative and unbelievable as Sharon's story of what she'd experienced – or hadn't experienced – that night in the basement.

Ultimately, though, from the Martenses' point of view, the ABC show was a great success. Their pre-trial motion to include Tom's fears about Jason killing his first wife had been rejected by Judge Lee – but now, millions of people heard Molly say she thought Jason had killed Mags, and that she was next.

Likewise, the Martenses had wanted to build their defence around the Dragonfly tapes, but the judge had ruled them inadmissible. The tapes leaked to ABC ensured millions heard Jack condemning his own father.

ABC played the section of the Pancake Tape where Jason slammed the kitchen chair and Sarah screamed at him and Molly to please stop fighting. The defence had not even tried to introduce that as evidence in the trial. But in the court of public opinion, it would become a leading exhibit.

Lastly, the Martenses got to poison public opinion about Jason and bolster sympathy for Molly as a victim of domestic and sexual abuse by claiming something neither had claimed when interviewed by police – that Molly was regularly choked during sex and had been strangled twenty times. Even if many didn't believe the claims, they were still discussing it, posting, sharing and commenting.* Doubt was sown.

Two days after the ABC interview was aired Molly's younger brother Connor went on WVLT8, his local television station in Knoxville.

Connor accused the district attorney of withholding key pieces of evidence – the children's statements at Dragonfly;

---

* The killing of Jason Corbett inspired online devotees on both sides. More than 20,000 people supported the Justice for Jason Facebook page in 2017. There were dedicated threads on Websleuths and Reddit. The *Daily Mail*'s website, then the second-biggest news site in the world, covered the case obsessively.

the explanation for why the brick was in the bedroom; and Tom and Molly's police interviews.

'My sister risked her life for years for those kids,' he said, but now she had lost everything. 'And my dad gave his life to the nation and risked his life to save my sister.'

Connor said his family had been 'financially gutted' by the case. In the interview he was sitting next to his uncle, Mike Earnest, who framed Molly and Tom's convictions as an American tragedy. 'These two really outstanding people,' he said, '[from an] all-American family, are innocent and now behind bars. And this can happen in America.'

The purpose of this interview was to publicize a new online fundraising drive by the Martenses. They raised $18,000 for their appeal before the month was out.

The following month, unbowed by mounting bills, the Martenses hired three new lawyers to defend the wrongful death lawsuit taken by Jason's estate.

The DA and detectives always suspected that Sharon had left the basement and played some role on the night of the killing. Jason's estate was going to test that theory in a civil court, where the burden of proof was lower.*

To counteract, the Martenses' new lawyers filed papers blaming Jason for his own death: 'Jason Corbett's death was the sole proximate result of his unprovoked violent aggression and his deliberate attempt to kill Molly Corbett and kill or seriously injure Mr Martens.'

Molly – prisoner number 1551729 – was struggling at the North Carolina Correctional Facility for Women. She claimed her hair was cut and dyed against her will and that

---

* In a civil action the burden of proof is on the balance of probabilities as opposed to beyond reasonable doubt.

she hadn't been allowed phone calls, or even a toothbrush, for the first nine days.

'Over fifteen people have passed out [with the heat] in her short time there,' Connor posted on the Martenses' GoGet-Funding page. 'There are no activities. On rare occasions, she gets to go outside, only to be reprimanded for walking too fast in her attempt to get exercise.'*

Connor accused the sheriff's office of 'ineptitude' and the DA of withholding evidence.

'It isn't even about whether they're guilty or innocent,' Connor said. 'At this point it is about every American, and their right to a fair trial.'

While their lawyers prepared their appeal, the Martenses' extended family continued the debate in the media. Bobby Martens' wife, Ely, insisted Jack and Sarah should still be living in America: 'I don't know how anyone can think this is best for Jason's kids. They really love Tom and Molly. We love them, they were at my house before they were taken and it is just very hard to believe because they were devastated when they were taken away.'†

Jason's older brother, John, a National Health Service worker in the UK, told Irish newspaper the *Limerick Leader* that the Martenses should have got the death penalty on a first-degree-murder charge. 'I wish them eternal pain and suffering in prison,' he said.‡

In September 2015 the Martenses filed appeal papers claiming jury misconduct and bias after two jurors told ABC they

---

* A prison spokesperson denied all Connor's claims.
† Interview in *Irish Daily Mirror*, August 2017.
‡ John Corbett interview with the *Limerick Leader*, published August 2017. The death penalty was reintroduced in North Carolina in 1977.

believed Molly attacked Jason as he slept; that there never was any abuse; and that Molly was bipolar.*

This enabled the Martenses' defence lawyers to appeal, because no argument about Molly's mental health was presented in court. Nor was there ever any argument in court that Jason was asleep when first hit. Therefore, the jury had deliberated on evidence that wasn't put before them.

According to the Martenses' defence lawyers, the jurors had also allegedly discussed the case among themselves before they were asked to deliberate.

Molly's lead attorney Walter Holton was confident that they could win an appeal and get a retrial, and if that happened, they could convince at least one of the new jurors to acquit Molly.

Holton's confidence was based on a canvass they had done of the jury after the 2017 trial finished. This revealed that during the trial two jurors had initially believed Molly.

After the first afternoon of deliberations, one female and one male juror were hold outs. They wanted to acquit Molly on the murder charge. Both then changed their minds overnight.

Holton, a former prosecutor, knew the DA would not risk such a situation repeating itself in a retrial. The DA would see the fact that two jurors initially wanted to acquit Molly as poor odds – a one in six chance that a future juror would acquit.

Holton could see a path to freedom– win the appeal, then negotiate a plea deal.

---

* Miriam Figueroa said: 'To me the choking did not occur.' Molly struck her husband first with the brick while he was sleeping. Jury foreperson Tom Aamland agreed: 'When he got up and tried to protect himself, I believe that's when Tom had to intervene.' Aamland said he believed Molly could control her personalities, regardless of her mental health struggles, 'whether it's bipolar or whatever'.

Tom's lead attorney, David Freedman, was equally confident that they would win at the North Carolina Court of Appeals. He had identified two new points of attack – Jack and Sarah.

22. Covid Complications

In February 2020, Tom and Molly won their appeal. The North Carolina Court of Appeals overturned their convictions and said they were entitled to a new trial.

Attorney David Freedman's decision to centre Molly and Tom's appeal on Jack and Sarah's statements at Dragonfly was vindicated. The court ruled by a two-to-one majority that the trial judge should have allowed the jury to hear the children's condemnation of their father.

If there was a retrial, Jack and Sarah, now aged fifteen and thirteen, would have to take the stand. They would face intense cross-examination and would have to reveal in open court what life was really like behind the closed doors of 160 Panther Creek Court.

For the Martenses, winning this appeal was worth it, of course, but if Tom and Molly had to face a retrial and fund a whole new defence, it would be financially ruinous.

It was little over a year since the Martenses had finally settled the wrongful death claim brought by Jason's estate.

In December 2018 lawyers for Jason's estate had told the Martenses' lawyers that if there was no settlement offer forthcoming, they would press ahead and request that a specific type of DNA testing be carried out on a pale yellow hair which had been found among the twenty-five adhering to the bloodied brick. As we know, there were already forensic findings which suggested the hair was Sharon's. Jason's estate believed that the additional testing would confirm this.

While the district attorney had decided not to pursue criminal charges against Sharon, the Lynches *were* pursuing her through their wrongful death case, where she was named as a defendant alongside Tom and Molly.

In 2019, a settlement was reached in the wrongful death case. The Martenses agreed to pay $180,000 to Jason's estate. Their insurance company agreed to pay $20,000. Under the terms of the settlement, Jason's $600,000 life insurance premium, frozen pending criminal and civil proceedings, would be paid not to Molly but to the trust established for Jack and Sarah.

The mystery of who owned that unidentified hair on the brick would remain unsolved.

The $760,000 proceeds from the sale of the Martenses' Folly Beach vacation home* went on the wrongful death settlement and the legal fees incurred defending Tom and Molly in the 2017 criminal trial.

The Attorney General of North Carolina asked the North Carolina Supreme Court to review the decision by the North Carolina Court of Appeals to overturn Tom and Molly's convictions for second-degree murder.†

In the meantime, Tom and Molly would remain incarcerated, and Sharon would need to raise several hundred thousand dollars for the Supreme Court review and a possible retrial.

Five weeks after the Martenses won their appeal, Irish schools were ordered closed to contain the Covid pandemic. Isolation from their friends can't have helped 15-year-old

---

* They bought 914 West Ashley Avenue in Folly Beach for $740,000 on 31 December 2012. They sold it on 20 April 2017 for $760,000.

† Because their appeal victory was by a majority (two to one) and not unanimous, the Attorney General of North Carolina was required to ask the North Carolina Supreme Court to review the decision.

Jack and 13-year-old Sarah as they contemplated the daunting prospect of testifying against Molly in a retrial.

When Jack and Sarah's grandmother – Tracey and Jason's mother, Rita – died of Covid complications two months later, only twenty-five mourners were allowed at her funeral.*

The North Carolina justice system ground to a halt during lockdown.† Tom, now seventy, applied for compassionate release, arguing Covid was lethal at his age. He was refused.

A year passed before the North Carolina Supreme Court voted on 12 March 2021 by a margin of four to three‡ to uphold the Martenses' appeal. The Martenses were entitled to a retrial. And they would be freed in a matter of weeks.

The *Winston-Salem Journal* described the prospect as 'The Greatest Show on Earth, the Sequel', before questioning whether locals were ready for the national and international media bringing the 'circus' back to town.

If this article was the first hint that the DA was testing public opinion about a possible plea deal, Molly's brother, Connor, let the cat entirely out of the bag. He revealed on TV§ that Molly and Tom were discussing a plea deal.

Jason's family was against a plea deal because it would mean the Martenses escaping murder charges and only accepting their guilt on a lesser charge of voluntary manslaughter. As the Martenses had already served three years and eight months for second-degree murder convictions

---

* Rita Corbett died on 17 May 2020. She had survived a heart attack the previous August.

† Governor Roy Cooper subsequently faced a slew of lawsuits from bars, restaurants, churches, strip clubs and gyms over the state's Covid lockdown.

‡ The North Carolina Supreme Court ruled on 12 March 2021 to uphold the findings of the North Carolina Court of Appeals.

§ In a TV interview with WATE 6 channel.

that had now been overturned, they would likely escape with very little extra jail time, if any, should they agree to plead guilty to voluntary manslaughter.

One week after the North Carolina Supreme Court ruling overturning the Martenses' convictions, Tracey, David, Jack and Sarah arrived in North Carolina, where the children were to be interviewed separately by Detectives Brandon Smith and Michael Hurd, who had led the investigation into Jason's killing.

With the Martenses' murder convictions now overturned, if there was to be a retrial, there would have to be a whole new criminal investigation.

The detectives had been unable to interview Jack and Sarah in August 2015 – other than setting questions for Brandi Reagan, the children's interviewer at Dragonfly House, to ask. If there was a retrial, the Dragonfly House tapes would be played for the new jury, so Jack and Sarah would be called as witnesses.

What the children said to the detectives now, on 29 March 2021, would inform whether DA Garry Frank believed he could win a murder conviction in a retrial.

Sarah was interviewed by Detectives Smith and Hurd for a total of six hours. The 14-year-old told detectives that Molly had threatened her into lying about her father. She said she was told she would go into foster care or would be put into 'some crazy person's house' if she didn't lie. She said her father was not the abuser, Molly was.

Sarah said Molly would regularly physically abuse Jack. She would punch and kick him. Sarah said she had seen Molly beat Jack up so many times she was terrified of what Molly would do if she didn't comply and lie to Brandi Reagan at Dragonfly, and to the other social workers who had interviewed her.

Sarah described one day when Molly became so enraged she took Sarah's treasured photograph of her mother, Mags, threw it down the stairs, and screamed: 'She is gone, she is not your mom. I am your mom – not her.'

Sarah said that after they all moved to America in 2011 Molly began to punch and hit Jack whenever Jason was away on business trips. Sarah told detectives about one particularly violent beating of Jack where Sarah had to drag Molly off Jack's back near the utility room and kitchen.

Molly began telling Sarah that Jason was abusive to her and that he had killed Sarah's mother. Sarah said Molly claimed variously that Jason strangled Mags, or that he smothered her with a pillow.

Jack was due to be interviewed by the detectives the same day, but Sarah's allegations were so extensive he was asked to come back the following morning.

Jack's interview began that next day, 30 March 2021. Equally intense, it didn't finish until seven that evening.

The 16-year-old told detectives that he lied about his father in Dragonfly and elsewhere because he was scared of Molly. She had just killed his father and he genuinely believed she could kill him. Even though he was afraid of her, she was still the only person he had in the world at that time, so he did what he was told.

Jack said that Molly would frequently physically assault him while Jason was away on business. He told detectives about Molly attacking him one time because on a phone call he told his father that he loved him. Afterwards, Molly chased him and ended up 'kicking the crap' out of him outside the utility room. Jack said Sarah had to help him fend off Molly.

Like Sarah, Jack was told by Molly that Jason had killed Mags. Jack said he was only six or seven years old when Molly first told him that Jason had strangled Mags or that he had smothered her with a pillow.

After the detectives had interviewed Sarah and Jack they briefed DA Garry Frank. Frank asked David and Tracey to attend a meeting at the DA's office at 4 p.m. the next day.

At this meeting, Tracey and David were shocked to hear that Frank had decided to offer the Martenses a plea deal. In return for pleading guilty to the lesser charge of voluntary manslaughter, the Martenses would receive a sentence in the following range: a minimum sentence of six years and eight months up to a maximum of nine years and eight months.

Given that they had already served three years and eight months, the plea deal, if agreed, would see Tom and Molly being sent back to jail for a minimum of three more years and a maximum of six more years.

Frank told the Lynches that the deal was already offered and the Martenses had been given one week to think about it.

Tracey decided to go public with her belief that the DA was not going to hold a retrial and that he intended to agree a plea deal. Jason's supporters in Ireland started a petition to stop the deal. More than 10,000 signatures were gathered.

Tracey wrote to every member of North Carolina's state legislature, the state senators, the attorney general and governor, demanding a retrial. John Corbett, Jason's older brother, wrote to President Joe Biden.* Jason's friend Brendan O'Callaghan wrote to the DA imploring him not to reach a deal.

'I sat there in silence,' he wrote, 'and looked at the horrendous photos of my friend naked and battered as he lay dead on his bedroom floor . . . What actually puzzles me is, what

---

* John Corbett wrote: 'Sadly, the justice system seems, in this case, to be working for the murderers, and not for the life they have coldly taken for their own narcissistic agenda.'

has changed? Jason is still dead and will always be dead, and you are allowing convicted murderers to walk free, but you still get your conviction.

'Realistically, I don't expect to hear from you, but I believe you are throwing away all the good work your office has done.'

The one-week deadline on the offer of a plea deal passed. One of two things happened – either the Martenses rejected the plea deal and decided to fight for their innocence if there was a retrial; or DA Garry Frank bowed to public pressure and withdrew the deal offer. Whichever it was, the deal was now off the table.

On 7 April 2021, Tom and Molly were moved to Davidson County Jail ahead of their release pursuant to the Supreme Court ruling seventeen days previously which had upheld the quashing of their 2017 convictions.

Jack and Sarah wrote to the judge begging him not to release the Martenses.

Tom and Molly were brought into court separately, each masked, cuffed and in ankle chains. Detectives later learned that a defiant Molly told a fellow prisoner that no matter what happened, she would never spend another day behind bars.

Prison had not been kind to Molly. Far from the manicured image she'd presented on *20/20* nearly four years previously, Molly was now dressed in brown scrubs and orange prison Crocs, her skin pale and pockmarked, with two small cuts and scarring visible over her right eye. The blonde dye had drained from her naturally brown hair.

Molly had not seen her father for three years and eight months, but there was little acknowledgement of one another as he sat less than 10 feet to her right in court.

Behind his Covid mask, Tom looked rested and healthy.

Dressed in an orange prison jumpsuit, the former FBI agent appeared thinner, his eyes furtive and smiling. Instead of looking at Molly, he kept his gaze to his right, on his wife, their three sons and their partners, who were sitting in the socially distanced gallery. A child could be heard crying. This was Lucy, Tom's new grandchild, who he had never seen before.

The Martenses' convictions were quashed, but the original charges of second-degree murder and voluntary manslaughter were not vacated. The Martenses had the right to a retrial and would be released on bail while the DA decided whether to proceed with that retrial.

Bail was set at $200,000, despite assistant DA Alan Martin asking the judge to set it at one million dollars. Tom and Molly had to surrender their passports and were banned from contacting Jack and Sarah. Otherwise, they were free.

Molly was released first. She was led out of the courthouse jail by Bobby. She avoided eye contact with the posse of waiting media and ignored all questions.

Tom didn't leave for another hour. One of his attorneys, Jones Byrd, and his son, Connor, helped him carry four large boxes of case files. While in prison, Tom the lawyer had been keeping a diligent eye on every filing and every cost.

The following month, in May 2021, *Elle* published an exclusive interview in which Molly sought to align herself to the MeToo movement, which had exposed the prevalence of hidden victims of male sexual violence and harassment. As behemoth abusers like Harvey Weinstein* were convicted, the MeToo movement generated public debate about 'toxic

---

* The MeToo movement reached its zenith in 2017, the year Molly was imprisoned. Weinstein was convicted in February 2020.

masculinity' and the millions of wives and mothers who silently suffered at the hands of brutish men.

Molly told *Elle* a story of abuse that began with a mother nurturing her children in the kitchen, having been strangled in the bedroom the night before. She suffered in silence.

'I realize, looking back now, that it [the abuse] was a whole lot worse than I thought it was. And I think that's true for a lot of domestic violence situations. You just convince yourself, "Oh, it's not that bad." Because you wake up in the morning and you have to keep living life. You have to go to work and you have to pack the lunches and you have to clean the kitchen, and so you've convinced yourself that, "Oh, I was strangled last night, but I'm okay."'

Molly admitted in the interview that she had lied in the past – including about having a dead sister – but this was just because she was insecure. 'First of all, everybody lies, that's true. And anybody who says that they don't, they're lying,' she said.

Molly denied describing Sarah's birth at book club. She insisted she had only described pregnancy, and she *had* experienced pregnancy. Others at that book club remember things differently.

Molly gave *Elle* a recording which she claimed was of Jason coming home drunk in late December 2013. *Elle* described it as 'compelling evidence that Jason was not just the "gentle giant" he's routinely described to have been'.

The magazine reported:

He finds the door locked and rings the bell repeatedly. She opens it within 39 seconds and apologizes. 'You never mean to do anything, do ye?' he asks angrily, then mocks her. Molly pleads, multiple smacking sounds can be heard, and she begins to whimper. 'I hate you,' she sobs quietly before the recording cuts out.

The *Elle* tape seemed to be different to the Pancake and Shower tapes. When *Elle* sought comment from Tracey, she asked to hear the tape first. Tracey said the magazine refused to provide it or to detail what steps the magazine had taken to authenticate it.*

Molly told *Elle* most of the secret recordings she made had been destroyed or lost, and 'the few that remain were given to the district attorney's office.' Tom's lawyer David Freedman was quoted saying that to the 'best of his recollection', this was true.

The *Elle* interview was Molly's second attempt, after her ABC interview, to litigate the case through the media. Her aim was to garner public sympathy for her as a domestic violence victim and consequently add pressure to DA Garry Frank so that he would not proceed with a retrial. As her conviction was now overturned, she was, once again, innocent until proven guilty.

No longer a felon, Molly successfully petitioned Facebook to reinstate her old account.

Tracey had spent years getting Facebook to take down photographs of Jack and Sarah which Molly had posted in the four months between the August 2015 killing and her indictment in January 2016. With Molly's Facebook account now reinstated, Molly's old posts, each accompanied by private photographs of the children with Molly, were now publicly available again.

If there was to be a retrial, the Dragonfly tapes would be shown to the new jury. So DA Garry Frank wanted to find out how the old jury, from the 2017 trial, would have responded had they heard them before delivering their verdict.

* After the article was published Tracey wrote to *Elle* seeking a right of reply. *Elle* did not respond.

Jury foreperson Tom Aamland told me he was shown a transcript of the tapes at the DA's office and asked if this would have altered his verdict. Aamland said it would not. He believed Jack and Sarah were coached to make those allegations.

Brandon Smith and Michael Hurd, the detectives who'd investigated Jason's killing, seemed fully behind a retrial of Molly and Tom. DA Frank, though, was increasingly sceptical.

The Dragonfly tapes did two things: they showed the children accusing their father of domestic violence and they offered an explanation for why the brick was in the bedroom.* Frank knew from canvassing the 2017 jury that the unexplained brick in the bedroom was critical. He also knew that up until the eleventh hour, two jurors had wanted to acquit Molly on the murder charge.

There was another important point to consider: when the Supreme Court had upheld Tom and Molly's appeal, it had also upheld the finding of the appeals court that Jason was the 'sole aggressor'. So, in layman's terms, Jason started it, and the Martenses acted, at least initially, in self-defence.

The DA could still argue that the Martenses' response to Jason starting the affray was excessive and not justifiable but, looking at things coldly in the best light for the defence, the Martenses' case in advance of any retrial was hugely strengthened by the Dragonfly tapes.

---

* Jack confirmed he brought the brick inside with the intention of painting it as part of some garden decorations they were planning. This essentially echoed what Molly had said in her police interview. Also, it was not included in Sharon's statement, but in Detective Nathan Riggs's 'case supplemental report' filed on Monday, 4 August 2015, he wrote that when he asked Sharon in the basement about the brick, Sharon volunteered, 'A few weeks ago Molly and Sarah mentioned seeing something on Pinterest about painting and decorating paving stones.'

Who would the new jury believe?

The now 16-year-old Jack and 14-year-old Sarah would be compelling witnesses, but they would be subjected to extensive cross-examination. The jury would hear the Martenses' defence lawyers make the case that Sarah and Jack had been brainwashed out of their earlier views by Tracey and the 20,000 supporters of the Justice for Jason Facebook page. The jury would see the tape of the visitation meeting where Jack and Sarah clung to Molly and wrote her notes telling her how much they loved her.

DA Garry Frank feared for what Jack and Sarah would face if they went into the witness box. Jack would be cross-examined about the phone call he made begging Molly to keep fighting. Were these the actions of someone who hated Molly, someone abused for years by her?

At a retrial, the defence could also introduce a raft of new witnesses – the five women whom Molly confided in about ongoing abuse. The defence would tie what these women heard to what Jack and Sarah admitted seeing back in 2015.

If DA Garry Frank proceeded with a retrial, he would have to rest everything on the shoulders of two teenagers. Aside from coldly weighing up the evidentiary value of what they might testify to, there was the bigger question of their psychological welfare. Sarah and Jack were still receiving counselling. They were still so young and vulnerable. There was a genuine risk of permanently damaging both children in pursuit of a conviction that was far from certain.

What if they went through all that and the jury didn't believe them? Their guilt would be compounded. A plea deal would save them from the trauma of giving evidence, take the risk of acquittal off the table, and yield a felony conviction on the lesser charge of voluntary manslaughter for Tom and Molly.

This was the bitter pill of giving the Martenses a plea deal:

they would likely only be returned to prison for a short period. The sugar of the plea deal was: they would be convicted felons, and as such would be held to account for their actions on 2 August 2015.

Davidson County had other murder victims' families who were also waiting for justice. The DA had finite resources. After twenty-three years as a DA, Frank was faced with the most difficult decision of his career.

23. A Reckoning

Tom and Molly had been free for almost a year. Covid delays had created a backlog of criminal cases before the North Carolina courts, so a court hearing on the next steps in the Jason Corbett homicide case didn't take place until Friday, 11 March 2022. Because the DA and the Martenses had failed to reach agreement on a plea deal, the matter was now brought back before the courts to set a date for a retrial.

Assistant DA Alan Martin led Jack and Sarah into the Davidson County Courthouse via an entrance normally reserved for the jury.

No one wanted the children bumping into their father's freed killers in the corridor outside.*

This would be Jack and Sarah's first time in Molly's presence since 20 August 2015, when they were crammed into a small room at the back of the courthouse for their final visitation. They had loved Molly then. Now, seven years later, they were determined to expose her for the killer and abuser they believed her to be.

Every justice system in the world can sometimes seem cold and procedural, but when Judge David Hall referred to Jason as the 'alleged victim', it upset Jason's family. There was nothing alleged about his death. He was most certainly dead.

By contrast, Judge Hall referred to Tom and Molly by name, or as the 'gentleman and lady' accused. There was no

---

* Earlier Molly and Sarah had briefly come face to face, when Molly emerged from a lift. No words were exchanged.

acknowledgement from the court of Jack and Sarah's presence. But why would there be?

Judge Hall was disdainful of the national and international media coverage, particularly any commentary around a prospective plea deal in the case. He issued a gag order on all parties. No one associated with the case could issue any public comment until its conclusion.

This was important because, in America, it is commonplace for plea deal negotiations to continue even when a retrial date is set. The previous prospective plea deal had leaked and led to a vocal international backlash. Judge Hall was determined to limit any further public commentary about the case whether it concluded via a retrial or a plea deal.

Legal and media experts in North Carolina were surprised by how wide-ranging this gag order was – it covered witnesses, law enforcement, lawyers, family members and anyone with an interest in the case. Production on a Netflix documentary that I was co-producing on the case was temporarily suspended to honour the order.

It was common in American trials for lawyers to give daily press briefings on the courthouse steps, so local network affiliates in North Carolina were shocked at the blanket nature of this gag order.

Tracey, as a prospective witness in the retrial, was silenced. If there was any renewed talk of a plea deal, she would be unable to start another campaign. Molly was also gagged. There would be no more ABC or *Elle* interviews for her.

Judge Hall was a fastidious man. This case would not be determined in the court of public opinion.

David Lynch took over correspondence with DA Garry Frank. Frank wrote to David later that month saying the Martenses had asked for a meeting to discuss 'plea possibilities', but he had declined.

Sarah grew frustrated with the gag order. She tweeted: 'So the person who murdered my dad, abused me, shared all my images and my private notes to the whole world is ok to do so but I can't talk. Where is my protection? My freedom of speech? I will speak the truth about MY life!'

By the time of the next administrative hearing, in September 2022, Jack was eighteen and Sarah sixteen.

At the hearing, Judge Hall again referred to Jason as the 'alleged victim'. He said he had been made aware of statements made that came close to violating his gag order. Without naming Sarah, he warned: 'If it happens again, there will be a hearing . . . a contempt hearing.'

Judge Hall set 26 June 2023 to hear pre-trial submissions.

Sarah tweeted a photo of her dad, writing: 'His name is JASON.'

Three days before Christmas 2022 – Jack and Sarah's eighth without their father – Molly and Tom applied to move the retrial, claiming they could not get a fair trial in Davidson County.*

Supporting documents claimed that the judge's gag order had been breached within twenty minutes of the previous September's court hearing. This seemed to be an oblique reference to Sarah's tweet.

Ruling that Tom and Molly could not get a fair trial in Davidson County due to the attendant publicity, Judge Hall moved the retrial to Forsyth County, a more affluent area.†
In Forsyth County, 35 per cent of residents were educated to bachelor's degree level, compared to 20 per cent in Davidson

---

* They had unsuccessfully tried to move the trial in 2017, too.
† The median household income in Forsyth County was $4,000 greater than in Davidson County.

County. Jurors from Forsyth would be less inclined to view Tom as arrogant, and more inclined to empathize with Molly, especially her most recent iteration as a MeToo mum in executive trouser suits.

Privately, prosecutors viewed the decision as preposterous – in the internet age, news didn't stop at county lines; tweets were not birds flying into some invisible glass dividing Davidson from Forsyth County. It took eighteen minutes to drive the 10 miles separating the Meadowlands crime scene from Forsyth County Courthouse.

The sheriff in Forsyth County was an ex-FBI man. He was part of a group of retired FBI agents who called themselves the G-boys. Tom was a G-boy himself, and word got back to Davidson County's sheriff, David Grice, that Tom had asked this G-boy group of former FBI agents to give him public backing. They refused.

The DA had bigger problems to worry about. The Martenses had hired two experts who found that Mags did not die of an asthma attack. The DA had hired his own expert in response, and he agreed. This was a major shock – Mags had been dead for almost seventeen years and, in all that time, no one had questioned the Irish autopsy findings that she had died of complications pursuant to an asthma attack. Now, the Martenses were seeking discovery of Mags's medical records.

Assistant DA Alan Martin wrote to Tracey explaining that the Martenses were going to argue that Mags had been choked to death by Jason. The DA's office would dispute this, but Tracey needed to source any medical records that could corroborate Mags's history of asthma difficulties or provide an explanation for the sudden death of an otherwise healthy young woman.

What had started as a seemingly spurious claim by Tom in his police interview was now being officially given legal and medical credence. The DA, Garry Frank, going on the appraisal of his own expert, was now agreeing that Mags's death was at least mysterious.

Getting medical records for Mags nearly seventeen years after her death was not easy. Jack had to make a Freedom of Information application as next of kin. The records were sourced and sent to North Carolina, but Tracey was unable to get records relating to a visit Mags had made to a GP in November of 2006, just weeks before her death on the 21st.

Tracey recalled Mags complaining of feeling fatigued by flu-like symptoms and of having a rash on her chest. Tracey believed she had gone to a doctor about ten days before she died, complaining about headaches and a pain in her arm. A pain down the left arm is often a warning sign of cardiac problems. The doctor, however, was unable to locate records for this or any other visit by Mags.

GPs were only required to keep records for seven years. This doctor that Tracey recalled Mags visiting had moved premises, and her records from 2006 were not digitized. After deploying people to search through old appointment card indexes for three days, the doctor was unable to find any paper record of Mags having attended.

A retrial date was finally confirmed – 6 November 2023. Jack and Sarah barely had time to digest this news, however, when the DA brought their world crashing down.

Seven weeks before the retrial was due to start, DA Garry Frank circulated an email to every member of Jason's family who had been in touch with the DA's office, stating that he had agreed to a plea deal. There would be no retrial.

Tom would plead guilty to voluntary manslaughter. Molly would plead 'no contest' to the same charge. A no-contest plea means that the defendant refuses to admit guilt but accepts punishment as if guilty. The legal import was the same as a guilty plea: Molly would be considered a convicted felon.

In the same email, Frank said the range of possible sentences for Tom and Molly would be from three years and two months up to nine years. Though Frank didn't spell it out, the Martenses had already served three years and eight months, so there was a chance they would walk free with no further jail time.

Frank finished his email with a warning not to reveal this plea deal to the public or make any comment that would breach the gag order imposed by Judge Hall. Anyone who did faced 'serious negative consequences'.

After eight years fighting for justice, Tracey was finally silenced. If she sought to organize another campaign against the plea deal, she would find herself dragged before Judge Hall for contempt.

24. The Mother of Invention

Eight years after the killing, Tom and Molly presented themselves in court on 30 October 2023 to accept felony convictions. If the plea deal was meant to spare Jack and Sarah the ordeal of being witnesses and being subjected to cross-examination, DA Garry Frank underestimated the ferocity of the Martenses.

Once the hearing got under way, it was clear they intended to pursue every avenue possible to avoid more jail time – even if that meant putting the victim of the killing on trial and using Jason's children as the principal weapons in the assassination of their father's character.

Standing less than 8 feet from Jack and Sarah, Molly stood with her hand on the bible and entered a plea of 'no contest' to voluntary manslaughter. She would not say the word 'guilty'.

Tom stood and entered a guilty plea. He sat back down with his shoulders open and his right arm draped over his seat. He was Mr Calm. And he had a plan, too.

Tom would turn seventy-four in two months' time. It had taken his retirement nest egg to fight the case all the way to the North Carolina Supreme Court and win. That ruling was priceless, not just in overturning Tom and Molly's murder convictions. The ruling had also made it legally official – Jason was the sole aggressor.

All talk of murder one, of premeditation, of Jason being drugged with trazodone, of Jason being killed for the life insurance policy, or because he wouldn't allow Molly to adopt Jack and Sarah, or because he planned to return to Ireland without Molly – all these theories were now irrelevant. He hadn't been killed for any of these reasons. There was no premeditation or malice; Jason was killed solely because he started the violence that night.

That was the cold, majority finding of the appellate court and the Supreme Court. DA Garry Frank could have retried the case and challenged that conclusion. But he chose not to.

The plea deal meant the State of North Carolina now accepted that the Martenses had been forced to defend themselves. The plea deal was based on the premise of 'imperfect self-defence'; though entitled to defend themselves, Tom and Molly's response had become, at some point, unreasonable and excessive.

Once the Martenses had entered their pleas, the only remaining matter was the length of sentence the judge would impose. Legal sources in North Carolina told me that in the normal course of events, if a defendant pleaded guilty to voluntary manslaughter, sentencing would take place within the hour. Here two weeks were set aside for the prosecution and defence to call witnesses.

The Martenses' strategy was to establish that they believed Jason had killed his first wife and this caused such fear for their own lives that 'extreme mitigating circumstances' applied, enough to excuse their excessive, unreasonable response, and set them free under the Probation Act.

Because this was now a sentencing hearing, not a trial, the Martenses could argue in possibilities and probabilities. Jason *could* be a killer. Jason *might* be a killer. They didn't have to prove it beyond reasonable doubt. There was no jury to convince, just the judge.

As Tom knew full well, the rules of evidence did not apply in sentencing hearings in North Carolina. This allowed the Martenses to present testimony and exhibits which were not permitted in the 2017 trial: the police interview with Molly, the Dragonfly tapes, the Pancake Tape and the testimonies of Molly's multiple Meadowlands confidantes who backed her allegations of Jason's abuse.

The aim was to use this selection of evidence to put Jason in the frame for killing his first wife.* Whether Jason had killed Mags or not was not critical to the Martenses' case. All they needed to show was that Tom and Molly believed Jason had killed Mags, and that Molly was next. Thus, the sentencing hearing became a trial by insinuation. And there was only one person in the dock: the victim.

As previously described, Jason's family was told before the hearing that the Martenses faced a minimum sentence of three years and two months, and a maximum of nine years. Judge Hall, however, reminded the parties at the beginning of proceedings that he had the power to override that, and to impose the Probation Act if there were extreme mitigating circumstances. Given that this judge had referred to Jason as the 'alleged victim' throughout pre-trial hearings, Jason's family steeled themselves for the onslaught ahead.

It was far worse than they could ever have imagined.

To get the lowest sentence possible, Molly would spare no expense and take no prisoners. She intended to use Jack and Sarah to destroy not just their father's name, but their mother's, too.

Jack and Sarah were robbed of redemption through a retrial. They were Tom and Molly's get-out-of-jail card – the principal

---

* Their strategy was one David Freedman had planned to use in 2017, when he filed the 'statement of intent' document. Freedman intended to argue that Tom believed Jason had killed his first wife. He did not intend to argue that Jason actually killed Mags. The strategy was abandoned when the trial judge refused to allow the jury to hear Tom's 'self-serving' story.

reason they won their appeal. Their words had damned their father and freed his killers.

Jack and Sarah had poured their hearts out to Detectives Brandon Smith and Michael Hurd in March 2021, exhuming painful memories. They wanted to testify against Molly in a retrial and expose her for all the abuse she, not their father, had subjected them to.

Two and a half years later, nothing had happened as a consequence of their new statements. Instead, they had been silenced by the DA's secret deal, gagged by the court and threatened with contempt.

Eight years had passed since Jack and Sarah were prised from Molly. That day, as they were taken from Bobby's house, the children screamed at the social workers to stop the car, to take them back. But there was no going back.

Now aged nineteen and seventeen, Jack and Sarah were still asking for everything and everyone to just stop. Just listen to us. Instead, the orphans were the ones forced to listen silently as the Martenses desecrated both their parents in the sentencing hearing.

Doug Kingsbery, Holton's replacement as Molly's lead attorney, attacked from the off, saying, 'Molly confided in multiple witnesses that she had growing concerns that he [Jason] had killed his first wife and the same fate was going to befall her.'

Kingsbery said experts for both the defence and the prosecution agreed that Jason's first wife did not die of an asthma attack. 'Homicide by strangulation is a possibility,' he said, virtually writing the ensuing headlines. There was a history of domestic violence in the Meadowlands home, he went on, and Jack and Sarah had told social workers this in the immediate aftermath of the killing.

Sharon, now seventy-three, sat across the aisle from Jack and Sarah. She stared ahead and avoided eye contact with her former 'grandchildren'. Sharon was flanked by her brother, Mike, and two of her three sons.

The Martens family attempted to present a united front, but over the 8-day hearing I saw Molly and Tom talking to one another outside the courtroom on just a few occasions. Otherwise, they tended to stand more than 10 feet apart, each surrounded by their own cohort of supporters. During lunch breaks, Molly took to walking, straight-backed and fast, around the courthouse, circuit after circuit, on her own.

Inside the courtroom, however, Tom and Molly's stories coalesced as neatly as those of the five women in whom Molly had confided. The five were due to take the stand, after which they would be cross-examined about Molly's 'long and complicated relationship with the truth'.*

Before that, however, the court would see and hear, for the first time, exactly what Molly had said in her video-recorded interview with Lt Wanda Thompson hours after Jason's killing.

In that interview, Molly said it all started with Sarah having a nightmare. 'She [Sarah] woke up, so he was angry that he was woken up . . . I said she'd just had a nightmare. He choked me. Told me to shut up. I screamed.'

As the police interview played to a hushed court Molly was heard admitting that she hit Jason with the brick: 'He tried to hit my dad and might have missed, and I, and I hit him on the head with a brick.' In her 109-word written statement – which was all the jury heard in the 2017 trial – she only admitted 'trying' to hit Jason. There was a second discrepancy here, too: Molly said Jason tried to hit her dad and missed.

But Tom never mentioned Jason trying to hit him with the bat. In fact, he conceded under cross-examination from assistant DA Greg Brown during the 2017 trial that when Jason

* This phrase was used variously by assistant DAs Alan Martin and Marissa Parker.

stood opposite him, now in control of the bat, Jason had not deployed it. Even though he had been struck by the bat at least two times at that stage, Jason did not deploy the bat once it was in his control – hardly the actions of the 'sole aggressor'.

These two discrepancies were surely not lost on the three assistant DAs at the sentencing hearing, but the plea deal, and the Supreme Court designation of Jason as the sole aggressor, had made these points moot. The only side interested in relitigating the case and prolonging the sentencing hearing, it seemed, was the defence.

The defence had made dramatic claims in their closing statements at the 2017 trial about evidence being withheld from the jury. Connor Martens and Mike Earnest, when trying to raise money for the Martenses' appeal, had subsequently described the convictions as a 'miscarriage of justice' and an American tragedy. One of the main pieces of evidence 'withheld' from the jury was this interview between Molly and Thompson, now being shown at the sentencing hearing.

At the end of Molly's interview, Thompson is heard on camera telling Molly: 'At this point, having talked to your dad, and talked to you, it looks like this is going to be self-defence, okay? I don't think there's going to be any issue with that.'

Thompson later explained to me that she was just following protocol.* However, this on-camera concession was

---

* Thompson said protocol dictated that investigators should believe victims who report domestic violence in the first instance and look at all the evidence in the best light of the defence before challenging them. 'People made a big deal of the fact that I said to Molly that it sounded like self-defence. But I have dealt with hundreds if not thousands of cases of domestic violence and it is our job, on hearing allegations of domestic violence, to believe the victim and try to substantiate the claims they are making. If in the course of investigating those claims, questions arise that take the investigation in another direction,

probably why the DA chose not to enter the interview as evidence in 2017. David Freedman and Walter Holton, the Martenses' lawyers, would have claimed that the head of the Criminal Investigations Division – the most senior detective on the case – thought Molly acted in self-defence, and that she has 'no issue' with what Tom and Molly did.

Thompson had been retired for five years by the time of the sentencing hearing. She was not called as a witness. Detectives Smith and Hurd were present for every day of the sentencing hearing, as they had been for every day of the 2017 trial, but neither was called as a witness.

This meant the judge was provided with no context or critique of Molly's police interview – no one asked, for example, why Molly failed to mention in her police interview the twenty instances of strangulation she later alleged in her *20/20* interview. Just as she did at her criminal trial, Molly chose not to take the stand here, either. As keen fishermen like DA Garry Frank knew – only fish with open mouths get hooked.

When Judge Hall called a 10-minute recess after hearing Molly's police interview, Molly rushed from the court, heaving in tears. Pushing past me, she cast aside her uncle Mike Earnest's attempts to calm her, then ran off down the hallway outside Courtroom Six to be alone with her thoughts.

Jack and Sarah remained stoic, outwardly unemotional, as the court heard from investigative social worker Sheila Tyler.

Tyler described how when she interviewed the children at Bobby Martens' house two days after the killing they told her

---

then you follow those leads. But, first and foremost in the early part of the investigation, you are trying to stand up the domestic violence claims, trying to verify them.'

that Jason pushed and hit Molly and that he was angry and controlling over small things, like lights being left on, or bills not being paid on time.

Tyler had interviewed Molly that same night, Monday, 3 August 2015. Molly told Tyler that Jason would choke her during forced sex, placing his hand over her mouth and nose so she couldn't breathe. Tyler told the court that Molly said, 'Each time, he would keep his hand over her a little bit longer. She passed out and she didn't know how long she was out [unconscious] for.'

The defence strategy was building to the question: if Jason choked Molly to the point of losing consciousness during sex, then did he kill his first wife in this way?

The claims of Molly's female confidantes – Shannon Grubb, Melissa Sams, Billy June Jacobs, Helen McCormac and Jennifer Turner – were never aired in the 2017 trial. But now, one after another, they took the stand and knitted a coherent, plausible tale of ongoing domestic violence in Jack and Sarah's home.

While readers will recall much of what follows, it's important to report on what was said in court to assess the kind of impact it may have had on the judge.

Shannon Grubb was the star witness. She told the court about the five occasions – four of which we've heard about previously – that showed Molly's marriage was abusive.

First, there was the 1.01 a.m. phone call on 12 October 2014. 'Jason was very angry and Molly was screaming, "Please don't do this to us,"' Shannon told the court.

The second occasion of abuse was a social outing where neighbours had hired a limousine and Shannon saw Jason pull Molly's arm because he was jealous over male neighbours looking at her as she exited it. The third instance involved a social gathering where Molly took out a blood-soaked tissue from under her hat. She was 'visibly bleeding' and claimed Jason had caused the injury.

The fourth example involved Sarah. Shannon Grubb said Molly called her and asked her to bring shoes to a local park for Sarah. She had been forced to flee the house after a fight with Jason and had left without Sarah's shoes for school.

The fifth incident was at Shady Grove vacation bible school. 'Jason had car trouble,' said Shannon. 'Molly was in the car beside me and Jason reached in my window and grabbed the car keys from her. That was the first time that I saw his anger.'

Shannon was asked about the party in her house two days before the killing where other witnesses had heard Molly abusing and insulting Jason, who then left. Shannon said she had never witnessed Molly abusing or insulting Jason.

Under cross-examination of Shannon, it emerged that Molly had been enraged when Shannon and her husband, Charlie Grubb, originally gave statements to detectives. Molly told a mutual confidante – Sara Neeves – that Shannon was just naïve and her statement made no sense.

Shannon and Charlie subsequently contacted detectives to change their statements. It was not revealed in court what the Grubbs' original statements were, or what specific changes they made in their second statement.

Assistant DA Marissa Parker said detectives had taken statements from approximately fifty people, many of whom were in Meadowlands, but of those fifty statements the only people to question the detectives' accuracy in taking statements were the five Molly confidantes.

Parker cross-examined Shannon about Molly's lies. A flyer was produced for the court. It had been distributed around Meadowlands promoting Molly as the swim coach. The flyer stated Molly had been on the Clemson swim team. Shannon was not aware that Molly lied about this.

Shannon was also unaware that Molly had invented a sister who died from cancer. Parker listed some of Molly's many other lies.

'She lied to her bridesmaids that she was Jack and Sarah's birth mother. In bible club she lied about how complicated the birth of her daughter [Sarah] was. She claimed she helped care for Jason's first wife. She claimed Mags told her that she was dying and she wanted Molly to take on the role as mother to the children. So all those were lies; do you have any concern for Molly's truthfulness?'

Shannon Grubb replied: 'I do not.'

Billy June Jacobs told the court about her frequent walks with Molly and how Jason would call and text repeatedly. Billy June heard him yelling, demanding to know where Molly was and who she was with.

Molly told Billy June she was worried about how Jason's first wife had died. She said Jason would sometimes cover her face with a pillow or strangle her during sex. Molly claimed to have passed out on numerous occasions. She told Billy June that she worried that she would die like Mags.

Jennifer Turner told the court that one day, after shopping in a mall with Molly, they got back to the car and Molly's phone rang repeatedly. There were nine missed calls from Jason. He rang a further three times before Molly answered. Turner said she could hear him shouting, demanding to know where she was and who she was with.

Helen McCormac, Bobby Martens' next-door neighbour, said Jason would control Molly: what she wore and who she spoke to. If Molly was talking in a group and there were men there, Jason would come up behind her, put his hand on the nape of her neck and guide her away.

Helen had heard Jason screaming at Molly over the phone, calling her 'a bitch' and warning that she would 'pay for it'.

Helen said she could hear this because Molly 'fumbled' with the phone and turned on the speaker by accident.

Melissa Sams told the court about the system of code-words and secret recordings she had set up with Molly eight months before the killing. Melissa advised Molly that she could use the secret recordings to apply for an emergency custody order. The recordings would need to show that Jason was a domestic abuser or a drunk and that the children were in danger.

Melissa referenced the Shower Tape, produced a week after hatching the recordings plan. This tape was not played for the court, suggesting it was, as Thompson had assessed, of absolutely no evidentiary value. However, Molly produced another tape for her lawyers. The Pancake Tape, recorded on Shrove Tuesday 2015, was certainly of evidentiary value. There was no physical violence, but when played in open court it added credibility to the preceding claims by Molly's five confidantes that Jason was an angry, controlling husband.

Recorded six months before the killing, it captured Jason berating Molly in a frustrated voice and checking her phone. He loses his temper over not being able to have a family dinner with his wife and children. He is heard slamming a kitchen chair.

Jason shouts: 'You have made it very clear you want to separate me from my kids.' Sarah tries to calm everyone down, and Jason says, 'Shut up, Sarah.'

Sarah asks them both, 'Please stop. It's very upsetting.'

Molly's attorney, Doug Kingsbery, said the Pancake Tape was evidence of an angry, abusive and controlling husband who was frightening his wife and children.

Assistant DA Alan Martin said Molly had made numerous tape recordings for one reason only – to 'manufacture evidence'. The DA's office was only ever provided with two or three tapes. 'This [the Pancake Tape] may be one bad instance out of 150,' he said.

It was notable that the *Elle* tape recording – which the magazine claimed was audio of Jason coming home drunk and possibly hitting Molly in December 2013 – was not produced or referenced in court.*

Like ambiguous illusions – photographs or objects that present the viewer with two equally valid interpretations – the Martenses had presented the five female confidantes and the Pancake Tape as a mosaic for Judge Hall to interpret.

A less enquiring mind than Hall's might have instantly concluded that Jason presented as the violent, controlling man Molly said he was. Those who looked more closely at the mosaic could see a single source for every piece: Molly.

Stage two of the ambiguous illusion took Judge Hall back in time to 6 August 2015, the day Jack and Sarah attended their father's 'funeral' – the memorial service that had taken place with an empty coffin while Molly and Sharon negotiated with Tracey over the release of Jason's remains.

After the memorial service the children went to Dragonfly House. Judge Hall watched intently as the Dragonfly interview videos were played in open court.

In American accents, Jack and Sarah, then ten and eight years old, tell Brandi Reagan how their father pushed, punched, slapped and hit Molly. How, sometimes, Molly and Jason could fight for two hours. How Sharon set up the Russian doll and the codewords for when it got really bad.

Yes, Molly's lawyers said, the children had recanted these allegations once back in Ireland, but Jack had continued to side with Molly. Molly's lawyer produced a transcript of a

---

* It was listed among the defence exhibits but it was not discussed or heard in open court.

voicemail and text message which a desperate and confused Jack had sent to Molly just after she was indicted in January 2016 on second-degree-murder charges.

As described earlier, Jack had tried to call Molly nine times and left this message. 'Hi Mom, this is Jack. This cannot go public. I miss you and I love you. Keep fighting really hard. I want to know how you are. I love you so much.'

Jack had told me years before about these calls, and how Molly had actually answered some of them. She could hear him, but she said nothing in reply. So, in the end he left the voicemail and sent a text message. That image, of Molly staying silent on the line to this confused and lonely child she professed to love, to this child she had been pleading to speak to for months, was unambiguous.

After five days of hearings, the court rose for the weekend on 3 November 2023.

For Jack and Sarah, the worst was yet to come.

25. Possibly, Probably

The Corbett and Fitzpatrick families never doubted the findings of Mags's autopsy. An Irish pathologist, Dr Elizabeth Mulcahy, had found 'death was most likely due to an acute cardiorespiratory arrest secondary to bronchospasm in a known asthmatic.'

Mags had suffered her entire life with asthma. She kept inhalers and a nebulizer in her home. She had awoken in the early hours of 21 November 2006, unable to breathe, telling Jason and her sister, Catherine, who lived with them at the time, that she thought she was going to die.

Until Tom Martens told Detectives Brandon Smith and Michael Hurd in the sheriff's office that he believed Mags's death was 'mysterious' and that she had died of asphyxiation, no one had ever questioned Mags's death as being anything other than a tragedy.

Now, seventeen years later, the Martenses were alleging that Jason killed Mags. They produced two experts to say Mags had not died of an asthma attack and it was possible she had been strangled. One of the experts went further, finding it was 'likely' she died of homicidal asphyxiation.

As we've seen, DA Garry Frank's own expert witness agreed that Mags did not die of an asthma attack. He agreed with the defence's two experts that the Irish autopsy did not meet American standards of forensic pathology, and, as a result, the cause of death could not be determined. There were any number of possible causes of death, he said, so asphyxiation was one possibility. There was, however, no *scientific basis* for saying that asphyxiation was possible.

The Martenses had hired renowned experts. Dr Bill Smock had given expert testimony in the trial of police officer Derek Chauvin for the murder in 2020 of George Floyd – a homicide which prompted riots and global 'Take the Knee' protests against police brutality.

Based in Louisville, Kentucky, Dr Smock was the only police surgeon in the United States,* a position that paid $180,000. He also trained and provided consultancy to the FBI, police, judges and doctors in how to apply forensic medicine to living patients, with his speciality being survivors of strangulation.

Dr Smock said a lesion on Mags's airway may have caused her death, and that such injuries may have been caused by manual strangulation. 'And [if] that was the case, it would be homicide,' he said. The autopsy found 'the deceased's face was pale with blushing around the nose and mouth.' This was one of the 'hallmarks' of someone whose airways were being blocked. 'It's consistent with strangulation,' he told the court.

The defence's second expert to testify that Mags didn't die of an asthma attack was Dr Thomas Sporn, Adjunct Associate Professor of Pathology at Duke University School of Medicine and a former assistant chief medical examiner for the State of North Carolina. Dr Sporn said asthma would cause a hyperinflation of the lungs, where they fill up like balloons, because the person having the asthma attack can breathe in but not out. There should also be evidence of 'mucus plugs'. However, the Irish pathologist had found only a 'mild hyperinflation of the lungs and no significant mucus plugging'.

The first expert had said it was possible Mags had died of

* Dr Smock is the director of the Clinical Forensic Medicine Program for the Louisville Metro Police Department in Louisville, Kentucky.

manual strangulation, but Dr Sporn went further. He said it was 'likely' Mags died an 'asphyxial death' caused by manual strangulation, smothering or suffocation.*

Under cross-examination by assistant DA Alan Martin, Dr Sporn admitted: 'I am not in a position where I could testify that to any degree of medical certainty.'

'In fact,' Martin responded, 'you introduced the scenario of possible homicide because that was the only possibility upon which you were asked to pontificate [by Molly's lawyer, Kingsbery, who had paid him as an expert witness].'[†]

Martin said the DA accepted the cause of death was undetermined. The DA also accepted that manual strangulation was one of a number of possibilities. However, Martin said, there was no scientific or physical evidence from the autopsy to make a homicide even remotely probable.

Martin suggested a much simpler explanation: Mags had a long history of asthma, had been hospitalized previously and used asthma inhalers and a nebulizer. Mags had gone to the doctor previously complaining of chest pains[‡] and pain down her left arm – a classic sign of possible heart problems.

Martin said the toxicology report showed that Mags had taken her asthma medication, albuterol, and this in turn increases the heart rate. Cardiac arrest was a possibility, too, he said. However, because the heart was not examined sufficiently at autopsy, we would never know.

---

* In his letter to Molly's lawyer, Doug Kingsbery, dated 17 February 2023, Dr Sporn only said it was 'possible'.

† Kingsbery asked him to consider two things: was the cause of Mags Fitzpatrick's death asthma, and whether it was possible that her death was a homicide, death resulting from injury to her upper airway.

‡ In the absence of some medical records, the DA relied on anecdotal evidence from Tracey that Mags had visited a GP close to her death complaining of these cardiac symptoms. Mags Fitzpatrick's only documented GP visit for chest pains and arm pain was in the period 1991 to 1995.

Martin then called the prosecution's expert, Dr William Bozeman, a professor of medicine who also trained police Special Weapons And Tactics (SWAT) teams and bomb squads. Dr Bozeman agreed with the defence experts that it was a possibility that Mags had died of manual strangulation, but he said this was not the same as being probable. 'I do agree it [manual strangulation] is potentially the cause of her death but I can't get to the word "probably". It is plausibly but not probably the cause of death.'

As the DA pointed out, there was an eyewitness to what happened in Jason's house on the night Mags died: Mags's sister, Catherine Fitzpatrick. Despite being willing to attend the sentencing hearing, Catherine was not summoned as a witness. Mags's mother, Marian, told me they would have borrowed money to travel and testify, but they were not asked.

With Judge Hall's previous gag order no longer in force, the media on both sides of the Atlantic seized on the expert testimonies and splashed headlines about Jason possibly killing Mags.

Mags's family issued a statement expressing their full support and love for Jason.

What the Martenses claimed is totally inaccurate and untrue. Jason woke Catherine and he called an ambulance and ran out to take her to the hospital. He revived her in the car. He did everything he could to save this person he adored.

Mags was a great daughter, the rock in our family, a loving wife and mother. We miss Jason dearly. He was a part of our family and continued to be after Mags died. He was Mags's soulmate. All we want is peace and closure for Jack and Sarah. We want the world to know the depth of Mags and Jason's love. Nothing can tarnish the love between Mags and Jason.

The Martenses' legal team had done a quite incredible job. After five days of hearings, the man whose skull was crushed, whose head was beaten with a baseball bat and brick in ten different locations, was on trial – even though the hearing's sole purpose was supposedly to sentence the two people who admitted killing Jason Corbett.

Alan Martin attempted to steer through the smoke and mirrors and return the focus to Tom and Molly.

The root cause of Jason's death, he said, was Molly's sense of entitlement to his children. Molly planned, prior to marrying Jason, to take the children from him. This was the finding of psychiatrist Dr David Adams, whom the defence hired to interview and psychologically assess Molly.

The court heard that Dr Adams concluded she was driven to take his children: 'A primary focus of her existence from before she married Jason Corbett was to adopt these children, then divorce him and take these children.'

In court Martin said that Dr Adams's opinion chimed with something Helen McCormac, Bobby Martens' neighbour, had said. Before Molly left for Ireland to meet Jack and Sarah for the first time, Molly talked incessantly about them, so much that Helen felt she herself knew Jack and Sarah. At the time, Molly was recently released from a secure psychiatric unit.

Martin said Molly weaponized Jason's children against him, before 'bashing his skull' in when she learned he wanted to take the children back to Ireland and divorce her. She knew 'the endgame was coming' and took advantage of having her father, a former FBI agent, in the house on the night of the killing to unleash an explosive and lethal event.

Dr Scott Hampton, an expert witness in domestic violence, was asked to review Dr Adams's psychological assessment of Molly. Martin put it to Dr Hampton that adopting the children was Molly's number-one desire and she would lie and deceive and stop at nothing to achieve it.

Dr Hampton said he didn't like the word 'lie' because there were good lies too, when someone is not telling the truth for what they believe are good reasons. He said: 'Molly was all about the kids, and everyone knew that.'

This opened the door for Martin to outline Molly's multitude of lies and ask what good reason she had for lying that she was a foster parent. Dr Hampton suggested these lies were innocuous and were about 'future-pacing'. 'This is what I want my life to be and I'm going to talk about it until it happens,' said Dr Hampton.

Martin countered by asking how manufacturing a fake sister who died of leukaemia fitted into Molly's grand plans.

Dr Hampton replied that some people create non-factual events because they 'want their life to be better'. In other words, it was okay to lie so long as you were just manifesting or wishing into existence a life you didn't have.

'So,' Martin responded: 'I'm going to fake a sister who died? That's bordering on delusional.'

Dr Hampton said when Molly lied at the bible-study group about Sarah's difficult childbirth, this was just 'wish-fulfilment'.

Martin replied that Molly had told friends that Jason's first wife had begged her: 'If anything happens, take care of Jason and Jack and Sarah. She had never met Mags. We know all these things are false.'

Dr Hampton claimed that Molly was highly motivated to save Jason from dying on 2 August 2015. 'If Jason is killed, she hasn't adopted the kids, so she won't have access to the kids. How to decide how much force to use and keep that balance of keeping Jason alive is very challenging.'

Martin showed Dr Hampton photographs of Tom and Molly at the scene with not a mark on them. Then he showed him pictures of Jason's autopsy where his skull was bashed in with such violence chunks of bone fell from the back of his head on the autopsy gurney.

'Does that look like a reasonable amount of force to you?'

'I believe it's a measure of how terrified Tom and Molly were,' said Dr Hampton.

This drew gasps of disbelief from Jason's family. So the spotless attackers who crushed Jason's skull with a series of descending blows to his head were actually terrified, desperately trying *not* to kill him?

The following morning, a number of character witnesses took the stand for Tom.

You could tell they had worked in law enforcement or the FBI even before they opened their mouths. They dressed the same – suit and tie, side-parted hair – and they carried themselves with a conservative, upright deportment. Tom was part of their tribe.

His former colleagues spoke of a man who was eternally calm in all the years he had enjoyed a Q-level security clearance while heading up crime task forces in Cincinnati and Knoxville. Over the course of his thirty years at the FBI Tom had what his second defence attorney, Jay Vannoy, called a stellar career.

Vannoy didn't elaborate on something which Lt Wanda Thompson believed was important. When I interviewed her after the sentencing hearing she told me Tom's legal expertise was highly sought after in the FBI. He trained FBI and DEA agents in how best to conduct interviews with detainees, how to spot the evasive tactics used by suspects, and how to interpret the evidential narrative of crime scenes.

Thompson and her fellow detectives believed Tom had used all these skills to manage his police interview hours after the killing.

Dr George Corvin, a forensic psychiatrist, interviewed Tom in January 2023. He told the court that he found Tom to be 'meticulously responsible', rules-driven, a man who liked order and organization, but that he wasn't particularly emotive. 'He was deliberate and analytical – a classic type-A personality. He prefers to use logic over emotion and he follows the rules rigidly,' he said.

Dr Corvin's expert opinion chimed with the views of various character witnesses who portrayed Tom as a loving father who would work ten to twelve hours a day but always found time to go to his children's sporting events. These various witnesses had never seen Tom lose his cool.

Mike Earnest said his sister had found 'the perfect match' in Tom. 'I remember Sharon bringing Tom home to meet our parents. I would say we have been quite close in the fifty-three years since.'

Mike had been on hand the day after the killing to help Molly try to cash in Jason's life insurance. He accompanied Molly to Jason's workplace, looking for all his possessions. He had taken Molly to the Department of Social Services after she secured the emergency custody order and outlined to social workers how Jason's brothers were in the IRA.

Mike was present in Bobby's house when social workers and police came to take Jack and Sarah away. His daughter had spread the first online stories about Jason being a violent domestic abuser. He had stalked Jack and Sarah in Ireland, going on radio shows and trying to hire planes to fly over their school.

Mike didn't detail any of that for the court, however. Instead, he spoke glowingly of Tom, how he refused to cheat at golf, and how he had mastered all kinds of cuisine styles since taking up cooking in prison.

Mike then joked that Tom had recently learned how to use a smartphone and could now google how to make a vindaloo.

Even when cooking, he diligently observed the rules, never deviating from the recipes. No one asked Mike if it was really believable that a man who had spent thirty years in the FBI and eight more in counterintelligence fighting online and other attacks of foreign spy agencies had suddenly mastered google and smartphones while making vindaloo.

Mike described Tom as a dedicated father who coached his four children's swim, soccer and T-ball teams. When his children were growing up, he read them bedtime stories, and then, later, books by Tolkien.

Tom's son Stewart then took the stand. Tom's third-born child described Tom as a dedicated grandfather. Stewart now had two children of his own and Tom would get involved, 'even in the diaper changes'.

Tom's oldest son, Bobby, was not asked to be a character witness. During the guardianship hearing in 2015 Tracey's lawyers had asked Molly about Bobby's arrest for driving while intoxicated. Perhaps Tom's lawyers were worried that the Inland Revenue Service agent would be challenged about things Jack and Sarah were about to claim in their victim impact statements, things they had seen in Bobby's house.

Before the judge handed down sentence, he invited Jack and Sarah to step forward and read their victim impact statements.

For eight days, Jack and Sarah had sat in the court and listened to their father and mother's reputations being destroyed. The funny, gentle giant, whom they both loved, was depicted as an out-of-control domestic abuser who choked both of his wives during sex, killed Mags, and would have killed Molly but for Tom's heroic intervention.

Now, more than eight years after their father's killing, Sarah and Jack finally had an opportunity to tell the court how it felt to lose their dad. They never got the opportunity to take the stand as witnesses, but they were both determined to be heard through their victim impact statements.

Sarah rose and began delivering hers to a hushed court-room.

She laid bare the carefully cultivated persona of her former stepmother, stripping Molly of the facade she and Tom had created over the past eight years. Breaking down occasion-ally, and crying softly throughout, Sarah's statement had the devastating finality of a cell door closing. 'They have pleaded guilty to voluntary manslaughter. I have seen the bloody handprint on the door in the bedroom, there was nothing voluntary about my dad's death. I know in my heart he tried to leave that room.'

Sarah silenced the court, apart from Molly, whose weep-ing threatened to drown out Sarah's accusations.

'Can you imagine being eight years old in your first days at a new school, in a new country, your father has been killed by your stepmother, and everyone is looking at you, the new girl? Can you imagine trying to make friends when you are the troubled girl? A friend of mine, a girl who sat next to me in school, was contacted by Molly Martens when I was in 6th class. I was nine years old.'

When the judge heard this, he stared down at Molly, who had collapsed into dramatic heaves, before finally resting her face sideways on the table in front of her.

This was the exact pose she adopted at the end of her police interview on 2 August 2015. Some saw tragedy in the symmetry; others just saw through it.

Some heard Molly's weeping and empathized with a woman who just desperately wanted to be a mother, a woman will-ing to endure sexual and physical abuse to stay in a violent, dangerous situation because her love for Jack and Sarah was so profound. Others saw Molly's courtroom response as just another exposure of the real Molly, a woman prone to rage and dramatics in equal measure, a woman who abused both Jack and Sarah, and then sacrificed them for her own freedom.

'Sitting inside of this courtroom has been a traumatic experience,' Sarah continued. 'Listening to adults twist and manipulate the words I said out of fear as an eight-year-old child has been extremely difficult.

'Your Honor, I would like to give you an example of how our truth is being twisted. When Shannon Grubb testified about the park incident where I had no shoes going to school, there was no fight with my dad. My dad had already gone to work well before we got up for school. Molly had beaten Jack again and that is why I was hysterical. Molly had left Jack at home instead of bringing Jack to school. She left in such anger, she forgot my shoes.

'I didn't want Molly to go home on her own, as I was afraid of what she would do to Jack if I wasn't there to stand up for him. This is an example of how the true situations of my life have been manipulated. You can take any story the defence has created and I can tell you the true horror of what actually happened.'

The Martenses' tactic of mirroring – projecting on to Jason allegations which had been made against them – had traumatized the teenager.

'While my friends are out having fun and going to parties, I am in therapy learning how to live with the fact that I lied and helped their case. I was eight years old.'

Sarah spoke of never having a father-daughter dance, never getting to show Jason her future children, never experiencing his hugs or wonderful laugh again. Then, Sarah delivered a line which must have stabbed at Molly's heart.

'I do not love Molly and she is not my mother . . . I was used by her. All I have ever been is a piece on her chessboard. She taught me how to shoplift, how to vomit, and how to be the most convincing liar. I thought Molly loved me but I was just her entertainment, someone who would do anything she said, and be like a doll she could dress up.'

Sarah told the judge that after Jason was killed, Molly took off her wedding ring almost immediately and, within days, told Sarah to stop crying and 'get over it'.

'She turned me and my brother against each other, being nice to one of us one day and awful the next day, making us compete for her love. When I was five years old, Molly Martens began her mind games. What kind of mother tells a five-year-old girl that her father killed her birth mom?

'When I was six years old, Molly would sit in the bath for hours. She hit herself with a hairbrush and had me take pictures. What kind of mother hides recording devices all over the house? When I was seven, Molly told me I was allergic to gluten and dairy so all I could eat was veg. I'm not allergic to any food groups.

'Her way of punishment was starvation – she just wouldn't feed us if we did something wrong, like, for example, not swimming fast enough in our heat. She would stop speaking to us or turn to violence.'

Then Sarah spoke of the many times she had to drag Molly off Jack to stop her hitting him.

'One time, she was hitting him so hard that I jumped on her back using all my body weight to pull her off him, but she grabbed me and threw me to the floor and started screaming at us both. I am telling you this to demonstrate the power and control she had over my life.

'I treasured a framed photograph that my dad got me of him and my birth mom, Mags, on their wedding day. Molly threw it down the stairs and screamed at me that "She is dead. I'm your mother, that woman is dead." I was seven years old.

'She broke my family down piece by piece and then killed my dad with no remorse. I loved my stepmother even after all the abuse she put me through. I didn't know anything else. I thought that was just how all families were back then. It was only when I went to live with Tracey and David in Ireland that I knew the true meaning of family. I now know what a loving mother is. I've always known a loving father and Dave is that now, too.'

Sarah then spoke directly to the judge who had so enraged her with his insistence on calling Jason the 'alleged victim'. In a calm, measured voice she said:

'I am begging you to restore my faith in justice, in humanity, and give me time to heal without sharing the free world with my father's killers. On the 2nd of August, 2015, I said "Goodnight, Daddy, love you." And when I woke up the next morning he was gone forever. Just like that I had to leave house, home, community and country. I will never come to terms with that. I will never get to hug him one last time or hear my dad say "I love you, Princess" to me again.'

Sarah was conscious to repeat Jason's name when asking for the maximum sentence to be imposed. She added:

'Judge, you didn't have the pleasure of meeting my dad, Jason Corbett. Two weeks before he died, we pulled up at a Sheetz. There was a woman there and her three kids were crying. She had no money. My dad filled her car with gas and bought her groceries for her children. When I think of him, I remember his kindness. I am proud to be the daughter of such a kind and gentle man. I am proud to be Jason Corbett's daughter.'

Jack's experience was equally wrought, his statement rendered with the same powerful simplicity.

'I was a liar. From the age of four to ten years of age I was taught how to lie and manipulate people by Molly Martens. During this time, I was abused by Molly Martens in every way you can imagine and then some.'

Jack said he contemplated suicide.

'The bright boy and happy kid everyone used to see was buried deep inside of me and I don't know if he will ever come out again. The tragedy and trauma I have had to deal with growing up destroyed me.

'Every day I wake up, I have the constant feeling of never being enough, and punish myself in ways that I know I don't deserve, but I can't stop myself. I never felt I could call someone my own since I lost my dad. I am drowning every day in pain.

'When I was a young teenager, I used to think sometimes it would be easier if I wasn't here any more and at least that way I could be with my dad and my mam and apologize and feel safe.'

Speaking with a calm and bravery that belied his nineteen years, Jack said:

'Your Honor, don't be fooled by this mask of civility of Molly Martens. There is a monster lurking underneath the exterior. She systematically broke me down and drip fed me untruths. I want to be clear: I never witnessed my dad hit Molly Martens – ever. I am not under duress now; I want you to look at me standing here today and know the truth.'

Tom's sons lowered their heads as Jack alleged a broader conspiracy by other members of the Martens family.

'The fact that my father's phone, laptops, computers and hard drives were in Bobby Martens' house in evidence baggies and not found or admitted to evidence just shows that the entire Martens family is complicit in the cover-up of the killing of my father.

'It is a travesty of justice that Molly Martens wasn't charged with first-degree murder as was considered by the DA. Molly Martens needs to be locked away for as long as possible so she cannot do this to another family, another child. It is my biggest fear and gives me nightmares. She will do it again if she finds the opportunity.'

Weeping could be heard from both sides of the aisle, but if Judge Hall was moved, his sentence was still lenient. Molly would face just seven more months in jail.*

A sheriff stepped forward and placed handcuffs on Molly. Judge Hall asked that she be placed on suicide watch and that she receive a psychiatric assessment.

Moments later, Tom showed no reaction as he received the same sentence. He stood, calmly took off his coat, removed his wallet and handed both to his son Stewart. Sharon leant forward and whispered in his ear.

Tom told her: 'Everything is going to be okay.' Then he was cuffed and led away.

Molly and Tom were released on 6 June 2024 after serving seven months.

Molly, forty, was photographed leaving the Correctional Institute of Women in Raleigh, North Carolina, wearing a blue-and-white striped summer dress and white sandals, smiling broadly now that her ordeal was finally over.

Tom, seventy-four, was released a few hours later, collected by his son Bobby from Caldwell Correctional Center, a minimum-security prison in Lenoir, North Carolina.

Tom came home to Sharon, his wife of fifty-two years. For several months, Molly was prohibited from sharing a home with Tom, as North Carolina prisoner-release regulations prohibit felons sharing a dwelling.

However, this restriction was ultimately lifted, and Molly moved back to Tennessee, intent on completing an associated science course she had begun in prison.

* They were both sentenced to a minimum of 51 months and a maximum of 74 months. They had already served 44 months, so in reality, they would be out in 7 months or less.

26. Manifesting Molly

In September 2024, almost one year after the sentencing hearing, I travelled to Washington, a small town four hours east of Davidson County, to meet Wanda Thompson, by then retired six years.

Thompson still wishes she had known that Jack and Sarah were not Molly's children that morning in Meadowlands. She regrets the decision to leave the children in the care of their father's killers. Maybe, if they had been put into temporary emergency foster care while the custody issue was resolved, the murder case might have ended differently.

For Thompson, there remains a lack of resolution to the Jason Corbett case. She outlined for me how some of the parts of this story still didn't fit neatly together.

I had been working as a journalist on this story for five years by the time I met Thompson in Washington. I, too, found the story still fractured, the narrative unaligned in parts because the people present at 160 Panther Creek Court in Meadowlands in the early hours of 2 August 2015 still had such contradictory perspectives.

In this final chapter, I outline these fractures in the narrative.

I also outline some new lines of enquiry and evidence that I uncovered over the years, through interviewing various participants in the story, and through my analysis of thousands of pages of documents, expert reports, search warrants, witness statements, the case notes of detectives and social workers, and the crime-scene photos and video.

*

At the sentencing hearing the court was told of a report by forensic psychologist Dr David Adams, who had been hired by the prosecution to interview and psychologically assess Molly.

As previously discussed, Dr Adams found that Molly's plan all along – before she had even arrived in Ireland in 2008 – was to marry Jason, adopt his children, divorce him and take Jack and Sarah.

Reflecting in September 2024, Thompson agrees the children were Molly's primary motivation from the moment she came into their lives as their nanny. Sheriff David Grice was told by Jason's family that Molly had slept with Jason within four hours of meeting him. Jason had told his best friend, Paul Dillon, and his sister, Tracey, that he felt guilt over this, but he was lonely, still grieving heavily, sixteen months after the loss of his wife.

In those first months, Molly had long phone conversations with her old friend, Susie West, about how she was falling for Jason. We've seen how in email correspondence with Jason five months into their relationship Molly is the one pressing for a long-term commitment. Jason is openly expressing his fears that he's not sure if he's ready. He states that he doesn't want to commit too soon to Molly in case things don't work out. He's worried Jack and Sarah will get too close to Molly. He can't stand the thought of them losing another mother.

But, like Rebecca De Mornay's character in *The Hand that Rocks the Cradle* – a movie about the slow infiltration of a family by a woman posing as a nanny – Molly was obsessed with another mother's children.

Why did Molly choose *The Hand that Rocks the Cradle* by Robert Tine as one of her book-club recommendations two months before the killing? The book had been published twenty-three years earlier, when Molly was nine years old. In the story, the nanny attempts to kill the mother by emptying the asthma inhalers she kept around the house.

Mags kept multiple inhalers, too. Jason had told Molly that Mags died following an asthma attack. Among the expert reports submitted by the defence at the sentencing hearing but not read out in court, I discovered a macabre claim by Molly that Jason would choke her during sex, at times using Jack's nebulizer to cover her mouth.

Thompson believes Molly drew inspiration from *The Hand that Rocks the Cradle*, and also from the movie *Gone Girl*, the other book she had recommended at book club shortly before Jason's killing.

I noted that *Gone Girl* – a story involving fake pregnancies, life insurance scams and a wife who enlists neighbours' support by spreading fake stories about her husband's abuse – premiered in the United States on 3 October 2014.

Nine days later, Shannon Grubb's phone rang at 1.01 a.m. and she heard Jason shouting on the phone. This call came two months before Melissa Sams encouraged Molly to make secret recordings if she wanted to take Jack and Sarah from Jason via an emergency custody order. But, both Wanda and I wondered, was she already recording Jason before Melissa's advice?

In defence exhibit 48, Melissa Sams says that Molly told her that she 'had recorded Jason in the past'. Billy June Jacobs said they discussed Molly making recordings in spring of 2014, six months before the call to the Grubbs' house.

I wondered if Shannon and Charlie Grubb had heard a live argument between Jason and Molly at 1 a.m., or had Molly called Shannon's number and played a recording of Jason and Molly arguing? And had the inspiration for this come from watching the recently released film *Gone Girl*?

*

Lynn Shanahan, Mags's former business partner and best friend, gave a statement to prosecutors ahead of the 2017 trial. Ultimately, the statement did not feature in the 2017 trial, but when I saw it later I realized it was potentially significant.

The statement said that Molly had been spreading stories of Jason's abuse in the neighbourhood prior to July 2013.

Molly's behaviour at Myrtle Beach in July 2013 – where she told Lynn she didn't love Jason any more but wouldn't leave him without Jack and Sarah – alarmed Lynn. Lynn sought reassurance from Jason that the children were safe. Jason said Molly would not hurt them but she was inflicting bruises on herself, taking heavy medication and, sometimes, disappearing.

Jason believed she was spreading lies about him because 'he was starting to get looks by the pool'. He described Molly taking to bed for days or spending hours in a bath crying. She was abusing over-the-counter medications. Lynn had said in her statement: 'He [Jason] said since this started, he used to ring her all throughout the day to make sure she was alright and the kids were being looked after. Some days, Molly would just decide not to answer the phone or [to] ignore text messages and then he would be rushing back from work to see if they were okay.'

Thompson had factored Lynn's statement into the detective's timeline of events leading up to the killing. She believed Molly was spiralling, behaving just like she had with her former partner, Keith Maginn, in 2008.

Two to three months after Jason's heart-to-heart with Lynn, Molly turned up in front of Helen McCormac, 80 miles from home, in Charlotte. Helen, Bobby Martens' neighbour, heard Jason over the speaker on Molly's phone demanding to know where Molly was and why she had left Jack and Sarah alone. Helen heard Jason call Molly a bitch and warn that she would 'pay for it'.

I wondered if this was one of the occasions, referenced in Lynn's statement, where Jason had rushed home from work to find Molly missing, his young children alone, and Molly not answering her phone?

About six months later, in March 2014, Jack and Sarah's Green Card applications were approved. Molly stepped up her walks with her neighbour Billy June Jacobs. They talked about Molly's intention to stay in the marriage for another six years, until Sarah was a citizen and thirteen years old. They discussed making secret recordings.

Jason applying for Green Cards for Jack and Sarah would indicate that he was not intending at that point to return to Ireland for good. However, two months after the children were granted Green Cards, Jason clashed with Bobby Martens at Bobby's house in Charlotte and he threatened to take the children and return to Ireland.

This is one of those occasions where the story fractures – the Martenses having one telling, and Jack and Sarah another. Both sides agree there was a confrontation that day between Jason and Molly's brothers.

Sarah and Bobby differ in their recollections of what exactly happened and when. In Sarah's recollection, they were at Bobby's house for Molly's youngest brother Connor's twenty-first birthday party. He was twenty-one on 10 May 2014, a Saturday.

Bobby had told social worker Sheila Tyler about this incident but was unsure of the date. Molly later told a psychiatrist that this incident happened on Memorial Day, which was 26 May 2014.

Sarah witnessed a young man in his early twenties, whom Sarah believed was one of Connor's friends, berating Jason over something that happened in the hot tub. Sarah recalls

Molly had been in Bobby's hot tub with a number of Connor's friends.

In Bobby's recollection, Molly was with 'kids' in the hot tub and Jason got in a jealous rage. He threatened to take the children's passports and leave. There were conflicting reports that Jason drove off, then returned, or that he ended up sleeping in his car outside the house.

In any event, relations between Jason and Molly were clearly fractious at this time.

Two weeks after this incident – if Sarah's date is correct – Jason sent a formal email to Molly in her role as the children's swim coach. He complained that, unlike other parents, he was not being notified of swim events. Though they were husband and wife, Jason felt the need to implore Molly in writing:

'It is with great sadness that I now have to resort to email for communication regarding the kids . . . I would also like to be included in school events. It was brought to my attention the other day about upcoming events regarding father's [*sic*] that was [*sic*] also kept from me for some reason that I cannot understand. I would just like to know whats [*sic*] going on and since you will not or forget to tell me, maybe copying me on email might help. Thanks. P.s. . . . don't focus on the grammar.'

The email lays bare a relationship so fraught with tension Jason has to email asking to be kept involved in his children's lives.

Three months later, in August 2014, Jason, Jack and Sarah returned to Ireland for a holiday. Molly did not go with them. She was undergoing infertility treatment in America.

Jason confided in Tracey during this 2014 trip that he had financial concerns, having spent $25,000 on infertility treatment. He told Tracey about Molly's multiple miscarriages and that he was unsure if they were real, if she was ever actually pregnant.

It was two months later at 1.01 a.m. that Shannon Grubb's phone rang and she heard Molly pleading with Jason, 'Don't do this to us.'

What was Jason threatening to do to 'us'? Was this a recording of one of Molly and Jason's frequent arguments over adoption and his plans to return to Ireland?

Thompson told me the detectives considered it very telling that Shannon Grubb did not call 911 after receiving that 1 a.m. phone call. 'If you were so concerned about it, why didn't you call 911? Why didn't you call the cops and have the cops go there if you were so concerned about her safety? Nobody in that whole development [Meadowlands], no matter what she told them, nobody ever called.'

Three other women – Jennifer Turner, Billy June Jacobs and Helen McCormac – had heard Jason shouting and threatening Molly on the phone. In each case, they said they could hear because he was shouting so loudly, or because Molly had accidentally put the phone on speaker.

What if *Gone Girl* inspired Molly to spread false rumours of domestic abuse, and then Melissa Sams inadvertently showed Molly in January 2015 that there could be an endgame, a hope of one day leaving Jason and getting the kids, without adopting them?

'I think Sams planted the seed in Molly's mind,' Wanda Thompson told me as we discussed the intricacies of the case in late 2024. 'Molly put recording devices around the house, but in eight months, all she produced was two tapes. Sure, he raises his voice, and he doesn't sound good on the tapes, but there is no violence. We can't arrest every husband and wife who have words. Show me a married couple who don't raise their voices once in a while.'

Assistant DA Alan Martin had told the sentencing hearing in 2023 that Molly may have accumulated up to 150 hours of recordings; yet prosecutors were given less than an hour of audio. The rest, according to Molly's lawyers, were 'lost or destroyed'.

Given that Sarah saw recording devices in the master bedroom and bathroom, it's possible the actual killing itself was recorded. Thinking about this, I could not help but recall those dresser drawers that had been opened and shut in a hurry in the master bedroom. The doors to storage space under the sink in the bathroom were open, too. Sarah remembers Molly used to keep a recording device in both of these locations.

Molly must not have been recording that night – otherwise, the tape would be her best defence. Or, she was recording but the killing tape doesn't match her story. Or, maybe the tape was among the many inadvertently destroyed or lost.

Had Molly planned to provoke a confrontation on the night of the killing, one that would finally prove the case she had been trying to build for emergency custody?

The secret recordings had yielded Jason raising his voice and losing his temper. There was no physical violence – apart from him angrily slamming a kitchen chair. Having Tom in the house as an unwitting witness would certainly have helped Molly's case if, for example, she provoked a confrontation and fled to Tennessee with the children, where she could apply for an emergency custody order with Knoxville's former FBI supervisor as her chief witness.

Thompson told me: 'I can very easily see [a situation] where she initiated confrontation. She made sure her parents got there that night, so she had back-up. She instigated an argument with Jason and that argument got out of hand.'

We know that in the final week of Jason's life Molly was frustrated about Jason not letting her adopt the children, to the point of complaining about it within hearing of Jason's brother, Wayne, while they were all staying with Mike and Mona Earnest in Washington.

From early on, the detectives believed something happened to make Molly summon her parents from Knoxville in a panic on Saturday, 1 August 2015.

Thompson believes Molly found out Jason was leaving her. She called her parents. Tom cancelled dinner plans with his boss, and, suddenly, drove four hours to North Carolina. 'It must have been a real family emergency for him to cancel dinner with his boss. You might let friends down, but when your boss is a former CIA chief, that dinner was important. Why did he drop everything?' Wanda Thompson wondered when we spoke in 2024.

I had discovered something which indicated that Molly did know Jason was planning to leave and return to Ireland for good. In July 2015, one month before the killing, Jason told his best friend, Paul Dillon, that he wanted to come home. Paul told me: 'I asked if he had spoken with Molly about it, to which he replied, yes, but it always ends in disaster. That was one of the last conversations I had with Jason.'

Paul doesn't recall if it was during this conversation or another call, but he remembers Jason telling him over the phone from the US that he had an escape plan – he would bring Jack and Sarah to Ireland and go back to divorce Molly. He said this while driving, as Paul recalls hearing the navigation issuing directions, which provoked him to rib Jason about still needing directions to work after four years in America. This little detail could be vitally important, given what I discovered next.

Jack and Sarah had been getting flashbacks, some more detailed than others. Jack told me and detectives that he had a clear memory of his father paying him five dollars to clean out his car. While doing this chore, Jack discovered a recording device taped with Velcro under the passenger seat. He told his father.

Jack remembers Jason going inside and loudly confronting Molly. Then Jason put Jack and Sarah in the car and asked them about going back to Ireland for good, without Molly. Jack was all for it. Sarah was unsure.

Neither Jack nor Sarah is certain about when Jason suggested leaving America and Molly, whether it was months or just a matter of weeks before the killing. Either way, having found the recorder, Jason knew Molly was secretly recording him and plotting to take Jack and Sarah from him.

He also knew something even more significant – that it was likely Molly had been listening to his conversations in the car with Paul Dillon and knew of his escape plan. She would have heard Jason telling Paul that he planned to bring the children home first, then go back and divorce Molly.

This theory fits neatly with Thompson's belief that Molly discovered Jason was leaving and summoned her parents for help; and with assistant DA Alan Martin's synopsis at the sentencing hearing: 'She knew the endgame was coming.'

Search warrants for Tom, Sharon, Molly and Jason's phone records reveal interesting exchanges on the day of the killing.

Molly had twenty calls on her cellphone on 1 August, beginning with a 2.21 p.m. call from Tom. It lasts fifty-nine seconds. Fifteen minutes later, Tom tries to call Jason, twice. The second of these calls gets through but is cut off after six seconds and forwarded to Jason's messaging service. Four minutes later, at 2.30 p.m., Tom makes two further calls to Jason. The first is not answered. The second lasts thirty-seven seconds and is forwarded to Jason's messaging service.

While Tom is trying to reach Jason, simultaneously, Molly has a 2-minute call with Sharon. We know from her behaviour at the cornhole party in the Grubbs' house that Molly was spiralling less than twenty-eight hours before the killing, publicly insulting and abusing Jason about his weight. What did Molly tell her mother that Saturday to prompt the change in dinner plans; to prompt Tom to call Jason, the son-in-law he hated?

About an hour later, the Martenses set off for North Carolina. During the journey, there were eleven calls between Sharon and Molly. Was this flurry of calls about Jason leaving? Molly's records show two calls to Shannon Grubb and a call to an unidentified number in Charlotte. Detectives never learned what those calls to Grubb and the number in Charlotte were about.

Detectives were also left wondering about the voicemail Tom left on Jason's phone. It, like Jason's laptop and home computer, was mysteriously missing. Without having the physical phone, detectives would never know what that 37-second voicemail was about.

Thompson told me that police television dramas have given a distorted view about what can and can't be retrieved with electronic data: 'The jury see stuff on television. We call it the *CSI* effect. They watch it on TV and it doesn't register with the juror and most of the public, that's Hollywood, some of that technology doesn't even exist today, and if it does, do you think Davidson County can afford to use it? We don't have the money or the services to be able to do that, so some technologies that are available to, let's say the FBI or the secret service, are not necessarily available to local law enforcement agencies in North Carolina.'

Jason's phone was registered with AT&T. Thompson said each of the different phone service providers have different policies, so when search warrants are issued the data each provider releases is different.

'If we had the physical phone and the code for getting

into it, it certainly would have been easier. We would see what recent internet searches there were on [Jason's] phone, whether he had searched for flights. We could see if anything was downloaded. We could see text messages and hear voicemails.'

There was other suspicious activity, too: a neighbour, Mitch Klass, had seen a car leaving Jason's house around 2.15 a.m., an hour before the 911 call.

Klass was up, tending to his ill daughter, sitting looking out the window directly opposite Jason's house. He saw the headlights of a car driving up out of Jason's steep driveway. He couldn't provide a make of car, however, and despite detectives scanning CCTV, they were unable to confirm a car had left the house.

When I examined the crime-scene video and photos I zoomed in on what appears to be a laptop under Jason's nightstand. It was not listed in the evidence log of items seized. The Martenses were driven home to the crime scene less than seven hours after the 911 call. Did they find Jason's laptop after the police had gone?

A week after the killing, and after lobbying by MPS's corporate lawyer, Tom's lawyer handed over a Dell laptop to Detective Brandon Smith. This was Jason's work computer,* not his personal laptop.

Jack told detectives in March 2021 that his father sometimes kept his personal laptop under the nightstand by his bed. Detectives were shown the crime-scene still I had isolated showing what appears to be Jason's personal laptop at the scene. The computer remains unaccounted for.

I also discovered something else strange. When I reduced

---

* Detectives examined two terabytes of data on his workplace laptop.

the background noise on the audio of the 911 call I was able to identify some mystery audio – an incoming call, eight minutes into Tom's 911 call. Another phone was ringing in the house. It cuts off quickly.

Who would be calling the house at 3.10 a.m.? Was this incoming call related to the car that was seen leaving the scene an hour before the 911 call? Did this car ferry away the items that were missing from the house after the killing: the Nike bag Jack had seen in the master bedroom, Jason's phone, wallet, desktop computer and servers?

We will never know.

While there are clearly numerous unanswered questions about the events of 2 August 2015, some key claims by the Martenses do stack up and can be corroborated by the evidence at the scene.

Thompson believes Sarah's Dragonfly testimony that she woke from a nightmare, frightened that the ballerinas on her sheets were spiders. Photos taken by Lt Frankie Young in Sarah's bedroom show the exact sheets Sarah and Molly had described. They were bundled on the floor near Sarah's bed.

The physical evidence corroborated other parts of the Martenses' story, too. It was widely reported in mainstream media, on social media, and in Tracey's book, *My Brother Jason*, that Jason was first attacked when lying in bed.

The claim was repeated by two jurors, Miriam Figueroa and Tom Aamland, in their interviews for ABC's *20/20* programme in 2017, and again when I spoke to them in September 2024.

This claim, repeatedly attributed to Stuart James, the blood-spatter expert, is untrue. James never said that Jason was first attacked when lying in bed, either in his report or on the stand. James said the initial bloodshed occurred on 'the south side of the bed in the master bedroom'.

He called this Area A – towards the end of the bed, on the right side (as you face the bed). Blood found on the underside of the quilt, and on the box springs, showed that an 'impact incident' took place there. 'It may well be where bloodshed first occurred,' James told the 2017 trial. Area A is exactly where Tom said he first struck Jason.

So, the first blow took place where Tom said it happened; and the inciting incident – Sarah waking from a nightmare – also seemed to be proven by the crumpled sheets. So, what does Thompson think happened next?

Thompson believes Molly was telling the truth about Jason waking up and becoming annoyed when Sarah came down having woken from a nightmare: 'He had been drinking, so when he awoke, he most likely got up to use the bathroom. It's the first thing most people do if woken in the middle of the night. He is naked. He comes out and they argue.'

Detectives believe Tom heard this argument and rushed upstairs. Thompson surmises that, being naked, Jason's natural instinct when confronted by his father-in-law coming into the bedroom in the middle of the night would have been to draw Molly in front of him, so she's covering him.

Then, things escalated, either through Tom swinging the bat for Jason's head – as Tom testified – or through Molly grabbing the brick from the nightstand and smashing Jason across the head.

Whichever weapon Jason was first hit with, he didn't die. He was bleeding and disoriented. He was trying to get out of a darkened room. He stumbled down the hallway bleeding – hence the transfer stains on the walls either side of the hallway. He was hit again, either in the hallway or just before he entered it, because there is impact spatter on the east wall and two clumps of scalp and hair halfway down the hallway.

Tom told detectives he wasn't sure if he hit Jason in the

hallway, just that he tried. It's barely 3 feet wide; it would be difficult to swing a bat, but not a brick, and its coarse edges would be more likely to detach two parts of Jason's scalp than a bat.

The detectives found the bathroom light switch was blood-smeared and cracked, and 11 inches above it there was an oval white gouge mark in the paint. Detectives suspect this gouge mark was deliberately made after the killing, in an attempt to stage the scene, and match the narrative that Tom would tell detectives at the sheriff's office.

However, the gouge mark did not have any blood in it. Tom had told detectives that he had already struck Jason at least once before they got to the bathroom. Therefore the bat should have had blood on it when it made that gouge mark, and the blood should have been transferred. Instead the gouge mark was pure white. There was a second white oval-shaped gouge – at a height of 5 feet, on the south wall of the bedroom.

Assistant DA Greg Brown had argued at the 2017 criminal trial that these gouges were evidence of staging. Tom's attorney Jones Byrd responded in court that the gouges must have pre-existed that night, because otherwise small bits of plaster or masonry would have been collected from the carpet and the bathroom floor that same night.

After enlarging the crime-scene photos of the south wall, I spotted an indentation in the paint, its jagged edges forming the perfect facsimile of a brick. This indentation was an inch above the skirting board. It would be some coincidence if that brick-shaped indent in the wall had been made some other night. There were no bits of fallen plaster beneath that indent, just coagulated, jellied, dried blood and brain matter.

For me, and for detectives, this raised the prospect that Molly had done all the damage with the brick – there were twenty-four of Jason's hairs on the brick, and only two on the bat – and that Tom had come along afterwards and frantically created a narrative that would match the crime scene.

Molly's mental illness was cyclical.

The first signs of troubled behaviour came before Molly was even a teenager. Detectives told me she was caught shoplifting as a child but no charges were brought.

After the family moved to Knoxville in 1994, when Molly was eleven, she began to miss school for long, unexplained periods. A psychologist diagnosed her as bipolar aged fifteen.

The following year, she began a high-school romance with Jonathan DeBerry, the ex-boyfriend so beloved of Sharon and Tom. Molly's turbulent teens stabilized when she was DeBerry's girlfriend. But aged twenty, she had another breakdown at Clemson University, and, as previously discussed, Tom and Sharon decided to withdraw her from the university after she was discovered sitting fully clothed in a shower.

Suffering bouts of depression and anxiety after leaving Clemson University, Molly saw a psychologist in Knoxville.* When afterwards Molly lived for a year with Susie West, her future maid of honour, she would have long periods of manic happiness, followed by bouts of depression during which she refused to leave the house.

Molly's next boyfriend, Keith Maginn, witnessed her transform from a chirpy, beautiful, interesting first date into a morose, suicidal fiancée.

She would spiral and crash again in Ireland – Jason had

---

* Molly saw a clinical psychologist, Dr Connie Cole, in Knoxville in November 2003, when she was twenty.

told Paul Dillon about her lying in darkness, pulling her hair out. Paul had told Jason to run.

There is evidence that Molly was spiralling and mixing medications from different doctors in the weeks leading up to the killing.

On 19 May 2015, ten weeks before the killing, she attended Novant Health Medical Center in Kernersville complaining of a 4-day-long headache. She was feeling spasms in her head several times a minute. She denied trauma, substance abuse or being a victim of domestic abuse.

The nurse noted she was texting on her phone throughout the consultation. Her right eye was twitching. She was discharged after being given a 30 mg injection of Toradol, an anti-inflammatory, whose advisory sheet warns that it should not be mixed with lithium. Readers will recall that an empty bottle of lithium was found by Lt Frankie Young among various prescription medications at the scene.*

Jack told me that two or three days before the killing Molly told him to put the brick beside her bed. Lieutenant Young photographed sixteen bricks outside the back door, beside three large plastic containers of potting flowers. This photo

---

* By the time Molly consulted a different doctor on 31 July, two days before the killing, she was requesting a sleep aid and had discontinued the 100 mg Seroquel dose she had been taking daily for bipolar disorder. Records state she was taking this drug between 2009 and 2012, which contradicts evidence she gave, under oath, at the guardianship hearing, where she claimed she had not taken bipolar medication for seven or eight years. As of 31 July 2015, she was taking Imitrex for migraine, ibuprofen and aspirin. When the doctor prescribed trazodone, she was warned not to mix it with Imitrex. Her records at Kernersville list Molly as having a baby sister who died. They also state she held a bachelor's degree. Given these lies, could Molly be trusted to tell the doctor the truth about what medications she was on?

corroborates Molly's story that they intended to paint the bricks as a garden decoration.

Molly said they took the brick inside in case it rained. In August, Davidson County typically enjoys temperatures in the high eighties and at least twenty-four rain-free days.* Most of the bricks photographed outside were shadowed by a wooden balcony overhead. They would have been protected from rain anyway. What was so special about that one brick? One painted brick would have proved a pretty mundane decoration. Why instruct Jack to put it on her nightstand?

Jack, who was ten years old, had to heave it through the living room, past the entrance to the kitchen and the stairs to the basement, to go to the master bedroom.

'I held that brick, and it was heavy,' the jury foreman Tom Aamland told me, recalling how 'it had blood and hair on all six sides'.

Sarah had recalled several dark incidents in her victim impact statement, two of which, she told detectives in March 2021, occurred in the final week.

In the first incident, as we've heard, Sarah had to pull Molly off Jack to stop her beating him.

Sarah told me that later that evening an enraged Molly screamed at Jason in front of Sarah, saying Jason had killed Mags, suffocating her with a pillow.

Sarah recalls sitting with her father on the stairs the following day, and how upset he was as he reassured her that he would never do anything to hurt Mags or anyone else. They were alone at the time because, according to Sarah, Molly had gone out to buy a dress for the cornhole party in the Grubbs' house that Friday night.

* Weather Spark tracks data in Davidson County and found the probability of rain in August is between 31% and 43% over the course of the month.

As Sarah recalls it now, Molly stayed up all night after the Grubbs' party. If accurate, this would be consistent with Molly's previous behaviour when spiralling – Keith Maginn had experienced Molly staying up all night in the final days before he took her to the psychiatric unit in Atlanta, Georgia, in February 2008. If Molly did indeed stay up all of Friday night, it may have contributed to her volatility on the following night, when Jason was killed.

There is a common misunderstanding that circumstantial evidence can be dismissed.

In court, at the 2017 murder trial, Freedman explained the difference between direct and circumstantial evidence thus: if you witnessed somebody trudge through snow and throw a brick through your window, that would be direct evidence that the window was broken by this person. However, if you woke up and saw footprints in the snow leading to and from a window that was now broken, there is circumstantial evidence that the window was broken by the person who left the footprints.

I was always struck by the little consistencies introduced by Molly's confidantes, the seemingly innocuous details several of them had added in their second statements. The five were the only ones out of an estimated fifty people interviewed who demanded to change their statements in the lead-up to the 2017 murder trial.

The new details they added explained things like why the brick was in the bedroom and Jason being tight with money. Several of the five confidantes mentioned how Jason would get mad when Molly bought fruit, for example. In and of themselves, these mundane details were irrelevant, but when several of the women were echoing each other and Molly the statements started to form into a cohesive whole. Together the five women formed the footprints in the snow.

But, I discovered, these were not the only women who had given statements that Molly was a victim of domestic abuse. Among Detective Smith's case notes, I found a reference to Tori Adkins, Sarah's horse-riding instructor.

Sara Neeves, who had given testimony in support of Molly at the guardianship hearing fifteen days after the killing in August 2015, had called Smith and suggested detectives should talk to Tori. Smith noted that he called and couldn't get through.

There was no further mention of Tori Adkins throughout the court cases. She didn't give evidence at the 2017 murder trial or at the sentencing hearing in 2023. Given that Tori Adkins had seen Molly and Sarah on the afternoon of Jason's final day, surely she might have something interesting to say?

I contacted Tori Adkins, and we met at her barn at Lantana Drive, near Shady Grove Baptist Church, out in the North Carolina countryside in September 2024. She showed me the horse, Luke, which Sarah used to ride, and Molly's horse, Adriana. Sarah and Molly began riding there around November 2014.

Though Tori did not know Molly, she soon found herself as her confidante. One of the first things Molly said to her was never to call or text her, that Jason couldn't find out about her lessons. She paid for Sarah's lessons with a cheque from her joint account with Jason, but she paid for her own lessons with a yellow cheque from her own savings account.

'She said, "This is my emergency money,"' Tori told me.

This mention of Molly's emergency money tallied with something else I had discovered. Three weeks before the killing, changes were made to a savings account held jointly in Molly and Jason's name.

Jason was earning $141,000, taking home $8,000 a month after tax. His salary was paid into a Bank of America checking account jointly held with Molly. Out of this, $1,500 a month would be transferred directly into a savings account. While the checking account emptied each month, the savings grew.

Three weeks before the killing – when there was $22,000 in the savings account – Jason and Molly both signed documents with the bank to change the status of the account. Now, if one of them died, the other would get whatever was in the account and it wouldn't go to the deceased's estate.

If Molly was planning to force the moment to its crisis by engineering a physical confrontation with Jason while her father was in the house, she had go-money ready.

Tori Adkins told me Molly and Sarah came for horse-riding lessons over a period of approximately ten months. Sarah attended on sporadic weekends, while Molly had just six lessons in total, all during weekdays while the children were in school. These were the six occasions where she and Tori spoke about Jason being controlling and abusive.

'She never said he was physically abusive,' Tori told me; but, as a victim of domestic abuse herself in a previous long-term relationship, the riding instructor knew that abuse took many forms.

Tori told me she was interviewed by Lt Wanda Thompson. 'The woman detective was very confrontational, like, why would Molly talk to you? You hardly knew her. And I told her, I said, "Listen, I was two-thirds of the way through a ten-year mentally abusive relationship, and my way of coping was I talked to everybody."'

Tori believes that the movie *Fifty Shades of Grey* prompted her and Molly's chats about abuse. The film was released on 13 February 2015, four days before the Pancake Tape, in which Jason can be heard shouting at Molly and slamming a chair.

'When *Fifty Shades of Grey* came out,' Tori said, 'I had a boy student riding with me. He was at that age where, you know, everything is about sex. He found it fascinating that I read these [types of] books. And he made a comment about *Fifty Shades of Grey*. And Molly [who was present for the conversation] said, "Why would anybody read that? Living it is horrible." That was when I went, there's more to this than just not letting her have any money.'

Over the course of six lessons, Molly told Tori how controlling Jason was. 'I had her on a long rope,' Tori recalled for me, 'and I made her ride around me in a circle and we talked. I remember that she said, "I don't have access to any money. I'm not allowed to leave the house. I'm not allowed to have friends over." And then that combined with the "don't call me, don't text me thing" – she was giving me the impression that he was controlling her, definitely.'

Tori said she saw no marks or injuries and didn't notice Molly wearing inappropriate clothing to cover up bruising. 'I have an antenna for that kind of thing. I remember when I read *Gone Girl*. I remember there was a real quick thought, in the back of my mind, could I have been part of a set-up by Molly? Did she do what that woman in that story did and create a network of lies? I thought, there's just no way. There was just too much consistency in my experiences with her.'

Tori gave a statement ahead of the 2017 trial, but she was not called as a witness. She told me that ahead of the sentencing hearing in 2023 she was approached and asked to fill out a questionnaire by Doug Kingsbery, Molly's lawyer.

Tori says Kingsbery asked her to change some answers. She couldn't recall the specifics of the changes she was asked to make, but she remembered Kingsbery asking her to remove one particular comment: one of Tori's answers to the questionnaire described the jury that convicted Molly in the 2017 murder trial as being 'too stupid to see the truth'.

I asked Kingsbery to confirm if he had asked Tori to

change any part of her answers, but he did not respond to my emails. Clearly, Kingsbery was not happy to put Tori on the stand as she was not called as a witness at the sentencing hearing.

As Tori and I made our way back through the stables, I asked her how Molly's acquaintance and supporter Sara Neeves came to be mentioned alongside her in the detective case notes. Tori said Sara was a client of hers at the time, and she was the one who introduced Molly.

Tori told me that after the killing, she remembers Sara Neeves telling her: 'You know, there's some speculation he killed his first wife.' Tori went on to tell me, 'She [Sara Neeves] said this around about the time when she called me to tell me that the detective would be calling me.'

So Sara Neeves was spreading rumours about Jason killing his first wife and was calling detectives telling them to interview Tori Adkins. Sara had also told another of the five confidantes, Shannon Grubb, that she needed to change her first statement, because Molly thought her first statement made no sense, that Grubb was 'naïve'.

When I contacted Sara Neeves in 2024 for comment, she refused an interview and said she did not know Molly well at all. I felt that this was a strange admission, given that Sara had testified about Molly being a 'supermom' at the guardianship hearing, and, evidently, had been gathering and briefing witnesses on Molly's behalf.*

At least three of the women Molly confided in alleged they had experienced domestic abuse in their own lives – Jennifer Turner, Billy June Jacobs and Tori Adkins. Was this coincidence,

---

* 'Ms Neeves told me that she knew the Corbetts but was not close to them. Ms Neeves went on to say that Molly had never told her anything' – from Detective Brandon Smith's case notes.

or was Molly deliberately confiding in women she knew would be empathetic?

Why did the five women who changed their statements wait up to eight months to do so? Why did the changes come after the defence lawyers received approximately 5,000 pages of documentation under discovery?* These changed statements were made around the time Jack recanted the allegations he had made against his father.

Why did Helen McCormac, the neighbour of Molly's brother, demand to have her statement – given in March 2016 – videotaped? She lived 90 miles from Meadowlands, yet she was aware that a number of people were complaining about statements being taken inaccurately. If Kingsbery asked Tori Adkins to change her questionnaire responses, as she alleges, were others asked to change theirs, too?†

Despite the district attorney reaching a plea deal, detectives still believe the crime scene was staged. The body was cold. The blood was dry. The Martenses had no injuries and clean hands. Detectives believe they delayed calling 911 and faked CPR while Tom constructed a narrative using all his experience of crime scenes.

Did the catastrophic injuries to the back of Jason's skull also indicate an attempt to cover up which weapon caused those injuries? At least two sites were struck more than once,

* Between January and March 2016, the DA's office released ten batches of documents to the defence lawyers under discovery, totalling 5,000 pages of documentation.

† Statements were changed on the prosecution side, too. While JoAnn Lowry later testified about Tom hating Jason, she made no mention of this in her original statement when interviewed on 19 August 2015, seventeen days after the killing. She only included the accusation that Tom hated Jason on 5 July 2017, just before the trial got under way. Detectives had received an anonymous call saying they should reinterview Tom's colleagues at Oak Ridge.

with such force the skull was crushed and the skin ruptured upwards in 2-inch spikes.

These repeated blows meant the medical examiner was unable to say whether the injuries were caused by a bat or a brick. With blood, hair and tissue on all sides of the brick, it had to have been deployed more than the one time Molly admitted. That brick shape indented into the wall an inch above the skirting board, coupled with the brain tissue and blood found on the lower legs of Molly's pyjamas, shows she was in close and down low delivering the blows. Just how many times the brick was used to crush the back of Jason's skull was hidden by the secondary blows.

Wanda Thompson told me in 2024: 'Before they [Molly, Tom and the officers driving them back to the house in Meadowlands] left the sheriff's office [after being interviewed] that morning, Tom said something like "I want to say we called 911 right away, but we took a couple of minutes to get ourselves together." He knew the body was cold. What he meant was they took a couple of minutes to get their stories straight.'

David Grice, the retired sheriff, told me that he agrees with Thompson. He believes Tom and Molly waited at least an hour before calling 911 and that they faked CPR.

Mike Earnest said the children could have testified at the sentencing hearing but chose not to because of the cross-examination they would have faced. Earnest said the children had been brainwashed by Tracey, and that Jack, in particular, would have faced intense questioning over changing his story – especially when he had made attempts to contact Molly, telling her he loved and missed her. Instead, avoiding cross-examination, Jack and Sarah made victim impact statements alleging Molly was the abuser, a 'monster' who manipulated them and Jason and subjected them to 'all manner of abuse'.

Jack concluded his victim impact statement by alleging a 'conspiracy' by the wider Martens family. He said he had seen his father's laptop, computer servers and cellphone in police evidence bags in Bobby's house. They were alongside a sheet of paper listing the Lynches' various links to drug dealers and the IRA.

Like the identity of the driver of the mystery car that was witnessed by a neighbour leaving Jason's driveway at 2.15 a.m., some forty-five minutes before the 911 call, Jason's missing personal items were never discovered. The jury was never told about them or the mystery car leaving the scene.

The Martenses say the children's latest claims are the result of them being brainwashed from the moment they returned to Ireland. But, even if that was the case, it doesn't explain the missing items. Molly signed a waiver form authorizing detectives to search her property that night without a warrant. They found the things they were directed to find, like the Russian doll and the ballerina sheets, but Jason's phone, laptop and home computer, like so many of the recordings, had disappeared.

As we've seen, search warrants were issued for Tom, Molly, Sharon and Jason's phone records. Detectives could glean the number of calls made, their duration and whether they had been diverted to Jason's messaging service.

There is a terrible pathos to the list of calls to Jason's phone after he was dead. Calls from family members and friends who have just been informed, but they can't quite believe it. These calls to a dead man were not in vain, though.

When Tom called Jason at 2.36 p.m. on the day of the killing, Jason's phone pinged off a mast at 3858 Gumtree Road, 1.3 miles from Jason's home. When Tom called four minutes later and left a 37-second voicemail the phone pinged off the same tower. That 2.40 p.m. call was the last to Jason's phone the day he died.

When you receive a call on a cellphone, provided the phone is on, it will ping off the nearest mast in a 3-mile radius. Tom's calls place Jason's phone at home in Panther Creek at 2.40 p.m. on the afternoon of the killing. We know he spent the afternoon in his next-door neighbour's driveway until Tom and Sharon arrived around 8.30 p.m.

When I examined Jason's phone records for the day after the killing I checked the incoming calls from Tracey, Paul Dillon and another of Jason's friends, Damian McCormack. Tracey called Jason's phone nine hours after the 911 call. By then, Jason's cellphone was on the move. It pinged off a mast 92 miles from Meadowlands.

When Paul Dillon called twenty-two minutes later the phone pinged off a different mast, still in the Indian Trail area.

Finally, at 1.25 p.m., Damian McCormack, who was Jason's best man at his wedding to Mags, called Jason's phone. The call lasted just twenty-two seconds but left an indelible trace. That call on 2 August 2015 pinged off a mast 6 miles south of Indian Trail, at 209 Jim Parker Road, in Monroe, North Carolina.

I travelled to that mast on 3 October 2024, a day before catching my flight home to Ireland from Charlotte Douglas International Airport, after spending three weeks in the US conducting research and interviews for this book.

After the killing someone had taken Jason's phone from the crime scene and driven it south for an hour and thirty-one minutes. The final mast that Jason's phone pinged off was less than 3 miles from 3004 Dewdrop Court, Monroe – Bobby's house, where Jack and Sarah were kept for fifteen days in the custody of their father's killers.

Jack had shocked the sentencing hearing in 2023 when he said that he had seen his father's missing phone, laptop, computer and hard drives in police evidence bags at Bobby's house. He was so sure he had seen his father's cellphone alongside recording devices at Bobby's house he was able to tell me the colour, make and model.

Now, I had proof that Jack had not been brainwashed into making this claim. The phone-mast data is indisputable. Jason's phone was in Bobby's house within eleven hours of the killing. It is, as Tom once said of Mags's death, mysterious.

Tom's 37-second voicemail, the last call on Jason's phone the day he died, is probably lost for ever. As with all those secret recordings made by Molly, Jason's phone disappeared like footprints in the snow.

Epilogue

In November of 2023 I met with Brian Shipwash, the judge who had presided in Jack and Sarah's guardianship case. Shipwash reflected on the weekend when he controlled the sliding doors of Jack and Sarah's lives. It was his decision whether their future would be in America with Molly or in Ireland with Tracey.

Shipwash had the authority to override Jason's will, which named David and Tracey Lynch as Jack and Sarah's guardians, and give custody of the children to Molly, but she unnerved him.

'She [Molly] had this deranged entitlement to the children. It was like, how could the courts not rule in her favour? For me, as a judge, it was the case that I will remember for the rest of my life.'

Shipwash, who resigned from his role as Davidson County's Clerk of the Superior Court in 2019, told me he was shocked that social services placed Jack and Sarah with their father's killers: 'I didn't have a fear that she would hurt the children physically, but more so psychologically . . . Molly wanted to adopt. There is a reason why Jason didn't let her adopt.'

That reason, in Shipwash's opinion, was Molly's ongoing mental health struggles. Shipwash believes Jason was trying to leave. 'In an unhappy marriage,' he said, 'timing is everything. I truly believe that Jason, behind the scenes, was waiting for the right time to return to Ireland. But that all got thwarted.' Shipwash believes the last-minute trip by Tom and Sharon indicates that 'something was going to go down that night'.

'She [Molly] felt she had laid down enough baseline

groundwork to show domestic violence. She was in the home that she wanted. She had the kids that she wanted. Everything was good, except for Jason.'

Shipwash is entitled to his opinion – Jonathan Babb, special counsel for the Attorney General for North Carolina, agrees with him, and argued before the North Carolina Supreme Court that first-degree-murder charges should have been brought.

However, ultimately the courts set aside the murder convictions and named Jason as the 'sole aggressor'. The plea deal accepts that there was neither premeditation nor malice, that the Martenses did act in self-defence but that their actions became excessive and therefore unjustified, warranting convictions for voluntary manslaughter.

It is remarkable to consider that Jason was the victim, whose skull was crushed in from the weight of twelve blows to the head, and that the Martenses were the perpetrators who left that room with no injuries, and yet, officially, Jason is now regarded as the sole aggressor who instigated the events which led to his death.

The public and the media's focus at the time of the North Carolina Supreme Court ruling was almost exclusively on the fact that the Martenses' convictions had been overturned. But the court's designation of Jason as the sole aggressor was equally important – it meant DA Garry Frank's hand was considerably weakened should he want to have a retrial.

The new jury would be told that Jason started it, and Tom and Molly defended themselves, as they were entitled to. The only argument would be over how they defended themselves, whether their response was malicious enough to constitute second-degree murder.

The Martenses' legal team made it clear to Frank in negotiations on a plea deal that if the case went to a retrial and Jack and Sarah chose to take the stand as witnesses against Tom and Molly they would be subjected to rigorous cross-examination.

Jack and Sarah had condemned their father in three separate interviews with three different social workers – with each interview conducted during the 15-day period in August 2015 when they were in the custody of their father's killers. The North Carolina Supreme Court ruled that the Martenses did not get a fair trial because the 2017 jury had not heard the allegations the children made about their father in their main interviews, which were video-recorded at Dragonfly House.

Jack and Sarah recanted all their Dragonfly allegations against their father in 2016, within nine months of returning to Ireland. They said that over time, and through counselling, they started to remember what had actually happened in Meadowlands, how Molly was the abuser, not Jason.

In March 2021, in separate interviews that took six hours each to complete, the children told detectives in Davidson County about Molly's extensive abuse of both of them.

The concept of trauma victims having repressed memories which can be recovered through psychotherapy is now largely discredited among the scientific community. In the 1990s there were multiple miscarriages of justice, particularly in sexual abuse cases, where people were wrongly convicted on foot of false memories induced during psychotherapy sessions.

The Martenses told the DA in negotiations on a plea deal that if the case went to a retrial they intended to argue that Jack and Sarah were not suddenly remembering events they had suppressed, they were remembering things because they had been brainwashed by Tracey and David Lynch since their return to Ireland.

Even after Jack and Sarah made their new statements in March 2021 the district attorney still decided not to proceed with a retrial. Frank did not believe a second-degree-murder conviction could be secured in a retrial.

Logistically, there were a lot of problems: the sheriff, David Grice; the head of the Criminal Investigations Division, Wanda Thompson, and the head of CSI, Frankie Young, had all retired, as had Greg Brown, the senior assistant district attorney who had led the prosecution case in 2017.

Assistant DA Alan Martin was still involved, but he would need to brief two new assistant DAs who would be starting on the case from scratch. Davidson County had a backlog of murder cases, due to Covid delays, and there was pressure on resources.

Lt Wanda Thompson told me: 'Logistically and financially, it was always going to be very difficult to have a retrial. The children would have had to give evidence because the Dragonfly tapes would be shown this time. You have to pay for your old experts to give evidence again, or pay for new experts. And in a second trial, the defence knows what's coming, so it just makes it harder second time round.'

Garry Frank weighed up the odds and decided not to risk a retrial and instead reach a deal. Even then, the Martenses rejected the first plea offer, which would have seen them return to prison for a minimum of three more years. Molly led the resistance, refusing to plead guilty or countenance another day in prison.

The Martenses bargained some more and got a better offer second time round – a plea deal agreed in September 2023 that offered the prospect of no more jail time if they could convince the sentencing judge that there were extraordinary mitigating circumstances.

As we have seen, the Martenses seized on this opportunity by presenting a hypothesis in court – that the autopsy conducted on Jason's first wife in 2006, seventeen years prior to the sentencing hearing, was flawed and failed to meet American standards of forensic pathology; that in fact, Jason's wife did not die of an asthma attack but was probably or possibly choked to death by Jason.

Because this was a sentencing hearing and not a criminal trial the restrictive rules of evidence governing what can and can't be put before a jury did not apply. There was no jury in the sentencing hearing. The only person the Martenses had to convince was Judge David Hall.

The Martenses did not have to prove beyond a reasonable doubt that Jason killed his first wife, they just had to show it was probable or possible and that this influenced their level of fear for their own lives on the night of the killing.

Thus, the Martenses successfully turned the sentencing hearing into a trial of Jason Corbett. Instead of accepting a sentence in the proffered range under the second plea deal offer – three years and two months (they had already served three years and eight months, so this was effectively zero extra jail time) up to nine years – the Martenses turned the sentencing hearing into a trial, and they turned the victim, Jason, into the accused.

The Martenses used Jack and Sarah as the principal weapons in the destruction of their father's character – assistant DA Alan Martin said the children were 'weaponized' by the Martenses.

It was an extraordinary feat – without presenting any evidence to a jury about domestic violence (no evidence of domestic violence was presented at the 2017 trial) – they had managed to turn the naked, battered and cold corpse into the aggressor, and themselves, the uninjured, almost unblemished perpetrators, into innocent victims of Jason, the man they killed.

To get the lowest sentence possible the Martenses destroyed the reputation of Jack and Sarah's father, and of their mother, Mags, whom the Martenses now depicted as a murder victim.

For Jack and Sarah, and for Jason's family and friends, and the family of Jason's first wife, Mags, this was the ultimate betrayal. Jason's relationship with Mags was sacrosanct; they were soulmates whose enduring love was evidenced by the many devoted messages left by Jason at her grave, which he visited almost daily for eighteen months as he struggled to survive without her, raising their two children on his own.

Jason brought Molly into their lives to help raise the children. Instead, she took his life, orphaned Jack and Sarah, and then used the children to destroy the reputations, and tarnish the marriage and love, of their parents.

The Martenses finished Jason's character assassination at the sentencing hearing, but they put him in their crosshairs from day one. They fought their case in the court of public opinion long before they fought it in any court of law. The Martenses proved relentless in both arenas.

The Martenses spent more than half a million dollars on legal fees, but their defence began long before they stepped into any courtroom. They used social media, in particular, to transform their image and Jason's.

Amanda Mui, Mike Earnest's daughter, made some of the first unproven claims on Facebook that Molly was a victim of ongoing domestic abuse. On 19 August 2015, two weeks after the killing and two days after Molly had lost her battle for custody of Jack and Sarah, Amanda posted on Facebook that Molly had been the victim of Jason's physical and mental abuse for several years and had only stayed in the marriage for the children.

Mike Earnest led the Martenses' media campaign, acting as the family's spokesperson at various court sittings and in interviews he gave, mostly to the *Irish Daily Mail*. Mike suggested Jason could have been leading a secret life and nobody really knew what went on behind closed doors in Meadowlands.

After Molly lost her custody battle for Jack and Sarah, it was Mike who led Molly's campaign in Ireland – trying to hire a plane to fly a message for Jack and Sarah over their new school, or contacting a radio station so he and Molly could give live interviews pleading for members of the public to contact two recently bereaved and vulnerable children whose father had been killed, by Molly.

Mike was a constant presence in the media as Tom and Molly brought their appeals, helping them to set up fundraising campaigns on the internet. It was he who declared their convictions as a miscarriage of justice and an 'American tragedy'.

Mike had been involved in the case from the outset – on Monday, 3 August 2015, the day after the killing, Earnest had called First Unum Life Insurance to enquire about Molly's right to Jason's $600,000 life insurance policy. In the days following, he was present when social workers at Davidson County's Department of Social Services were told that Jason's family members were in the IRA, on 'terrorist watchlists', and that Molly feared them.

Tom and Molly also proved adept at using the media to blacken Jason's character.

Molly and Tom's interview with ABC's *20/20* was instrumental in putting into the public domain two highly emotive allegations that were wholly unproven: that Jason may have killed his first wife, Mags, by choking her to death, and that Jason would regularly – up to twenty times – choke Molly during forced sex.

These allegations were aired to millions of ABC's viewers and subsequently shared and posted on social media, two days after the Martenses were convicted of second-degree murder in August 2017.

It had taken two years for the police and the courts to deliver justice for Jason. It took the Martenses two days to flood the media with claims that the man they beat to death with a baseball bat and brick was a monster who hit and choked Molly so often that she had lost consciousness on occasion.

These claims were never mentioned by Molly or Tom's lawyers in court when they were on trial with the next twenty-five years of their lives at stake. Instead, the allegations were made on Facebook, and the comments, likes and shares that followed delivered their own form of judgement.

When the Martenses won their appeal in 2021 Molly repeated the allegations of Jason abusing and forcibly choking her in an exclusive interview with *Elle* magazine. It should be noted that none of these allegations made in *Elle* were part of the Martenses' appeal hearing, or the hearing before the North Carolina Supreme Court. There, at least, the facts might be contested; on Facebook, there were no restrictions on what people could post and share about the victim.

We have seen in the political arena the nefarious influence Facebook and other social media platforms can have in determining elections. It is becoming increasingly obvious from cases like the Jason Corbett homicide that the defenestration of legacy media – reliable fact-checked newspapers or television networks that at least attempt to show some level of balanced, impartial reporting – has eroded the value of truth and facts in favour of extreme opinions, the more loudly voiced the better.

Here, in this case, theories floated on social media eventually became the basis of a hypothesis pitched before a sentencing judge. How much that hypothesis influenced the sentencing judge we will never know. But he judged that seven more months in prison was a fair sentence for taking Jason Corbett's life. In total, Jason's killers served four years and three months in prison.

*

Jack and Sarah say it was during four pivotal days in 2015, between the killing on 2 August and their Dragonfly statements on 6 August, that they were coached by Molly and Sharon; told to say their father hit Molly. Grice and Thompson both now concede it was a mistake, and a consequential one, to leave Jack and Sarah in the custody of the Martenses.

Thompson told me: 'The kids were in Monroe [at Molly's brother's house] and so we're like "Crap, we just let these two kids that are not US citizens leave with the family of the people that killed their dad, we're hanging out there." So, I was like "We need to get child protective services and get them right now."'

Child protective services did respond on Monday, 3 August 2015, but it took fourteen days before the children were handed over to Tracey and David Lynch. Thompson says that apart from the psychological damage potentially caused to the children, it was also hugely traumatic for Jason's family, particularly for Tracey and David.

'For me, one of the issues that has always stuck in my craw about the whole child custody case is the financial and emotional trauma that David and Tracey went through just to assert their legal authority.' Tracey wrote in her book, *My Brother Jason*, that they spent almost $500,000 in legal fees.

'It is absolutely appalling,' Thompson told me, 'that they got dragged through the courts and had to spend all the money when they had the legal authority right from the get-go, from day one when they landed in this country with Jason's will in their hand.

'Jack and Sarah are not US citizens, they're Irish citizens, they've got passports. David and Tracey have got a will that says the father wants the children with them. I was just appalled at the legal and financial trauma. I mean, they're dealing with their brother's death and his kids, and they've got to fight through that whole mess.'

When I met former sheriff David Grice in September 2024 he was still troubled by what happened to Jack and Sarah: 'You know, it's one of the biggest regrets I have in my career, letting them take Jack and Sarah that night. We had given them to the people who had killed their father.'

Grice personally witnessed the malevolence of the crime scene. In his opinion, the crime did not match Tom and Molly's version of events. Their story jarred with the blood Grice saw splashed across five walls, blood that flew from Jason's head with such force it carried 10 feet across the room and spattered the window blinds. Their story didn't explain Jason's crushed skull versus their clean hands.

Grice became Davidson County sheriff in 2004, taking over from his controversial Trump-style predecessor Gerald Hege, who had been brought down for corruption by the new DA, Garry Frank. Hege tried to stage a comeback in 2018, but Grice defeated him and was re-elected to continue his 14-year stint as sheriff. Grice is, therefore, well placed to comment on the politics of law enforcement in Davidson County. He rejects any suggestion that Tom's long career in law enforcement and counterintelligence influenced the criminal investigation.

He said he found Tom arrogant, certain he and Molly would escape charges: 'I remember Tom asking me at the house [back in Meadowlands], after [being interviewed at] the sheriff's office, what would happen next. He winced when he heard the case would go to a grand jury. He thought that they were going to float their self-defence thing, and we're just going to be done with that. I'm FBI, you know? I'm one of the boys.

'He thought we were country bumpkins. You got this attorney, an FBI agent, and that might have influenced the appeal courts, but not us. Local law enforcement called the FBI the "first bunch of idiots" or "famous but incompetent".'

I don't believe Tom Martens' FBI career influenced the investigation, but the Martenses' status – as wealthy, white defendants from a family steeped in law enforcement – ensured the media was interested in, and amplified, anything they had to say.

Were Molly not the telegenic daughter of a retired FBI agent, and had this crime not occurred in an upscale golf community, their story, and this crime, would have received a fraction of the coverage. The media gave the Martenses a platform, and they exploited it expertly.

The Martenses' wealth was also influential. Less wealthy defendants could not have sustained an 8-year legal campaign all the way to the North Carolina Supreme Court. Money can, and does, influence the outcomes of criminal trials. Lawyers earning $400 an hour give you a chance at freedom that public defenders do not.

As we have seen, highly paid lawyers are expert enough to exploit the rules of evidence to ensure a jury never gets to hear, for example, the opinion of the 911 operator that CPR was being faked, or the opinion of the first officer on the scene that the blood was coagulated, indicating a probable delay in calling 911.

The jury never got to hear about the mystery car leaving the scene or the items, like Jason's phone, which mysteriously disappeared after the killing.

Ultimately, the Martenses' wealth and status allowed them to force the distillation of this case down to one question: who do you believe, Jack and Sarah, or the Martenses?

Five days after I signed off on the final page proofs of this book, an email arrived. I had been waiting for this email from the Davidson County Sheriff's Office for about six months. And now here it was – notice that my public records request was finally complete. It would take another week, but I was promised a digital trove running to ten thousand pages. It was everything I had hoped for, but five days too late.

My publisher had warned me that once the final page proofs were sent, I would not have another opportunity to change the text. After years of borderline obsession with this story, I felt a little sadness letting it go. I was invested in its veracity. I had worked stubbornly and diligently on the story as a journalist for the *Irish Times*, as a producer for Netflix, and now as the author of this book for Penguin. I had asked every question I could think of that might get me closer to the truth of what happened that night in Meadowlands. Now, it was time to move on. The proofs were sent, my job was done. But what if there was something new in these documents?

A week later, I was sent log-in details and a password for a portal link to ten thousand pages of detective case notes, witness statements, forensic reports, social worker case files and expert witness submissions. Even though the deadline for the book had passed, I wanted to be sure there was nothing of consequence that I had missed. It took me ten days to go through it all, line by line. I had previously seen or heard most of the information disclosed, but there were some very interesting new details, which I have been allowed to list here in this postscript.

- Molly's parents took her out of Clemson University, where she was studying Pre Health, after she was found sitting fully clothed in a shower in her dorm room, consuming soup and chips. Witnesses described to detectives how the whole dorm had filled with steam as the shower had been running for more than two and a half hours.

- Molly hatched a secret plan to buy 'black market sperm' on the internet in a bizarre attempt to get pregnant by another man. In July 2014, just over a year before the killing, Molly asked a neighbour, Jerusha Maddock, to store fertility drugs, which Molly said she had purchased using $10,000 sent to her by her father, Tom. Molly said she intended to combine the black-market sperm with the fertility drugs so that she could get pregnant by an 'upper-crust man', one with superior DNA to Jason. In contemporaneous emails, Jason describes how Molly belittles him over his 'loser sperm'. Jason sent himself an email, as an aide memoire of this abuse. It read: 'Molly says I'm so sick in the head. Bitch I wished dead. I need more of the bed because I'm so fat. My boobs are bigger than hers. Loser sperm, loser sperm. Kids probably aren't even mine because of my loser sperm . . . Physically attacked me. Drawing blood from my arm. Told me I'm disgusting.'

- Molly told a neighbour that she met Jason in a bar in Ireland, had a one-night stand, became pregnant and was forced into exile on the west coast of Ireland by Jason, causing her to lose the child. According to a memo filed by assistant district attorneys Greg Brown and Ina Staunton: 'Molly was locked away on the coast of Ireland for her pregnancy. Molly went into labour and had to walk to the hospital. Molly lost the child. This occurred before Molly and Jason came to the US.'

- Detective case notes reveal that Molly discussed putting night-vision recording equipment in the master bedroom. She told a neighbour, Billy June Jacobs, that she was using an app she had seen on the *Dr Phil* television show that would record violence or abuse and automatically call an emergency number.

- Just hours after killing Jason, Molly contacted his twin, Wayne. At this point, none of Jason's family in Ireland knew that he was dead. Wayne missed Molly's first call, so he texted her: 'Molly are you looking for me?' Molly replied a minute later: 'I missed a call from you, I assume it was an accident.' Wayne responded: 'I must have pressed your number by mistake, all good down in Lahinch.' A minute later, seemingly nonchalant, Molly replied: 'Have fun on your holidays.' Wayne replied: 'Cheers.' It was two and a half hours later before Wayne received another call from Molly's phone. This time it was Sharon on the line. She told him that Jason was dead. The call lasted less than a minute.

- Four weeks after Jason's death, Tom covered up Molly's involvement in a car crash. Molly drove through an intersection in Knoxville, at 11.30 a.m. on 31 August 2015, two weeks after losing custody of Jack and Sarah. She crashed into a neighbour's brick mailbox, causing thousands of dollars in damages. Detective case notes and witness statements show that Sharon and Tom arrived on the scene and convinced their neighbour and another witness, a former emergency medical technician, not to report the incident to police. The former EMT told Detective Michael Hurd that he believed Molly was 'out of it', but he did not smell alcohol, and she denied taking drugs. He had been so concerned for Molly's welfare that he asked her if she had been attempting suicide. She insisted she had not been drinking and was not suicidal. Detectives believed this event showed Tom's willingness to clean up after Molly, and to intervene on her behalf to stymie a police investigation. An insurance claim was paid out to the Martenses, despite the absence of any police report on the crash.

- Weeks after Jack and Sarah were returned to Ireland, Molly and Mike Earnest exchanged emails discussing how they could use an 'investigator contact' of Earnest's to smuggle a mobile phone to Jack when he was at school and away from David and Tracey Lynch's supervision. Mike Earnest wrote: 'Obviously this could only be conducted when Jack is away from T/D [Tracey and David Lynch] and at a time where Jack could be given a brief explanation. I know this idea has many obstacles and may not be possible, but I thought it might be something we could try. My idea would be that once Jack has the phone and the instructions on how and when to use it, that he would know only to do so when he could be absolutely certain that he would not be caught. Aside from just engineering this project, the biggest downside would be the possible repercussions to Jack and Sarah if caught.' Molly replies that she agrees with the plan.

In the end, all these vignettes of minor detail coalesced to underscore what I believe is the central truth of this story: Molly has been a mercurial, often malevolent, personality from an early age, prone to wild flights of fantasy and delusions of grandeur. When not medicated, her descent into mental illness is inevitable, and it draws those around her into the vortex. The details outlined above illuminate Molly's obsessive, unhinged character, but they also reveal Tom and Sharon in the shadows, constantly vigilant, ever protective, willing to step in to do whatever it takes to protect their only daughter. Now forty-one, and living back home in Knoxville, Molly is free to begin a new life. The story continues.

Acknowledgements

In journalism, they call it the 'death knock'. I still remember my first time having to call to the home of strangers and talk to them about a loved one who had died. It was 1995, and I was a junior reporter for the *Kerryman*, a local newspaper in Ireland. I was amazed that the family of this teenage boy invited me into their home and spoke for hours about him, giving me an array of photographs that captured his personality. The family explained that they didn't want their son to just disappear, they wanted his presence in the world, however short, to be felt, and his absence to be acknowledged. It was that family's way of saying: our son lived, he had value, and he is missed.

A year after my first 'death knock' I got an insight into how it must feel to be on the inside, when journalists like me are calling to your door at the most traumatic time of your life. Det. Garda Jerry McCabe was killed by the IRA in June 1996. Jerry's son, Ian, was, and still is, one of my best friends. Jerry's killing was the lead item on news bulletins and journalists were calling to his house looking for photographs and comments. To be honest, even though those journalists were polite, respectful and professional, it still felt intrusive. The truth is, there is a very fine line between reporting what's in the public interest and what's of interest to the public. How many of us can drive past the carnage of a car crash without craning our necks for a closer view? We look out of human curiosity, of course, but also out of empathy for whoever's life was lost, and for their families. We can imagine the fallout for them, and feel a guilty gratitude that today, at least, their cruel fate has not befallen us.

Now, thirty years later, having reported on murders, rapes, kidnappings, terrorism and all kinds of tragedies, I can see a consistent theme of ordinary families cast involuntarily into extraordinary circumstances. Some want to speak and share their memories; others prefer to stay silent and keep their grief private. Occasionally, when the death is high profile and the victim's reputation is being debated and dissected publicly, the family of that victim will feel compelled to speak for them, for their memory and their legacy. The challenge is always to find the right balance between telling someone's story as fully and accurately as possible and also telling the other side.

I recall covering my first murder trial, a couple of years after my first 'death knock'. I spoke to the lead detective on the case and remarked upon how normal the person accused of the murder appeared. The detective smiled at my naïvety, and asked in reply: 'What did you expect? They don't have horns on their heads.'

It was a valuable insight. I have spoken to murderers and rapists over the years. They have families, too. They have people who love them, too. Their families will occasionally also choose to speak out because they, too, want to paint a more rounded picture of the person they know. It doesn't excuse their crimes, or absolve their guilt, but it's important that the families of the perpetrators get the opportunity to put forward context or mitigation, in addition to addressing hard questions about the particular crime and its consequences.

In this context, I'm particularly grateful to all those who spoke to me, both on and off the record, for both sides of this story. From minute one, the facts of this story have been fiercely contested. However, Jason Corbett's family and the Martens family agree on one thing: there are no winners here. I have tried to present a balanced and comprehensive telling of the story here, and have left it to the reader to reach their own conclusions.

I would like to acknowledge the original reporting of Ralph Riegel of the *Irish Independent* and of Catherine Fegan of the *Irish Daily Mail*. Both reported on the case from the outset and each uncovered different elements of the story. I discovered my own new leads through my own research over several years, but the building blocks of this story were laid in their initial reporting.

I would like to thank my agent, Tim Hays, whose literary agency in New York immediately saw the appeal of this story for an international audience. A former journalist, Tim has been a mentor and friend as much as an agent, and when I hit roadblocks or wandered down dead ends, he made me laugh, turned me around and set me on my way again.

I would like to thank Adrienne Murphy, who edited this book, for her wise and always insightful suggestions. Brian Looney, my first editor at the *Kerryman* and later at the *Irish Examiner*, told me that editing was as much about what you leave out as what you put in. Adrienne guided me expertly along that fine line. I would also like to thank Deputy Publisher, Patricia Deevy, and Publisher, Michael McLoughlin, at Penguin Sandycove, for believing in this book and my capacity to tell this fractured story of a transatlantic tragedy in a comprehensive, cohesive and balanced way.